SAIL *for the*
MEDITERRANEAN

SAIL *for the* MEDITERRANEAN

HOW TO PREPARE FOR YOUR DREAM CRUISE

Claire James

ADLARD COLES NAUTICAL
London

Dedication

To my beloved husband

Published by Adlard Coles Nautical
an imprint of A & C Black (Publishers) Ltd
37 Soho Square, London W1D 3QZ
www.adlardcoles.com

Copyright text, illustrations and photographs
© Claire James 2003

First edition 2003

ISBN 0-7136-6249-2

A CIP catalogue record for this book is available from the British Library.

A & C Black uses paper produced with elemental chlorine-free pulp, harvested from managed sustainable forests.

Note: While all reasonable care has been taken in the preparation of this publication, the author and publisher take no responsibility for the use of the methods or products described in the book.

Design by Susan McIntyre

Typeset in 11 on 13 pt Minion

Printed and bound in Singapore by
Tien Wah Press Ltd

Contents

Maps

Acknowledgements

Many people have helped me with this book, and I would like to thank them all. In addition to Adlard Coles Nautical for publishing it, I'd like to say a big thank you to:

- David Teall for a vast amount of help with the computer (without which the book could never have been written); and to both David and his wife for reading the complete manuscript, and offering many ideas for improving it.
- Eric Bell, and the late John Brissendon, for initial help with the computer.
- Peter Price for help on the subject of electrics.
- Lynne Harrison for offering ideas for improvements.

- Pat for some help with typing when my tennis elbow was at its worst.
- Anne Hammick for advice about getting a publisher.
- The many people whose yachts I photographed.
- And the countless other people who gave general support and encouragement.

Finally, I must thank my long-suffering husband Jimmy, not only for constant help and support – he read and advised on every version of each chapter, and gave me much guidance concerning the various technical sections – but also for putting up with, as he once described it, having a computer instead of a wife for three whole years!

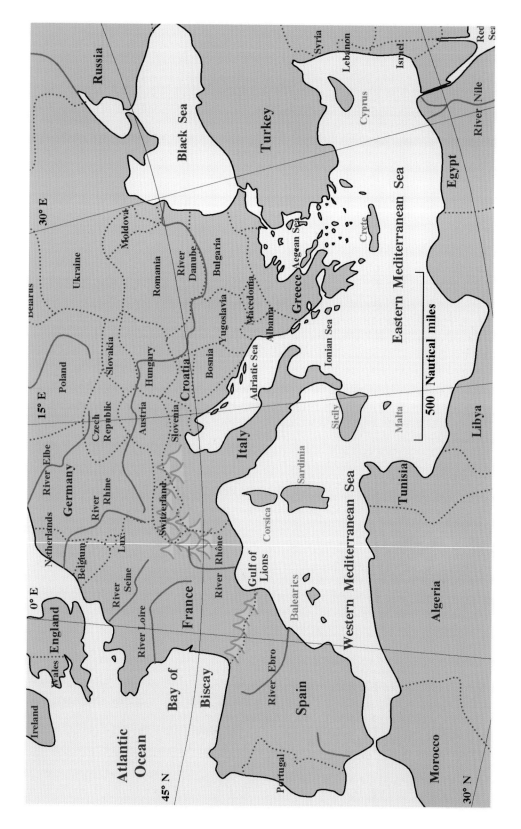

Introduction

Setting sail for the Mediterranean in 1992 was a completely unknown venture for me and my husband Jimmy. True, we had been sailing for many years, but never for more than a few weeks at a time. Live-aboard cruising is a different matter altogether. We knew no one else doing the same thing, and were totally dependent on books to guide us. But though there were books on selling-up-and-sailing the oceans, and books about sailing *in* the Mediterranean, there was very little on making preparations for cruising there. So having spent three years reading everything we could find, we then spent the next six years discovering from bitter experience all the things our reading had missed out.

I felt that a book specifically designed to help people who were setting sail for the Mediterranean for the first time was badly needed. More and more people seemed to be heading that way (all in the same state of ignorance as we had been), and I found my notes in such demand that I could hardly keep up with the photocopying. The only answer seemed to be to write the book myself – so here it is. It's not intended to be an 'everything you need to know' type of book. The aim is to supplement other books, not to replace them, and I have concentrated on three types of information:

1 Things that are specific to the Mediterranean.
2 Things that we had to learn the hard way.
3 Things that we see other yachts having constant problems with.

One aspect of this book is unusual, if not unique – I have attempted to include a *complete* packing list of boat equipment and stores to give a head start to anyone planning their own. As I unpacked after our first cruise, I made a list of everything on board that we would need when fitting out the next yacht. This I found so useful that I have included it in the book.

The vast majority of *long-term* Mediterranean cruisers are middle-aged or elderly couples, British and other north Europeans, who have some experience of yachting and who want to spend their retirement sailing in the Mediterranean; they typically choose a sailing yacht between 10 and 12 metres; they normally have a pension to live on, so do not need to earn money along the way. It is therefore with such couples in mind that this book has been written, though clearly it will have plenty of useful information for the many people who do not fall into that category. For convenience, I will refer to 'the skipper' and 'the wife', but in reality this latter term could cover a wide range of crew – generally indicating the weaker, less experienced, or less keen half of the partnership (indeed, of either sex).

Our experiences are of the northern half of the Mediterranean (from Gibraltar to Turkey), plus Tunisia. So when I talk of 'the Mediterranean', it is to this area that I am mainly referring.

But what are our 'qualifications and experience' for writing such a book? In 1998, when I started writing this, I was 50 years old and had sailed all my life, though only occasionally until I met Jimmy in 1978 and started racing with him. I had suffered a stroke when I was 15, leaving me with a weak right leg and a paralysed right hand, but this doesn't affect my sailing much when I'm with Jimmy because he does the heavier and more awkward work. He is 20 years older than me and spent his working life in the Royal Navy, as a shipwright. He has sailed naval yachts all over the world and, on retiring from the Navy, ran a small boatyard; he then became a yacht surveyor until 1991. During these 13 years we owned various racing yachts in Plymouth; but the highlight of each year was our two or three weeks' summer holiday, cruising France and the Channel Islands.

In 1989 I gave up my job as an educational psychologist. This freed us to venture farther afield and for longer periods – and finally to follow our dream of cruising the Mediterranean.

Our first cruiser was a Trident Voyager 38 (photo page 173) that we called *Phœnician Voyager* after the ancient Phœnician explorers. We started fitting her out in the autumn of 1990 and set sail for the Mediterranean (via the Atlantic coast) some 18 months later – in the spring of 1992. All yachts are compromises, and *Phœnician* was no exception. Voyagers are bulky deck-saloon yachts, and this created both her best and her worst characteristics. She was a wonderful boat to live aboard, but she had a lot of windage. It was very difficult to climb aboard from a low quay; and weighing anchor was a real chore, with her 45lb anchor and ⅜ths chain. It was *because* of this, and since everything about her seemed to be getting bigger and heavier as we grew older, that after five wonderful years in the Mediterranean we decided to sell her and continue cruising in a slightly smaller yacht. So in 1997 we came home through the Canal-du-Midi

and (reluctantly) put *Phœnician* on the market.

For our new cruiser we chose a much sleeker yacht, a Moody 376 – a foot shorter, a foot lower, and a foot narrower than *Phœnician* at deck level (photo page 27); she was also 2 tons lighter, with a 35lb anchor and ⁵⁄₁₆ths chain. We called her *Phœacian* (which we pronounce 'Fayshon') after the race of master mariners who finally managed to get Odysseus home despite the antagonism of Poseidon, the God of the sea.

In *Phœnician* we had mostly gone home for the winter, although we had spent one winter in south-east Spain which we had really enjoyed, finding both the weather and company excellent. But in early 1998, while we were buying *Phœacian*, Jimmy announced that he was finding the British weather so debilitating (one or other of us seemed to be ill all the time) that he didn't ever want to spend another winter in England.

That left us only four months for fitting out if we were to get away by early July and be back in the Mediterranean by the very next winter. I do **not** recommend fitting out a yacht for long-term cruising so quickly! Doing it in 18 months the first time had been bad enough: this was infinitely worse – four months of utter panic. In fact, it couldn't have been done at all if our home-based arrangements hadn't already been in place, had we not known from experience exactly what we wanted and had we not already got half the required equipment (transferred from *Phœnician*). In fact, we had no time to do anything else but concentrate 100 per cent on the task in hand. Despite this, many things were left undone – and I'm still hoping that, one day, all the modifications recommended in this book may yet be completed!

1
Initial Planning and Preparation

SETTING THE SCENE

Setting off on your first long-term live-aboard cruise is the most tremendous adventure. Everything is new; everything is fascinating; and difficulties are just there to be overcome. The preparations are exciting at first, but they become a desperate race against time as you approach your leave-by date, and the mountain of work still to be done tends to obscure the excitements lying beyond. However, once you leave, all the hassle is immediately forgotten; you are off and away on the adventure of a lifetime, and life seems very, very good – it is a wonderful way of life for those it suits. However, it's not for everyone; and even those whom it does suit need to get it right.

Two types of cruising folk

There seem to be two quite different types of cruising people – those who like ocean cruising and those who don't. The ocean types enjoy long periods at sea, and the gentle routine of trade wind sailing. They rarely get seasick, happily spending hours relaxing in their bunk with a book, and treat storms at sea as a natural, if

unpleasant, part of life. There is nothing to hurry for, because being at sea is, in itself, the life they like. They adore wild anchorages and like to be able to view the sea from where they anchor, because if bad weather obliges them to leave, they can do so in the dark by steering out on a set bearing. They don't mind rolly anchorages, and regard sailing in areas with few decent charts or weather forecasts as an exciting challenge.

We have listened with horror to such people's stories, a few of which make my blood run cold! For example, there was the couple who told us of eyeballing their way among uncharted coral reefs (finding the deep channel by the colour of the water) into 'fantastic anchorages, teeming with tropical fish' – only the sky then darkened, the wind got up, and they needed to leave in a hurry, but couldn't find the way out because all the water had turned a uniform grey.

This is *not* the kind of cruising I want to do. We belong to the other category, the coastal cruisers – as do probably most couples who cruise the Mediterranean long term. We don't like long sea passages because we get either sick, tired – or simply bored. I don't mind a few hours out in a rough sea. It can be enjoyable and stimulating, especially if the sun is shining, so long as I can be sure that the rough sea isn't going to follow me into the anchorage – and that means an anchorage where you *can't* see out to sea. I like really sheltered anchorages (and good pilot guides to tell me where they are). I want reliable forecasts – so that we don't get caught out in bad weather, or go to an anchorage that's slightly open in just the direction the strong winds are likely to come from.

So what are the advantages of Mediterranean cruising for people like us – or indeed for anyone? What is it that draws us (and thousands like us) back again and again?

WHY THE MED?

• *The location* A big advantage of Mediterranean cruising for northern Europeans is that it's not that far away: it's not too difficult to get the boat there, or to get to and fro yourselves. There are international airports every few hundred miles, and flights are comparatively cheap.

• *Seasickness* This is a problem that puts many people (especially women) off long-term cruising – including me, since I get sick if I have to go below when it is rough. This made night passages a real worry, because one simply has to go below – to sleep and to go to the loo. But if you are prepared to take some longer routes, it is possible to reach Gibraltar, and cruise almost anywhere within the Mediterranean, in long day-hops.

• *Facilities* These are excellent, with many marinas providing water, electricity, showers, fax machines, telephones, and

The peaceful, buoyed anchorage on the nature reserve island of Cabrera in the Balearics.

sometimes even launderettes. Shopping is improving all the time, and many people speak at least some English. Postal services are pretty good now, and getting money from your bank is easy.

• *Weather* One of the main reasons that most people head south in the first place

is the wonderful sunny climate of the Mediterranean. Except near the notorious Gulf of Lions (Map 1 page 9), stormy weather is rare in the cruising season, and weather forecasting is fairly good; with the right equipment you can receive forecasts, in English, covering the whole Mediterranean.

• *Safety* A major advantage of the northern Mediterranean is that it is so safe. There are no pirates or hurricanes, and there's no more likelihood of theft, vandalism or terrorism than there is at home. There are sheltered harbours throughout the region, and excellent charts and pilot guides to help you find them. The water is almost always safe to drink, and there are very few dangerous animals, insects or diseases.

• *Historical interest* One of the fascinating things about the Mediterranean is the way in which its history is our history – the history of western civilisation. The Romans, whose blood flows in our veins, came north from the Mediterranean, and brought that civilisation to our shores. The Med is full of ancient sites that are wonderful to explore; wherever you go there are interesting places to visit and some of your excursions are likely to be the highlights of your cruise.

• *Cruising grounds* Finally, the Mediterranean is full of good cruising grounds, all within a reasonable distance of each other, and many of them extremely beautiful. (See back cover photos.) They vary greatly in style, but wherever you go you are never that far from a safe haven.

IS IT FOR YOU?

Live-aboard cruising is very different from weekend sailing, or even from a fortnight's summer holiday cruise. So no assumptions can be made about whether you will like it. You need to try it out in smaller stages first, and only go ahead with planning your main cruise when you are absolutely certain that you will not regret it – it was only when we found that we still didn't want to go home after six weeks that we decided long-term cruising was for us. There are a large number of problems – but, equally, many pleasures; it's a question of balancing one against the other to decide whether it's the life for you.

An idyllic lifestyle

Many aspects of the cruising life are quite idyllic – lazing in the sun, swimming in warm clear water, and anchoring in stunning surroundings. You can wander ashore, and climb a hill to take that ideal photo of your yacht nestling in a deserted cove, the palest blue water contrasting vividly with golden sands and green trees. As evening deepens into dusk in a perfect isolated anchorage, you sit in the cockpit with a glass of wine, listening to the cicadas churring and the waves breaking on the rocks at the entrance to the bay. If there are other yachts around, you can invite your fellow cruisers over for a drink and a yarn – there is no doubt that the social life is one of the great pleasures of cruising.

Or perhaps you feel like a little civilisation – a harbour surrounded by typical white-painted Mediterranean houses with terracotta roofs, over-hung with brilliantly coloured bougainvillaea, and artistically interspersed with palm trees. You can spend hours watching the comings and goings of other boats. In the evening you may wander ashore to enjoy the nightlife, or sample the delights of the local cuisine. Sometimes there will be ancient sites nearby, just waiting for a visit – a Roman amphitheatre, a fabulous palace, perhaps a flamenco-dancing show. Or maybe it is fiesta time and you can join in the merrymaking.

All these are just some of the many and varied pleasures of cruising – the 'plus side' as you might say. But what of the problems?

A rigorous lifestyle

Long-term cruising is a life of contrasts, and if the idyllic picture described above is one side of the coin, there is another, darker side also – the times when the seabed is

The superb Moorish palace, the Alhambra, in Grenada, southern Spain.

weedy and you cannot get the anchor to hold, though you haul it up and try again until your are completely exhausted; and the times when you anchor carefully just the right distance from everyone else, and some idiot anchors virtually on top of you just as it's getting dark. You may anchor in an east-facing bay with a forecast of NW3, only to be woken in the middle of the night by the yacht pitching and rolling to an easterly 5. Or you arrive in a marina in force 7, exhausted after a rough passage, to find it's siesta time so there's no one to guide you to a berth – and you daren't venture down the narrow gaps, since if there is nothing available you'll never get out again without disaster. Worst of all for us was the time when a sudden, vicious thunderstorm, in a previously peaceful anchorage, nearly put us on the rocks.

There are not many times in normal shoreside life when you are in actual fear of your life, or when your much-loved home is at sudden risk of destruction. A certain toughness is needed to be able to cope with such situations, but in the Mediterranean serious emergencies are rare, so for us the peaks far outweigh the troughs. Indeed, in a way, occasional problems enhance the enjoyment of the good times because of the contrast; they certainly add tremendous zest to one's memories.

A basic problem with live-aboard cruising is that mostly it implies short-handed cruising: and while this is great when things are going well, it can be quite a strain at times – which is why both partners should learn the necessary skills to be able to play a full part in handling the boat.

SAILING v FOREIGN TRAVEL – A WAY OF LIFE

In contrast with ocean cruising, a love of sailing *per se* is not essential in order to enjoy Mediterranean cruising – though obviously it's no good if you actively dislike it or are afraid of the sea. In fact, I myself find just 'going for a sail' rather boring, but as a means of getting somewhere it's quite different. When the sun is shining, the coastline beautiful, and you are dipping gently through the waves, the only sounds being the swishing of the water past the hull, and the cry of the seagulls – what could be a better way to travel? And it is the *travelling* that this life is all about. The real joy of Mediterranean cruising is having your own floating home: so you can wander where you like, explore interesting places to your heart's content, get away from the crowds, and find beautiful places to moor; in fact, a love of foreign travel is really more important than a love of sailing. So if that kind of life appeals and you have the necessary toughness to cope with the rigours of the life, it's then a question of whether you can also cope with being cooped up in the boat, away from your family and friends, for six months or so.

CRAMPED CONDITIONS

Even on a large yacht, living conditions are very confined on board, and this throws you into each other's company 24 hours a day – and for most people on land that's unheard of. Many find this impossible to cope with for long periods. Others find it's the cramped conditions themselves that get on their nerves – everything is awkward (and you lack many of the labour-saving devices you probably have at home). After a while, all this can lead to great frustration; and in marinas you tend to lack privacy from the outside world as well (you spend a lot of time in the cockpit, which may be rather too public for your liking).

Only experience will indicate whether you can cope with these problems. But it is also important to do what you can to alleviate them – choosing the right boat is critical here, as are the modifications you make. *Both* partners must be flexible and willing to compromise: it's vital for the success of the cruise for each to be sensitive to the needs of the other.

LEAVING FAMILY AND FRIENDS

Elderly parents can be a big tie, especially if you have no siblings. Leaving one's family is a big wrench for some people, though this can be alleviated by them coming out to join you. If this is important, then choose a suitable yacht. A related problem is leaving your friends behind. If you like a 'bosom-friend' to confide in every day, it may be quite a strain to embark on a roving life where the friends you make are likely to be met up with again only rarely. Probably the people who adapt best to this life are those whose best friend is in fact their partner. Emotional self-sufficiency as a couple is extremely important. (See Chapter 5).

KEEPING BUSY

Another problem is being bored, or homesick for your normal occupations. It is impossible to take with you more than a fraction of the books and activities you have at home; but you can replace them with other activities, which may be even more interesting. We certainly have no difficulty in keeping occupied – indeed, we generally run out of time. For a start, there are a large number of jobs that need doing (domestic, navigational, yacht maintenance, etc). Then there are the many pleasurable activities that are inherent in the cruising life: swimming, sailing, walking, cycling, reading, going on trips inland, chatting to other yachtsmen – not to mention just sitting and watching the world go by! In addition, there are your own particular hobbies. Obviously you will have to consider whether your special interests at home are 'transportable', or whether you can develop new, more adaptable, ones.

The art nouveau church of Sagrada Familia, Barcelona designed by Antonio Gaudi.

SEASICKNESS

Since we started Mediterranean cruising I have had progressively fewer problems for the following reasons:

- One is far less prone to seasickness when living aboard, because of getting used to the motion. This makes a huge difference – I don't even take pills now, except at the start of the season.
- There is more time available, so you have freedom to choose when to put to sea. Nowadays, if the forecast is poor we simply stay put until it improves; and if on getting out to sea we don't like it, we turn back.
- The entire cruise *can* be done without night passages. In addition, we've found that getting a few hours' sleep early and setting off in the small hours is much easier than spending the whole night at sea. Also the Mediterranean itself is often calmer at that time than during the day, since the wind tends to die at night.

ROUTES TO AND FROM THE MEDITERRANEAN

There are seven ways of getting your yacht to the Mediterranean, starting from northern Europe, though the first three are the most common ones:

1 The Atlantic route.
2 The main French canals.
3 The Canal-du-Midi route.
4 The Rhine/Danube route (dependent on the political situation in the Balkans).
5 By lorry.
6 Hiring a delivery skipper.
7 Buying in the Med (see Chapter 2).

If you have the yacht delivered (either by land or sea), the important points are:
● Get a recommendation for a suitable person or company.
● Check their qualifications and experience.
● Make absolutely sure that your insurance is in order for the delivery.

Because of the size limitations of the canals, it is essential to decide whether or not you wish to use them before buying your yacht. If your boat is too big, you will have no choice but to go there *and* back round the coast: and while going south that way is most enjoyable, returning against the Portuguese trades is not.

So, since both routes are very interesting, I would in general recommend going to the Med via the Atlantic and returning through the canals. I will briefly describe the alternative routes here in order to help you decide, but see Chapter 7 for further route details.

The Atlantic route

Many people consider this simply as a delivery trip – so many miles of ocean to cross before reaching their goal. This is a shame, because the route is most enjoyable, offering much beauty and interest, and some excellent, cheap cruising. But it does need a larger, well-found yacht and more experienced crew than for the canals. We took the whole of 1992 (five months) to reach south-east Spain in *Phœnician*, and wished we could have gone still more slowly. The route can be divided into four different sections:

The Biscay crossing The Biscay weather has a fearsome reputation, but in summer – for a modern, well-found yacht – I think it is undeserved. In our experience, in the sailing season the Biscay weather is no worse than that in the English Channel – in fact, usually better, and improving rapidly as you go south. The problem is the distance involved, which means that if you do hit bad weather, there's nowhere to hide – so you have to ride it out.

You can head straight from England to La Coruña (on the north-west tip of Spain, Map 1), but that is a minimum of 450 miles, and it's much easier to cross from France. However, even from north-west Brittany it is 325 miles – a minimum of two nights at sea. One *can* avoid the night passage by going right round Biscay, but this means calling at Arcachon (the entrance to which requires good weather and a fairly calm sea). Otherwise, you cannot reduce the long passage to much under 150 miles, say from Royan to Hendaye, which is on the Spanish border – but this is a great deal easier than going straight across. Either way, you have to avoid the firing range off Arcachon. Examples of possible routes are given in the table on page 10.

Reducing the single long passage clearly adds greatly to the total distance. However, west Brittany offers pleasant cruising, and

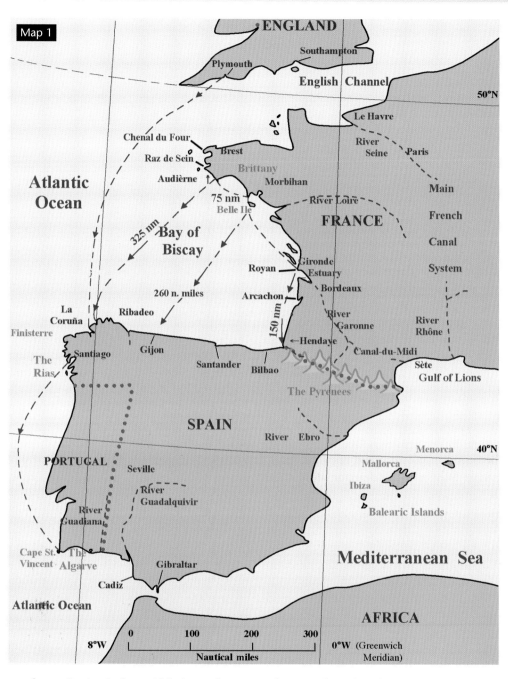

Map 1

ENGLAND

Southampton

Plymouth

English Channel

50°N

Le Havre

Chenal du Four

River
Seine   Paris

Raz de Sein   Brest

Brittany

Main

Audièrne   Morbihan

Atlantic
Ocean

75 nm
Belle Ile

River Loire

FRANCE

French

Canal

325 nm   Bay of
Biscay

Gironde
Royan   Estuary

System

260 n. miles   Arcachon

Bordeaux

La
Coruña   Ribadeo

Finisterre

River
Garonne

River
Rhône

150 nm

Gijon

Hendaye

Canal-du-Midi

The
Rias   Santiago

Santander   Bilbao

Sète

Gulf of Lions

The Pyrenees

SPAIN

River   Ebro

Menorca   40°N

PORTUGAL

Seville

Mallorca

Ibiza

River
Guadalquivir

Balearic Islands

River
Guadiana

Cape St.
Vincent   Algarve

Gibraltar

Mediterranean   Sea

Cadiz

Atlantic Ocean

AFRICA

0   100   200   300

8°W

0°W   (Greenwich
Meridian)

Nautical miles

northern Spain is beautiful (see photo page 113) – though lacking in yachting facilities.

The Rias of north-west Spain Few people seem to be aware of this delightful corner of Spain, though it forms one of the best cruising grounds we know. It's ideally placed for spending a couple of idyllic months on your way to the Mediterranean – yet most people go dashing past, determined to reach Gibraltar in record time.

Possible routes across Biscay

Route 1	Route 2	Route 3
From *Audièrne*	From *Audièrne*	From *Audièrne*
	75 miles to	215 miles to
	Belle Ile	*Royan*
325 miles *direct* to	Then 260 miles *direct* to	Then 150 miles *direct* to
	Gijon	*Hendaye*
	Then 140 miles to	Then 315 miles to
La Coruña	*La Coruña*	*La Coruña*
325 miles	**475 miles**	**680 miles**

Portugal This is a lovely country, but the west coast is rather inhospitable – less of a cruising ground than a route south. Winds in spring and summer are mostly from the north, and this tends to set up a continuous, south-flowing surface drift. Thus, normally, sailing south is easy; but heading north is an exhausting struggle.

The Portuguese Algarve and south-west Spain This coast offers far better cruising than west Portugal. There are some interesting rivers and lagoons to explore, new marinas to visit, and plenty of interesting trips ashore.

The French Canals

If you want to use the canals, you have two basic alternatives. The most usual is to cross the English Channel to Le Havre and head up the River Seine to Paris, thence through a multitude of branching canals, and finally down the River Rhône to the Mediterranean. This route can also be accessed from the canal systems of Belgium, the Netherlands and Germany.

The other alternative is a compromise, where you start the same way as for the Atlantic route, cruising down the Biscay coast, but at Royan you turn into the Gironde Estuary and reach the Mediterranean by the shorter overland passage diagonally across France via the Canal-du-Midi. Like the Atlantic route, the canals are so interesting that it would be a shame to miss them out: but there are a number of problems, especially for heavy yachts with weak crews.

Sections of all the canals are regularly closed in winter for routine maintenance; also, you should avoid the central canals of both routes in this season, since it's very cold, the canals can ice up, and there are few facilities open.

You will need to check the most recent 'maximum dimensions' – but note that the dimensions given are those of the *canal*: the boat itself must be smaller or otherwise you will get stuck! The Canal-du-Midi is the smallest, the maximum draught being 1.5 metres in 2002. The maximum air height was given as 3 metres, and this is due to one very low, arched bridge at Capestang. We actually measured this, and found that it was 3.2 metres at the very top of the slightly pointed arch, dropping to 3 metres at 1 metre out from the centre (thus giving 2 metres beam at 3 metres high); but it will vary with water-level.

The *very* low bridge at Capestang, Canal du Midi.

Maximum dimensions in the main canals vary, but some routes are much bigger than the Midi. A reliable engine is essential on all routes – and a powerful one if you'll be going *up* any rivers.

Take your time and, if appropriate, get friends to come and help. But don't be put off – the canals are beautiful; it is a fascinating experience, and one that you will never forget.

Conclusions

Both the Atlantic and the canal routes can be completed in only a few weeks if you are fit and strong, with a suitable boat and crew. However, both are far better taken slowly and savoured.

TIME-SCALE PLANNING

There are three different aspects:
1 An overall plan of where you want to go, and how long you want to take.
2 Organising your time between home and the Mediterranean.
3 Preparation time.

An overall plan
You need to decide:
- How much time you have available – a set number of years or as long as you like?
- How far you want to go – the western Med? The whole Med? Or to use the Med as a starting point for a more extended cruise?
- How fast you want to go. There are essentially three different modes of cruising:

Go-fast mode This is useful for getting from A to B really quickly. Get a strong crew, stock up thoroughly, wait for a good forecast, and then sail night and day until you get there. It's surprising how quickly you can eat up the miles this way (even averaging only 5 knots, you can do 100 miles in 20 hours); and if your route is along the coast, you can easily stop if conditions deteriorate.

Passage-making mode This is the normal cruising mode: when one is trying to get somewhere but not in any great hurry. We would aim to follow round the coast in day-trips, doing a passage of 30 to 50 miles every few days, with the rest of the time spent shopping, cleaning, preparing the navigation, exploring ashore, and (very important) relaxing. Your total estimated distance goes up quite a bit in this mode, and your actual logged mileage will be more still – possibly a quarter as much again as your estimate (depending on the care you take over the latter). So your 100 miles direct might become 160 miles estimated, and 200 miles actually logged, taking perhaps a fortnight; and this must be allowed for when planning.

In fact, though this is reasonably relaxed cruising for a month or two, trying to travel a long way in short hops becomes tiring. This is particularly so if you are covering new ground all the time, because of the extra work studying new pilot guides, the tension of constantly entering new harbours, and the difficulty of finding shops, etc in strange places – especially in new countries. Everything is *far* more relaxed when you are cruising an area you know. So, even though we don't like night passages, if we've got a long way to go in one season we've found it's really better to intersperse this mode with some longer trips followed by a few weeks of *real* relaxation. This bring us on to:

Pottering mode This is what you came for! You've reached your attractive cruising ground; you've all the time in the world; and you just wander, as slowly as you like. In this mode, a 100 miles could take forever.

Having considered the above points, you must formulate a tentative cruise plan. The following is what we and various friends have done:

A short sharp shock One young couple we know saved up some money, and took six months off work. They dashed south through the main canals in their small yacht (three weeks), worked their way down the Spanish coast until they could reach the Balearics in a day-hop (three weeks), spent the summer cruising the islands (three months), and then returned the same way (six weeks). They thoroughly enjoyed themselves – but you would have to be young to think it was worth the hassle of doing it so quickly.

Another friend (in a big, powerful yacht) pounded down the Atlantic coast and across to the eastern Med one year; he cruised there the second year; and returned home the same way the third. Again, an awfully long way to go for such a short time.

There and back slowly This is what most of our friends are doing. We originally planned a five-year cruise – to Turkey and back. Five years turned out to be far too short – we took six, and still we didn't have time to get more than a quick taste of the eastern Mediterranean. We spent all the winters at home except the last:

1992 Round the Atlantic coast to southeast Spain, including a long Channel crossing and a partial Biscay crossing (with a friend to help), and a month relaxing in the Rias. This was 2100 miles logged in five months: all new and wildly exciting.

1993 After our long cruise the previous year, we wanted to relax, so we spent the spring and summer in the Balearics and laid up in the south of France: 1250 miles logged in five months, with only one night passage. It was a very pleasant, quiet year.

1994 From the south of France to Turkey, via Corsica, Italy and Greece – 2150 miles logged in five months. This was too far and too fast, all short hops, all new ground, very hot weather, three new languages and a duff echo sounder – we ended up nervous wrecks!

1995 This was another relaxed cruise exploring south-west Turkey and back to western Greece. Only 1000 miles logged in four months, a lot of it over ground covered the previous year.

1996 A few weeks spent relaxing in Greece, then a hard slog coast-hopping to Sicily where we picked up friends to help with the two 200-mile passages to the Balearics. Then ten relaxed weeks were spent there, before spending the winter on board in south-east Spain: 1750 miles logged in five months – an excellent mixture.

1997 A hard slog up to the south of France, through the Canal-du-Midi, coast-hopping up north Biscay, across the Channel, and home – 1550 miles logged in four and a half months. The canals were far harder than we'd anticipated, but left us with some wonderful memories.

In total we logged 10,000 miles in the six years, with ten nights and six half-nights at sea – averaging 1700 miles per five-month season, or 80 miles logged per week (60 estimated), with some long hauls and pottering, but mostly passage-making.

However, we'd have enjoyed it even more had we done much more pottering, and not tried to go so far, so fast. The year

1994 was the real killer, where we were on the move more days than we stayed put, and I'm sure that was a large part of the problem. Now, each year we choose one or more good cruising grounds where we spend months pottering, with the in-between bits covered fast; this is far better.

So our second cruise has been as follows:

1998 A quicker version of 1992 (July to October), but wintering aboard in southeast Spain: hard going, but very enjoyable (2195 miles logged).

1999 Spring cruise to the Balearics and back; home for July and August, then wintered aboard: a very pleasant, quiet year (1280 miles logged)

2000 Relaxed spring cruise in the Balearics. We then left *Phæacian* ashore in Menorca while we flew home for July and August, sailed to Tunisia in September (500 miles, by ourselves, including two long passages), wintered aboard (Monastir), but went home for a month at Christmas. All in all, an excellent year (1310 miles logged).

2001 Sailed to Malta (two night passages) in March and spent a month there, then a hard month's slog to Croatia (600 miles, mostly very long day trips) and spent a wonderful summer cruising there. We left *Phæacian* there and flew home in September for Christmas. Another excellent year (1870 miles logged).

There but not back again Coming down the Atlantic coast in 1992, we made lasting friends with two couples who favoured this option. One decided that the Balearics was for them, and that they would keep their yacht there permanently, coming down for a few months at a time. The others shot straight across to Turkey in 1993, and have remained in the eastern Mediterranean ever since.

The wife of one German we met was still working as a teacher, so they spent her six-week summer holiday hard-sailing down to Tunisia, so that they could keep the boat there permanently.

The Med as a starting point Finally, friends we made on the way down with *Phæacian* went much faster than us and cruised the Balearics that same autumn, over-wintered in Tunisia, cruised the rest of the western Mediterranean basin the following summer, then headed across the Atlantic in the autumn.

It can be seen from this brief survey that the possibilities are endless; it is merely a question of finding a plan that suits your tastes. You probably won't stick to it anyway, but you do need to build some kind of new structure into your lives now that you are forsaking so much that you had built up in the past.

Organising your time

You have to decide:
- How much time you wish to spend in the Mediterranean each year.
- Which part of the year you want to spend in each place.
- Whether you will both spend the same amount of time on the yacht.
- How you intend to travel back and forth.

How many months in the Med? Some people like to have their yacht based in the Mediterranean and to go out there for a short holiday once or twice a year; others prefer two or three months at a time. To spend six months in each place is a common arrangement; or you could spend most of your time on the yacht and go home for 'holidays' (as we tend to do now). Or, alternatively, you could go for

real live-aboard cruising and not go home at all. Lastly, you could do something different each year.

Which part of the year in the Med? Most people come to the Mediterranean intending to cruise there during the summer, then lay the yacht up (and go home) for the winter – because that is the pattern they're used to. But it is not necessarily the best plan for the Med, since in July and August temperatures are far too hot, everywhere is terribly crowded, and marinas are at their most expensive.

We think spring is by far the best time to cruise the Mediterranean, though other people prefer the autumn (see Cruising weather, in Chapter 8); and although the winter weather in some parts of the Med is poor, elsewhere (particularly in the south) it's glorious, being *far* drier and sunnier than England – and who wants to spend the winter in the cold, damp, fog and snow? So what are your options?

One short cruise If you intend to spend only a few months cruising per year, then either late spring and early summer, or perhaps the autumn are best.

Five or six months on board If you want to divide your year half and half, then I suggest two options:
- Follow the common pattern – come out in the spring, spend the summer cruising, and go home in the autumn.
- Alternatively, lay up each year when it gets too hot, go home for the summer, spend Christmas at home with your family, and fly to the Med in January. Then spend some time in your chosen marina, enjoying the social life, before working your way towards this year's 'pottering ground'. The winter weather

in many parts of the Mediterranean is fine for marina-hopping so long as you keep an ear tuned to the forecasts.

Two short cruises Some people avoid the summer heat by having a spring cruise *and* an autumn cruise. We don't do this because it means doubling up on both fitting out and laying up, as well as on travelling (the aspects of this life we find most tiresome) – not to mention doubling travelling costs. But this method is better if you want more frequent contact with home.

Live aboard for most of the year With this option you will be going home for 'holidays' and there are two different times you are likely to want to do this:

- One is mid-summer to avoid the Mediterranean heat and crowds. Find somewhere cheap and secure to lay up for the hottest weather, and fly back home to sort things out, shop, and see the family; return to the yacht in the autumn, and wander on to your chosen over-wintering spot if you aren't already there. There are marinas all over the Mediterranean where yachtsmen congregate for the winter, and the social life is terrific. Then set off on a spring cruise whenever you like. You may want to have the family out to stay for the festive season. If there isn't room on the yacht to accommodate them, hotels and flats are fairly cheap in winter.
- Alternatively, you may want to spend Christmas at home with the family. So do your laying up for a month or two then, and cruise all summer. The disadvantage is that you catch the worst of the weather in both places.

Not to go home at all This is by far the cheapest option.

Will you both spend the same amount of time aboard? If you have *very* different views on how much time you want to spend in the Mediterranean, the only answer may be to spend different amounts of time there. We know a number of men who cruise by themselves most of the time, with their wives or partners joining ship just occasionally.

Travelling back and forth to the boat The norm is to fly, but train or coach are alternatives. Consider driving to the yacht to spend a few weeks during your first winter to bring down a car-load of gear, do a little maintenance work, and get away from the bad weather in England. Some people keep their car in the Med permanently, so that they have it with them when needed (using public transport to fetch it from place to place). They can then drive home and back in it too.

Preparation time
Planning Read all you can about live-abroad cruising and the Mediterranean. As you read, either make careful notes, or else mark the more important passages in the book so that you can find them again – it's most frustrating if you can't. We found *Ocean Cruising on a Budget* exceptionally helpful; *Mediterranean Cruising Handbook* is also excellent. There are some very useful suggestions in the appendices of *Brighton to the Med*, and also the last few chapters of *Leisurely Route to the Med*. These last two books also give you a good picture of the voyage to the Mediterranean via the Atlantic coast. (see Appendix 2 for full details of these books). Incidentally, *Leisurely Route to the Med* is of particular relevance to vegetarians.

It can also be helpful to go on some package holidays in the Mediterranean to enable you to visit marinas, talk to live-abroad yachtsmen, get ideas and to photograph equipment.

Choosing and buying your yacht (see Chapter 2) You probably need to allow a year for choosing and buying your new floating home, starting from the time you first start thinking and looking.

Fitting out your yacht (see Chapters 3 and 4) Allow plenty of time for fitting out – we took 18 months the first time. It's very time-consuming because:

- All work on boats is fiddly and takes twice as long as you expect – and it's even worse if you are getting things done by other people.
- Many complex modifications are needed (photo page 66).
- While some of these modifications will be obvious from the start, others won't become apparent until you've lived on board for a while. You will then need time to get on with the new work, try the boat out again to see how they've worked, and so on.
- Everything has to be done by a set date. Normally you make modifications over the years, but it's different when setting off on a long voyage. It's tempting to consider getting away sooner, and leaving part of the work for after you've set sail, but I don't recommend it for a number of reasons. Doing most work on a yacht involves disrupting part of it, which makes living aboard terribly difficult. Also there simply isn't time when you're always on the move. Either stay in one place for weeks at a time, or leave it until the following winter – and if you're going home for the winter, then forget it (it's difficult enough to cope with ordinary maintenance then). You will find

that getting things done and bought is infinitely more difficult abroad – as a visitor and a foreigner, you have grave handicaps such as: lack of knowledge of shops and services; inadequate tools and workshop facilities; lack of transport; and language difficulties.

So my advice is to finish everything you possibly can before you leave, especially anything that has to be done by someone else. If you do leave work for after you set off, make sure they are jobs that are really suited to being done under these conditions; and try at least to take the materials with you.

Shopping You will have a vast amount of shopping to do, and this tends to be a frustrating and time-consuming exercise. So again, don't try to rush it.

As time goes on and you approach your leaving date, the days will be more and more busy, and life becomes more of a mad panic than ever. So get the important things done as soon as possible, while life is still relatively calm.

SELL UP OR NOT?

Are you going to sell your property and leave for an extended voyage with few, if any, return trips? Or do you wish to retain a home base? You have four options:

Sell up and sail

This is the usual choice for people who've tried live-aboard cruising, know they like it, and want to go ocean cruising for an extended period of time without the worry and expense of a property left behind. It is a drastic step: we felt it would turn us into rootless wanderers over the face of the earth, which wasn't what we wanted at all. It is not something I'd recommend to people going long-term cruising for the first time.

Unfortunately, if your finances are limited, selling your home and investing the capital so that you can live off the income may be the only way you can afford to go cruising; but if this is the case, think about it very carefully. If you do sell up, you will of course have nowhere to live on visits home! There is also the question of being able to afford to buy a suitable property when you return as property prices have been steadily rising in recent years.

Letting your property

Keeping your home and letting it is a much less drastic step, and may be the better option financially. It also means you may have a loft in which to store possessions you want to keep. It is the usual choice for people who don't want to sell, but who need to augment their income. However, there are disadvantages:

- Short-term lets being far more difficult to arrange, you may well be unable to use the house yourselves on trips home.
- It's a great deal of hassle (unless you have an excellent agent – who then pockets some of your profits).
- In our experience, it leaves the house in a shambles. If your reason for not wanting to sell was that you have a lovely home – well, it probably won't be so lovely when you next see it!

However, the relative profitability, and the type of tenants you are likely to get, vary a lot with the area you live in, and many people seem to let more successfully than our family has done.

Leaving the house empty

We had a house we loved, and no desire either to sell or let it; and our original plan was to cruise in summer and return for the winters – so we really had no choice but to leave the house empty. (See Chapter 5.) This involved organising a gardener, a caretaker and a burglar alarm; but after the initial hassle of setting it up, it worked very well. It's by far the most expensive option, because you have all the costs of running your home, car, etc, which simply eat money, plus your costs of living in the Mediterranean.

Buying a pied-à-terre

However, there is a fourth, compromise option: sell your home and buy a small flat in an attractive place. This option has many advantages. It gives you somewhere pleasant to live during your periods home; it greatly reduces your running costs; it should give you some capital to invest (and thus increase your income); and it reduces the organisational difficulties of leaving a house – no need for a gardener, less work for a caretaker, probably no need to heat it in winter, etc.

EXPERIENCE AND QUALIFICATIONS

Only two formal qualifications are necessary for cruising the Mediterranean (or canals) – an operator's licence for your radio transmitter, and a qualification in boat handling. But what is far more important than formal qualifications is the training and experience that should go with them.

Boat handling

It is advisable for at least one of you to get the International Certificate of Competence

(ICC), since this is the qualification that is understood and accepted abroad – and it's fairly easy to obtain from the RYA (address in Appendix 3). A Yachtmaster's Certificate (though a much higher qualification) is no substitute. However, if you have passed Day Skipper practical or Yachtmaster, the RYA will issue the ICC without requiring you to undergo any further testing. The Certificate is issued free to members, but they charge for non-members. For using the canals you need to get the CEVNI endorsement on your ICC, which requires an additional short written test.

We see many yachts where a big strong man manoeuvres the boat, while a frail female struggles with the heavy work such as anchoring. This seems crazy to us! I think the problem is that women often lack the experience to handle the yacht in confined waters, and for some reason nothing is done to correct this – probably because boat handling is such fun that the man doesn't want to give it up (and his partner, not realising what she's missing, hasn't the confidence to insist). But it often makes sense to do it the other way round – after all, on average, men are considerably stronger than women.

In any case, regardless of who *generally* does the manoeuvring, when setting off on a project like this, it's essential that both partners should be *able* to do it, since in an emergency each one must be able to cope alone. Lack of experience can only be overcome by hands-on practice – a week's practical course in boat handling can be great fun, and is an excellent start.

Navigation

The same applies to navigation. Wives – do not think that because your husband is an experienced sailor you can just tag along and do the cooking. If you're going off on two-handed, live-aboard cruising

with him, you must be able to take over in an emergency – just imagine if he became ill at sea and you didn't know how to get the yacht back to port!

For an enterprise like this, we feel that *both* partners should be moderately competent; and if this is not the case, then the planning stage should be utilised for extending the experience of either partner in whatever directions that are deemed necessary. The basics are not that difficult. An evening class is an excellent way of learning the theoretical side of navigation (remember, they start in September), while the following summer should be put to good use trying it all out.

Engine and electrics

Ideally, somebody on board should be competent in these two vital areas. Engines need constant Tender Loving Care if they are to perform at their best (or, indeed, continue working at all) in the antagonistic marine environment. Electrics are always potential trouble spots for the same reason, and are likely to need frequent repairs or modifications. If necessary, go on courses to improve your understanding of these subjects – it will be time very well spent. The RYA run a Diesel Engine Course; and I believe Volvo and such companies run courses on their engines. Nigel Calder's book entitled *Boatowner's Mechanical and Electrical Manual* (Adlard Coles Nautical) is worth studying in depth and having on board as a reference.

Yacht maintenance

Most yachtsmen do much of their own maintenance, but this becomes much more important when abroad, where getting things done by other people is so much more difficult.

First aid

While you are never that far from a doctor in the Mediterranean, this is not the same as having an ambulance at the other end of an easy 999 call. You should both be competent not only to deal with everyday cuts and illnesses, but also to give immediate treatment in cases of more serious accidents and emergencies. At sea there is a constant danger of some sort of injury; and also, as we grow older, there is a growing risk of illness – cardiac for example. Remember, it could be your partner who needs help, and you, the only person available to give it. So you should *both* go on a first aid course – in any case, they're rather fun. The RYA can advise on specialised courses for yachtsmen.

Learn to cope with any health problems that afflict your partner: eg massaging a bad back, treating a diabetic attack if they become ill, or giving any necessary injections. The same applies during the cruise when you have guests – it's essential to check before you set sail whether they have any life-threatening condition, and to make sure that, *in extremis*, you will know how to treat them.

Radio transmitters

Except in an emergency, you should not use a VHF radio without possessing a Certificate of Competence. The courses are not difficult, so it's worth both of you going on one to avoid the skipper having to leave the helm at crucial moments in order to use the radio. Again, ask the RYA. You'll need a higher qualification if you want to use a marine-band SSB transmitter.

Languages

Away from tourist resorts, it's rare to find anyone who speaks much English, so it's tremendously useful to learn a little bit of the languages of the countries you will be visiting. Apart from anything else, it really pleases the people you meet, so they go out of their way to be helpful. (See Chapter 9 on the best way to do this.) Although language evening classes often tend to concentrate on the wrong things, they do get you used to the language and its pronunciation.

COSTS

To ask 'How much does it cost to go cruising in the Mediterranean?' is as meaningless a question as 'How much does it cost to live in England?' The answer to both is that it totally depends on your lifestyle. However, certain advice/information can be given.

Overall costs

Keeping a property in the UK and living on a boat in the Med costs no more than keeping a boat in the UK and living at home; in fact, often it costs less. So if you are managing on your retirement pension to run a yacht in in the UK, you should have no problems living on it in the Med. However, if you haven't yet got your own boat, or if your income is going to be much reduced, then you are going to have to think carefully – as indeed anyone does when approaching retirement. There are a number of ways of reducing costs:

- Generally restrict your style of living (avoid marinas, restaurants, using the phone, etc).
- Have a smaller yacht. The more you have to scrimp and save, though, and the smaller and more inconvenient your floating home, the more uncomfortable your life will be and the greater the chances of the project failing. However,

OUR EXPENDITURE:
spending six months at home and six on the yacht

Yacht expenses (annual – averaged over 6 years)

Harbour dues (summer): £37 per week x 26 weeks	=	£962
Yacht expenses (summer) eg chandlery, gas, diesel:		
£30 x 26	=	£780
Insurance	=	£600
Lay-up	=	£700
Equipment brought from home each spring		
(ours and the yacht's)	=	£2000
	Total =	**£5042**

Our expenses on the yacht (summer – averaged over 6 years)

Weekly: Food £50 + Restaurants £25 + Other £25		
= £100/week, x 26 weeks	=	£2600
Photography	=	£300
	Total =	**£2900**

Our fares home (averaged over 6 years)

Flights (etc) home and back for two people	=	£450
	Total =	**£450**

House expenses (whole year)

Insurance £530 + Council Tax £850 + Water £500		
+ TV licence £85	=	£1965
Electricity £300 + Phone £200 + Gas £250	=	£750
Burglar alarm (maintenance and monitoring)	=	£170
Gardener £625 + Cleaner/caretaker £625	=	£1250
Repairs/maintenance/new equipment (guestimate)	=	£2000
	Total =	**£6135**

if you are both keen enough, there should be no problem. We know many couples who really enjoy life in yachts that are well under 10 metres.

- Sell up and live permanently on the yacht. By doing this, and not going home at all, you could probably halve the yearly expenditure (see below).
- The best answer, if it would generate sufficient savings, would be the com-

promise of selling your property and buying a small pied-à-terre.

- Stay longer in the Mediterranean – we spend far more money when at home.
- Read Anne Hammick's *Ocean Cruising on a Budget* (Adlard Coles Nautical).
- If you have a skill that is readily saleable to other yachtsmen (eg sewing, carpentry, electrics, etc), you could earn some money during winters on board.

Car expenses (annual)

Insurance £250 Tax £150 Service/repairs £200	=	£600
Petrol (say, £50 a month while home + mini-holiday)	=	£400
Replacement (say, £6000 every 6 years = £1000 annually); if you have an older car, replacement will be less and repairs more.	=	£1000
	Total =	**£2000**

Our expenses at home (winter – guestimate)
Needed wherever we are:

Weekly: Food £60 + Restaurants £10 + Alcohol £27 + Other £33 = £130/week x 26 weeks	=	£3380
Our clothes (many from charity shops)	=	£300
Christmas £70 + Christmas & birthday presents £200	=	£270
Medicines	=	£100
	Total =	**£4050**

Not needed if we spend the whole year on the yacht:

Dinner parties £200 + dinner dances £130	=	£330
Subscriptions £320 + Charities £70	=	£390
Books £100 + Garden £150	=	£250
Mini-holiday (eg to France for wine; or driving down to work on yacht; or driving around visiting friends)	=	£500
Frittered away (probably underestimate!)	=	£300
	Total =	**£1770**

Overall total	=	**£22 347**

Keeping records

While still in the early planning stage, keep very careful records of a year's expenditure at home. For comparative purposes, I give in the table above a list of our annual expenditure (totalling £22,347). Compare your home expenditure with ours; then your cruising expenditure will probably differ from ours in about the same proportion.

Selling up

If we sold up and never went home, the equivalent total expenditure might be: yacht expenses (£5042), our summer expenses (£2900), plus our necessary winter expenses (£4050), totalling only £11,992 – approximately half the previous total.

COMPARATIVE COSTS IN DIFFERENT AREAS

Note: Highest and lowest figures in each category are shown in bold	No of weeks	Average expenditure per week for the two of us			Average cost of
		Overall total	Harbour dues	Food	Marina berths used
W Italy, Sicily, Sardinia (summer 1994/spring 1996)	5	**£250**	**£88.50**	£52.50	£23 (other typically £40
Med France (autumn 1993, spring 1994/1997)	9½	£247	£79	£60	£16
Canal-du-Midi (summer 1997)	6	£192	£21.50	£61	**£5.50**
Med mainland Spain (autumn 1992/1996, spring 1993/1997)	14	£184.50	£56.50	£46	£10
Balearics (summer 1993 & 1996)	23	£162	£29	£56.50	£20
Turkey (autumn 1994 & spring 1995)	10	£162	£43	**£32**	£17
Corsica/Madalena (June 1994)	4	£155	£32	**£67**	£20.50
Atlantic coast (summer 1992 summer 1998)	15	£146 £172	£24 £40	£41	£9.75
Boot of Italy (summer 1994 & spring 1996)	4	£142	£24.50	£47.50	£11.50
Greece (summer 1994/1995 & spring 1996)	20	**£126**	**£6**	£55	N/A
Overall averages	110½	**£171.50**	**£37.50**	£51	**£13.50**

Costs in different cruising grounds

The Mediterranean is considerably more expensive than many parts of the world – you have to pay for its convenience, safety and popularity. However, there is great variation even within the Med, so for comparative purposes I give figures of our weekly on-board expenditure in the different areas we've cruised in the table above.

For each area I give first our *total* weekly expenditure on board for the two of us and the yacht – all our normal day-to-day costs. In my accounts, this total is divided into seven different sub-categories. Of these, however, only harbour dues and food shopping vary noticeably according to area, so these are the only two I include here.

Average cost of	Comments
Meal ashore for the two of us	
£27.50 (restaurant) £16.50 (pizzeria)	Marinas can be exorbitant, so to avoid them we anchored in places we regretted! Therefore costs here are deceptively low. Pizzerias are much cheaper than restaurants.
£21	Few anchorages, so mostly marinas.
£23.50	Harbour dues figure includes the cost of the licence. Mast transport excluded.
£18	Few anchorages, but cheap marinas in south (average £10, Costa del Sol), getting gradually dearer as you go north (£26, Costa Brava).
£18 (1993) £22 (1996)	Expensive marinas but plenty of anchorages, even if only a few offer total shelter.
£12.50 (very variable)	Lots of super anchorages (though we used marinas a lot). Food prices subsidised.
£21.50	Plenty of anchorages (especially in Madalena archipelago in the south). Some marinas.
£16.50	Super anchorages in north-west Spain, but found recently that an increasing number of marinas in Portugal make it difficult to get a free night there.
As for western Italy	Few harbours on 'The Boot', but costs were bumped up by the amount of diesel used (since one mostly had to use the engine to reach the next harbour before dark).
£13.50	Very cheap cruising because very few marinas, but thousands of anchorages.
£18.50	

Harbour dues vary in three different ways:

- Typical price per night.
- How much you are obliged to use harbours because of a lack of anchorages.
- How much one chooses to use such harbours.

The weekly harbour dues figure depends on all three factors. So I give as well, the average nightly amount we paid per marina (for an 11.5-metre yacht).

The final figure is the average price we paid for a meal for two in a restaurant. We normally choose a not-too-expensive restaurant, and have the cheapest meal we like the sound of – with no extras other than a bottle of the house wine.

2
Choosing and Buying a Yacht

Before you can think about what type of yacht to buy, it is essential to decide on the maximum limits of your planned cruise. Are you going down to the Med via the canals and thereafter rationing yourselves to small day-hops? Or are you intending to cross Biscay and do some of the longer trips in the Med? Or will your Med cruise be the start of more extensive ocean cruising? If the latter is the case, you'll need a different type of yacht for this than the type most suitable for Mediterranean cruising – and you could manage with something different again if the plan is to stick to inshore waters only. Also, you need a much bigger, more comfortable yacht if you intend to live aboard most of the time as opposed to spending just short holidays on board.

This chapter should be read in conjunction with Chapter 3 (Modifying Your Yacht), because in choosing your yacht you need to check whether the required alterations are feasible.

TYPE OF YACHT

Motor versus sail
From a safety point of view, never restrict yourself to only one form of motive power

– even if you choose a motorboat, it should have two engines (preferably with independent fuel supplies).

Sails only I would not recommend cruising the Mediterranean in a boat without an engine, as there are far too many places where you are obliged to use marinas.

Sailing boats with auxiliary engines When passage-making in the Mediterranean, you usually need the help of the engine to keep up sufficient speed, because frequently there is not enough wind. However, it's wonderful to be able to sail rather than motor whenever the wind is co-operative; and when in 'pottering mode' and there's time to slow down, you really reap the benefits of a sailing boat. Conversely, there will be many times when your engine becomes the most important piece of equipment on board – such as when crashing to windward trying to get into port ahead of a gale – so you certainly need a powerful and reliable one.

Motorsailers The concept of a motorsailer (engine as primary power, and sails auxiliary) is OK, but you need to choose carefully. They won't sail well, and may be chunky with a lot of windage, but they are often very roomy and offer the chance of at least some sailing.

Motor yachts These range from traditional displacement hulls, through semi-displacement and deep-V, to planing hulls. Each of the two main types has advantages and disadvantages.

Planing hulls

- These are very fast in flat seas, so your daylight range may be extended by a factor of three or more compared with that on a sailing yacht. However, going at such a speed is very tiring. These boats are not able to use their speed in rougher conditions and tend to slam uncomfortably into waves – and some are even unsafe in heavy seas.
- They use a vast amount of fuel, which makes them extremely expensive to run.
- They will probably have less draught (yet greater interior volume) than displacement-hulled yachts of a comparable size.
- They tend to be very high out of the water. Thus:
  - they have a vast amount of windage, which reduces manoevrability and makes them difficult at anchor; indeed, we've noticed that such boats rarely spend the night in anchorages;
  - their sides and bows are usually too high to get ashore from easily;
  - they frequently lack good sidedecks – needed when walking forward to anchor or moor;
  - there are often ladders to upper decks, and these could be death-traps in rough seas (so make sure the yacht can be navigated from a safe place);
  - they may well have both the advantages and disadvantages of deck saloons (see pages 29 and 30);

CHARACTERISTICS OF MOTORBOATS

- Simplicity (lack of masts, etc) – hence less heavy work involved.
- They have the advantage of speed, but fuel is expensive.
- Motorboats tend to cost more than sailing boats of a similar size, but have less stowage space (probably because so much room is used up on engines and extra diesel tankage).
- Having more electric power, motorboats (and indeed, very large sailing yachts) tend to have a vast arrange of 'electrical goodies', such as deepfreeze, electric windlass, hydraulic passerelle, etc. But though these are wonderful while they work, the more complex the electrics are, the more likely they are not to work – and then you have a big problem unless you are an expert.
- Also motor yachts often have many luxuries requiring mains power, so when not in a marina you may have to run a generator for much of the time.
- Powerful engines will take much more maintenance than smaller ones (and you will probably have two of them to maintain), but you may well have easier access to the engines than on a sailing yacht.
- Finally, twin engines give good manoeuvrability.

CHARACTERISTICS OF SAILING BOATS

- No noise, smell, smoke or vibration.
- Flexibility of use (power versus sail).
- When sailing (and even motorsailing to some extent), the boat moves more gently – in harmony with the water, as opposed to crashing through it.
- Cheapness (the wind is free).
- Sailing is more fun than motoring at the same speed.

– they may be unable to use the canals;

– you will get a better view in marinas if surrounded by sailing yachts – but you may well be placed among even higher 'gin palaces'!

Displacement hulls

Such motor yachts are much more of a compromise:

- They are less fun than a sailing boat and more expensive to run; on the other hand, they will probably be quite a lot faster.
- They are considerably slower than the planing type, but the hulls tend to be more seaworthy, they may be more comfortable at sea, and they are much less expensive to run.
- They probably won't suffer from the above-mentioned disadvantages of height.

Berthing

In the Mediterranean you must choose between berthing stern-to-the-quay (front and back covers) or bow-to (photo opposite). Stern-to is often more convenient for access aboard, but it is a *far* more difficult manoeuvre. Unless the yacht turns on a sixpence in reverse, it's often impossible if there's any wind – we're constantly seeing yachts crashing into everything in sight trying to do it.

Also, you can't nose your way into a narrow gap if you go in blunt-end first; it can be dangerous for the rudder if there is rubble at the foot of the quay; and it leaves the cockpit very open to the interested gaze of passers-by. So I recommend buying a yacht that is suitable for bow-to berthing. (Put the yacht's name clearly at the chosen end, so marina staff can read it from ashore.)

Access on board

The shape of the fore-end is very important if you are intending to berth bow-to, since you have to climb over the pulpit to get ashore. Many pulpits are utterly impossible – they overhang the stem so that you have nothing to stand on outboard and ahead of them. If so, make sure that an adequate modification will be possible.

Equally important is the shape of the stern. We fitted a sugar-scoop on to *Phœnician* (photo page 30), and were so pleased with it that we vowed never again to have a yacht without one. The advantages were as follows:

Phœacian moored bow-to in a marina. From left to right: Stern mooring line; Air-Marine wind generator on tall pole; the lazy-line hanging down (when you are approaching a quay, this indicates that stern moorings have been laid so you won't have to use your stern anchor); solar panels above bimini; side, corner and front screens; large balloon fender (really useful); wind scoop.

- Its main use is for bathing, and this is supremely important in the Mediterranean where most people swim so much. Without a bathing platform, climbing back on board from the water is extremely difficult.
- It's easier to board from the dinghy, via a platform.
- It could save lives in a man-overboard situation.
- It's a good place to have a shower.
- It improved *Phœnician*'s looks.
- It increased her waterline length and

reduced turbulence, both of which increase speed.

If the yacht you are considering buying does not have a bathing platform, then think very carefully about whether it will be feasible to fit one (photo overleaf), with a permanent ladder up the transom and a rigid folding ladder down to the water. Look at the angle of the transom – if this overhangs it's very difficult to climb up any ladder mounted on it (see photo page 107).

This attractive bathing platform has a bar to hang on to when climbing out of the water. The ladder is a good length, with comfortable teak treads; a bar under the platform holds it at the correct angle. However, it should be bent to stow closer to the transom.

Height

- The higher your bow, the more difficult it becomes to climb up on to it from a low quay. Thus larger boats almost always have to berth stern-to, despite the problems.
- High windage (especially forward) can cause many problems, as we found with *Phœnician*:
  - such yachts fly around badly at anchor;
  - they have much more difficulty manoeuvring in marinas;
  - in the eastern Mediterranean, one anchors a lot with a long line ashore (photo page 153), which often means the wind is on the beam. This puts great strain on the anchor, which tends to drag under such circumstances (photo page 169).

Length As the size of your boat increases, finding and getting in and out of marina berths becomes progressively more difficult – and marinas become *very* much more expensive, especially on the change from under to over an even number of metres.

Draught Although shallow draught enables you to creep slightly deeper into shelter when anchoring, the difference is often minimal since mostly the bottom shelves fairly steeply. All the advantage really lies with a reasonably deep-keeled yacht, whose sailing performance is so much better, particularly upwind – you make much less leeway even when motor-

Size of yacht

For ocean cruising, in many ways the bigger the yacht the better. However, Mediterranean cruising is quite different. You'll be spending far more time at rest than at sea, and you will be going in and out of harbour every few days, which makes manoeuvrability extremely important. You won't be going far enough from land to require a yacht that must be able to ride out storms for days at a time (especially if you avoid the long passage straight across Biscay). All things are a balance of probabilities, but if you take good heed of the forecasts you are unlikely to encounter a severe storm when at sea during a cruise in the Med – and if you do, you will probably be able to find a sheltered harbour fairly quickly.

Most people can't quite afford the size of boat they would like, so the advantages of size are only too obvious. The *disadvantages* are far less apparent but need careful consideration:

sailing. However, I wouldn't want a draught that would stop me using the main French canals.

Surface area This goes up by the square of the length, so if you increase the length 1½ times, you increase the surface area by a factor of $\frac{3}{2} \times \frac{3}{2} = \frac{9}{4}$. So you more than double the area you have to clean, varnish and antifoul. The sail area also doubles and therefore the weight of wind in the sails, and the strength needed to control them, etc.

Volume/weight These go up by the cube: thus if you increase length by 1½ times, you multiply volume and weight by over 3 ($\frac{27}{8}$). This is an advantage regarding space, but the weight of the boat, sails and gear will also go up very considerably. So you'll need much more strength to fend off and you'll find that lifting everything will be *far* harder. You'll need a heavier anchor and chain, and you won't be able to raise them without an electric windlass (and these are notoriously unreliable).

For an ageing couple, these are factors that become more and more important – even if you have the strength now, you may not in a few years' time. So, think carefully about the size of your boat, and don't assume that for Mediterranean cruising the largest you can afford is *necessarily* the best.

Style of yacht
While old-fashioned yachts are often pretty, they don't make good Mediterranean cruisers. Modern yachts usually have much greater beam, which makes them roomier. Old-style yachts are likely to be much more work, since they usually contain a lot of wood. Gaff-rig means heavy work hauling up the gaff, and bowsprits are a real pain in marinas.

Clipper-style yachts tend to have an uncomfortable motion because the short waterline length makes them pitch more. Finally, most of these boats give very difficult access – both from the water and when end-on to a quay.

Regarding deck saloons, you pay for the view from the saloon – partly with higher windage and partly because they are hotter.

Twin forestays are common on ocean cruisers, but they aren't really necessary for the Med since you won't be doing long periods of downwind sailing. However, cutter-rig has the advantage that you can have two different sizes of foresail – a jib will be a much better shape than a rolled genoa; and if it is hanked on, you have a ready-made stay for the storm jib.

Ketch-rig adds complexity, but offers the advantage of being able to hoist a mizzen at anchor in order to hold the boat steadier to the wind. Catamarans don't heel, but tend to slam into waves.

Hull material
Books on ocean cruising often recommend steel yachts, because they are stronger and easier to repair in out-of-the-way places. However, neither factor applies to Mediterranean cruising. Charts and pilot guides are good, so you are unlikely to encounter uncharted reefs – in fact, you are far more likely to hit rocks in the murky and tidal waters back home than in the Med; should you be unlucky, there are facilities for repairing most types of hull.

Keel configuration and manoeuvrability
Manoeuvrability (especially when going astern) is terribly important in Mediterranean cruising, where you have to use marinas so frequently. One factor that

KEEPING COOL

Phœnician's scoop, plus our carefully-designed gantry. We had hung the bimini from the backstay but rapidly discovered that it needed rigid supporting bars. Note that the wind generator is not high enough above the bimini (which slowed the wind down considerably!).

So long as we kept the curtains drawn on the sunny side, *Phœnician's* deck saloon didn't heat up like a greenhouse – it was rarely more than a degree or so hotter than the shaded cockpit. However, in contrast, *Phœacian's* saloon in hot weather is often 2° or 3°C (5°F) cooler than the cockpit, partly because cabins below water level are cooled by the surrounding sea water.

However, whatever their actual temperature, cabins usually feel a lot hotter because they lack the cockpit's cooling breeze. Yachts built for northern climes never have enough ventilation, so consider whether it will be possible to add more. It is very helpful if some hatches open forward to scoop air in when you are at anchor. For ocean cruising, there is the worry about the security of these in bad weather, but they are ideal for the Med. If they are all aft facing, will it

be possible to turn some round? Are there any opening ports in the sides of the coachroof? These let in a wonderful amount of air. All windows should preferably have tinted glass.

Equally important is the need for shade in the cockpit. Unless you (and your guests) are absolute sun worshippers and don't mind the risk of skin cancer, then this is essential. A permanent bimini awning that can be kept up even when sailing (see photo) is a boon and a blessing – it shelters you from the sun (and summer days at sea can be scorching); it shields you from the downpours that often come with thunderstorms (when an over-the-boom awning might have to be taken down because of the wind); it stops the cockpit from becoming soaked with dew every morning; and when you arrive in harbour, and get hot

affects this is keel configuration. Long-keeled yachts are directionally stable – this is good at sea (and you won't need such a powerful, expensive autopilot), but means very poor manoeuvrability in harbour. Fin-keeled yachts are more lively on the helm and less directionally stable at sea, so you're more likely to have to hand steer in rough weather (particularly downwind) – but they are generally far more manoeuvrable in harbour: and I think this factor outweighs any other for Mediterranean cruising.

I see little point in bilge keels. You can't dry out on the mud because there are no tides; nor are there miles of shallow waterways for mooching about in (except the canals – and here you still can't get close to the shallow banks to tie up because of the angle at which the keels stick out). The only real advantage is stability when laying up ashore.

and tired mooring, you immediately have somewhere cool to sit, without the extra effort of putting an awning up. So ensure it will be possible to fit a bimini on the boat you have in mind.

White is by far the most suitable hull colour for cruising anywhere hot, because it's so much cooler. Some friends of ours actually had their dark-blue yacht resprayed, and were staggered at the difference it made; white is also far more visible at night. Not many yachts have hull and deck insulation or double glazing, but if they do, it's far cooler in hot weather – and of course warmer in winter as well. You also reduce condensation problems, which can be a problem when you are living aboard, because of the moisture in one's breath and the steam produced when cooking.

Performance of yacht

Good sailing performance is important because it's more fun! It's also safer – you have more control over the boat; you can also sail out of difficulties if the engine fails; and if you are caught out in bad weather, then your sails can supplement your engine to very good effect.

Good performance reduces passage time and increases your daylight range. This offers more choice of where to go, and reduces the number of night passages required (though obviously the power of your engine is important here too).

In the Mediterranean there are said to be only two winds: **too weak** and **too strong** – and though this is an exaggeration, you *will* spend an awful lot of time motoring if your yacht doesn't sail fairly well.

Some yachts lie quietly at anchor, but others sheer around when there is any wind. Both catamarans and non-displacement motor yachts tend to suffer from this, as well as some mono-hulled yachts. Others tend to roll a lot in wash or swell. Observe carefully which types of yacht seem to have which characteristics, and buy accordingly.

ON DECK

Reefing systems

For two-handed cruising you need the simplest systems. Theoretically, all reefing systems can be fitted after purchase, but changing in-mast furling is difficult and costly. You want the best compromise between the following:

- Convenience.
- Reliability – beware systems that were brand-new when the yacht was built, since these won't have had the 'bugs' ironed out.

- Good sail shape to improve upwind performance. This is where a roller-furling sail really loses out unless it can be fully battened.

Mainsail Slab reefing gives a much better sail shape; and stowing and reefing isn't too difficult so long as you fit full-length battens and lazy-jacks – these really make a huge difference. Even so, for an ageing couple in-mast furling is a lot easier – *when* it works: and that is the crux of the matter, they often don't – and when they jam half-in, half-out – oh boy, have you got a problem! Modern boats tend to have better systems than older ones, but it can still be a problem. A means of tensioning the luff-foil is apparently very important, as is keeping the bearing at the masthead lubricated and easy to turn. *Phæacian's* in-mast furling frequently jammed; so we have recently fitted a new Sanders furling mainsail with full-length *vertical* battens – which has so far been much better.

There are other mainsail reefing systems. Behind-the-mast furlers must also have a good means of tensioning the luff or the sail won't set well. We have no experience of in-boom or on-boom systems, but they are clearly much safer since, *in extremis*, you can lower the sail down loose.

Genoa Your foresail is a different matter altogether. A furling genoa is essential to avoid both the work of sail changing and the danger of going forward in rough weather – and anyway, you can't afford the space for the extra sails in a live-aboard yacht. All in all, the advantages of a roller-furling genoa far outweigh the disadvantage of poor sail shape; and the furling systems have been around long enough for most problems to have been ironed out.

Decks and toe rails

Proper laid-teak decks are attractive, non-slip and insulating, but can cause problems in a hot climate if they dry out and lift. Varnishing teak hand rails, toe rails and rubbing strakes is hard work – hand rails are quite enough, so try to avoid the others. Slotted metal toe rails are ideal, since they are maintenance-free – and extremely useful for fastening things.

At times you will need to go forward in awkward conditions, so consider if this will be difficult and whether you can climb on and off the cabin roof without slipping.

Cockpit

Whether you want centre-cockpit or aft-cockpit design will probably depend purely on the resulting internal layout; but if you are intending to berth stern-to, remember that, with an aft cockpit, even the cabin may be very open to view from the quay (and its hordes of interested passers-by).

What is very important is to have a big enough cockpit, since all year round it acts as an extra room. There should be enough space for you both to lie out in the shade of the bimini, and you will need room for visitors too. When at sea you'll want to stow lots of items on the cabin roof under the sprayhood – will this be feasible, especially with sprayhood down?

BELOW DECK

Sleeping arrangements

A permanent bunk (or bunks) set aside for sleeping is very important for live-aboard cruising – otherwise you will have to dismantle the saloon to make your bed each evening.

Whether you want a double or two

singles is a matter of choice – a double is cosy, but too hot in summer unless it is big enough for you to spread right out. Good width is essential if you like sleeping curled up – two people curled in opposite directions take up a lot of room; and if the edge of the bunk is a vertically sided locker, this makes things much more cramped than if it's the sloping side of the yacht. If you like sleeping stretched out, then bunk *length* is most important – check this out carefully, allowing for pillows.

If you like sitting up and reading in bed, then sufficient height and a headboard are essential. Central bunks are super for access – but also for falling out of! With a bunk at the side, you have to crawl over each other to get in. In the forepeak triangle, the bunk is often awkwardly high above floor level.

Other important features are:

- A shelf within reach of the bunk, for your drink, spectacles, watch, medications, etc.
- Adequate stowage for clothes including, if possible, a hanging locker.
- A dressing-table with drawers, and at least enough space for a mirror.
- Standing headroom.
- Somewhere to sit down while dressing.
- Privacy when you have guests.

The galley

You're not on holiday as such any longer, so you won't be able to afford to eat out every other night – you'll be cooking your everyday meals, night after night, just as you do at home. Therefore you need a good cooker, with an oven (and maybe grill); if the present cooker is old or inadequate, make sure there's enough space to install a better one (they vary in size). Standing headroom throughout the galley is important; and you must be secure at sea. A double sink is useful – and you'll need plenty of worktops, somewhere for a draining rack (photo page 83), and *lots* of stowage space.

While no single item can be counted as literally indispensable, there is no doubt that a fridge is pretty essential for Med cruising. However, the demands it makes on power also creates a big problem. If there's no fridge, make sure there's a big ice-box that could be turned into one (or a suitable space, with *plenty* of room for insulation).

An electrically pumped water system is very convenient (though it uses a lot more water). It enables you to have hot water easily from the engine via a calorifier, and from shore power via an immersion heater, which is even better. These can probably be retro-fitted, but you will need to check this.

Shower and toilet

A decent heads is a big plus on a live-aboard boat. If a wife is less keen on sailing in the first place, then having a large, comfortable heads may be something that will make life aboard bearable.

If you are in a marina, there will be showers ashore. However, to have your own on-board shower is very convenient, especially when marina ones are dirty, or if you're at anchor in cold weather (when you can't keep clean by swimming). However, steam resulting from hot showers can have a disastrous effect on head-linings if these are stuck up: they start hanging in loops (all over the yacht), and the work involved in rectification is enormous. Showers also make a mess of the heads, and the cupboards will get damp – leading to mould. Further problems with on-board showers when not in a marina are:

- They use a vast amount of water. (However, note that in Greece, where there are few marinas, it is easier to find water than a shower ashore.)
- Pumping the water out afterwards uses precious battery power.
- You won't have hot water unless you run your engine.

Accommodation for guests

Separate accommodation for yourselves and guests in comfort and privacy is ideal, but takes up room that is wasted when you are alone (though you can use it for stowage). The problem of visitors becomes acute on smaller yachts, with only one double berth. Some couples vacate their own berth in favour of their guests, and sleep on the saloon berths; this is not very satisfactory, though acceptable for short periods. Bear this in mind if you plan to have many guests on board.

A second toilet is wonderful when you have visitors, but is it worth the wasted space the rest of the year? It's also very useful on those awful occasions when the first one gets blocked – though another solution to this is a chemical toilet for emergencies.

Sea berths

Make sure that there are berths suitable for use at sea, as you'll need them on longer passages. This is a time when you may well have friends aboard to help, so two are vital, and three convenient. They should preferably be single berths amidships (check length and shape, and whether lee cloths can be fitted), but an aft-double isn't bad so long as you can wedge yourself in. The forepeak is normally far too bouncy in a rough sea.

Companionway

These can be deathtraps, and Jimmy usually modifies ours so that the ladder is much less steeply angled; make sure that there's room to extend it forwards.

Water and diesel tankage

Most yachts carry an inadequately sized water tank for live-aboard cruising. A tank that holds 100 British gallons is a nice amount (multiply by 4½ to get litres), giving 10 days' cruising at a comfortable 10 gallons a day (or you might squeeze 20 days if you're really, really careful). But when you've got running water (or worse, a shower) it takes a lot of discipline to keep down to 10 gallons a day. So if you only have 50 gallons, everything will be that much tighter. And all that, of course, is when you have no visitors. If necessary, you could perhaps add an extra flexi-tank somewhere – but there's not likely to be a space that you're willing to give up (unless you have a cavernous cockpit locker where the bottom half is difficult to get at and could thus be spared).

Diesel is less likely to be a problem, since diesel tanks normally give a few hundred miles' range, which is ample for the Mediterranean. But check this out, especially with regard to powerboats.

It is also important to know exactly how much water and diesel you have left. This should preferably be a *visual* gauge rather than the electric type, since these will fail in time (water gauges fail in the Mediterranean because they clog up with limescale).

Stowage

Stowage can be a really big problem for live-aboard cruising – particularly on small boats (after all, *you* need just as much gear, whatever the size of your boat), on old-

Built of stone, Croatian fishing harbours are often very picturesque.

fashioned yachts (which tend to have a narrow beam), and also on some modern designs where most of the volume is living space. The trouble is, yachts aren't designed to be lived in. New boats are designed to suit the market they are sold to, which tends to be charter companies or people who own boats as status symbols. As a result, one often gets dozens of berths, plus vast showers, dining tables and drinks cabinets, at the expense of large water tanks, plenty of stowage space, a good galley and sea berths.

The list of things you *need* to stow for long-term cruising is endless (let alone all the things you'd like!), and often the space simply isn't there. Many things may just have to go on deck (see Chapter 6). When you reach the stage of seriously considering a particular yacht for your venture, study the packing list in Appendix 1, and make a detailed check of whether there is space to stow what you will require.

AGE, CONDITION AND EQUIPMENT

The yacht

The state of your finances will probably determine how old a yacht you buy, but the newer the better because everything deteriorates, and the boat will be a lot older by the end of your cruise. If you are short of money, you may have to buy a boat in poor condition and renovate it yourself. But make sure she is structurally sound, and that the cost of repairs won't outweigh the initial savings.

A huge advantage of buying brand new is that you *may* be able to get modifications made while the boat is being built, which is infinitely easier than altering things afterwards; however, only some companies allow this. Unfortunately, many builders don't seem to operate adequate systems of quality control, so a new boat will have many faults that should have been corrected during building, but that will often be left to the purchaser to discover. It is worth asking to be put in touch with previous customers, so you can check both the construction quality, and whether the builders willingly put faults right after purchase. Allow plenty of time for corrective work; and, above all, don't accept the boat, or pay the final instalment, until thorough trials have been made of both yacht and equipment and you are completely satisfied. If you are buying abroad, things will be a lot harder than at home.

It goes without saying that the big disadvantage of buying new is the cost, especially as much essential gear will not be provided.

The engine

A powerful, reliable diesel engine is vital for Mediterranean cruising, so if the engine on the boat you are considering is small, old or in poor condition, think seriously about replacing it (and this is very costly). Don't even consider a petrol engine; these are far too dangerous in a hot climate.

If the yacht is poor at manoeuvring (especially in reverse), or has a lot of windage, then a bow thruster is a big advantage. They *can* be retro-fitted, but it is not easy – and it may even be impossible depending on the configuration of the bow.

The equipment

You will have to decide whether to buy a more expensive boat with a lot of equipment, or to choose a cheaper one and buy the gear yourself. The former will probably be cheaper in the long run; the latter will give you more precisely what you want, with new and reliable equipment – older equipment will have deteriorated in the

marine environment, even if it has been rarely used.

Electrics are so important on a liveaboard yacht, that unless you are an expert, any boat where the electrics are at all suspect should be avoided like the plague.

PURCHASE AND INSURANCE

If you get one of the RYA booklets on buying new/second-hand yachts (see Appendix 2), this will help you to avoid some of the worst pitfalls.

Before actually setting out to buy your boat, visit one of the major boat shows and study what's new on the market. This will suggest features you may or may not want, and builders you like or dislike. Some manufacturers build cheaply for the charter market, so quality may be low but the design good for hot climates; Others build yachts with the reverse characteristics. Make careful notes and take photos of yachts you visit, or you will get hopelessly confused.

For Mediterranean cruising it is essential to have a VAT-paid (or exempt) yacht, so check this carefully, ensuring that proof is available.

Where to buy

If you buy abroad, there may be considerable complications. You don't know the ins and outs of buying in a foreign country, and you may find that you have bought all kinds of legal liabilities with your boat. Buying from a compatriot abroad is probably safer than buying from a foreigner, and buy through a broker who knows the ropes. If necessary, use a local, English-speaking marine lawyer.

If the yacht is already conveniently in the Mediterranean, then she is very likely to be suffering from osmosis; and consider the difficulties of getting her surveyed and fitted out abroad.

Getting a survey

It is absolutely essential to get your chosen yacht surveyed by a competent marine surveyor for the following reasons:

- There could be something very seriously wrong with her.
- There will certainly be many, more minor faults, which the surveyor will point out.
- The surveyor's report will provide a work-list of things that need repairing.
- The faults found will provide ammunition to get the purchase price reduced – when Jimmy was surveying, it was very rare for a purchaser not to more than redeem the cost of his survey, and the saving was often considerable.
- Older yachts will need some kind of survey for insurance purposes.

Make sure you get someone good – there are people around calling themselves surveyors who are unqualified and incompetent. Surveyors *must* have adequate indemnity insurance, and should preferably belong to the Yacht Designers and Surveyors Association (or equivalent professional body). It is also wise to get someone who has been recommended to you.

Discuss your cruising plans with the surveyor, so he can make appropriate recommendations.

Insurance

Marinas require you to have third party insurance. However, I strongly recommend comprehensive insurance – after all, it's your home and way of life that is at stake. If you think you can't afford it, remember that it's people with the least money who in fact need insurance the most.

There is no point in going for the cheapest option if, when the crunch comes, the insurer fails to pay out. So ask around and find which firms are reliable when it comes to the point. (We had two claims with Pantaenius, and they paid promptly both times.)

Singlehanders have great difficulty in getting insurance, but there's much less problem if there are two of you, especially if you are both experienced (if one of you is not, then all the more reason to become so). Crossing Biscay two-handed is the trip that insurers may be awkward about, in which case the answer is to get a friend to come with you – we always prefer this anyway.

3

Modifying Your Yacht

You are setting forth on a voyage in which, for the most part, you will be sailing short-handed; and you are probably at an age where weakness will begin to take its toll before the end of your cruise – even if it hasn't already! So plan your equipment with this in mind. Many modifications involve stainless steel, so you need to find somewhere good to get this done. If convenience is more important than cheapness, then write off for the Besenzoni catalogue (see Appendix 3). They are an Italian firm who specialise in making 'convenience' items for yachts – passerelles, stern platforms, hydraulically operated equipment, etc. I've seen a number of their products, and they're super.

GETTING ABOARD FROM THE QUAY

You will be getting on and off the boat countless times for months on end, so this must be made as easy as possible.

Gangplank or ladder?

When moored stern-to you need a passerelle (gangplank). However, things are different if you moor bow-to. When the quay is about the same height as the bow, then a passerelle is fine (photo page 40). But it will often be lower – and a floating pontoon will be considerably lower still. You thus have to climb up rather than walk aboard, and for this a ladder will be needed – the photo opposite shows how Jimmy still has to stretch, even with a ladder. Test this out in your home marina.

Moored stern-to

Passerelle This can be anything from a simple plank to a complex piece of hydraulically operated equipment: hauled up and down, shunted in and out, or simply moved by hand. Amel-Yachts have a neat (though rather short) passerelle that doubles as a swimming ladder (photo opposite). Note that:

- A passerelle must be very light if you're going to operate it completely by hand.
- If you are going to rest it on the quay, it needs a universal joint at the inner end, and wheels (preferably pivoting) at the outer end to allow for movement in a surge or wash.
- But it is in fact preferable for it not to touch the quay at all, since this is noisy when it moves and encourages unwelcome visitors such as cockroaches.

▲ Jimmy stretching to climb *Phœacian's* old bow ladder from a low pontoon; it would be easier if the ladder were longer and set at a slight angle. A point to note: if we had been anticipating a surge we wouldn't have used the snubber on a doubled warp as it would stop it expanding.

▲ *Phœacian's* pulpit modification and new bow ladder, better than ladder (seen left) because it folds and can be fitted at a good angle and you can easily step over the pulpit.

▲ Climbing aboard via the anchor and modified pulpit – an easy method when the quay is high enough. The anchor is very firmly tied so that it is safe to step on.

▲ This (rather short) stern passerelle becomes a ladder on removal of the plank – a neat idea from Amel Yachts. Note the supporting halyard and side ropes.

Fig 1 *A passerelle hung from a halyard showing how you can fasten a handrail – suspending the passerelle above the quay gives a quiet night and deters cockroaches and other pests.*

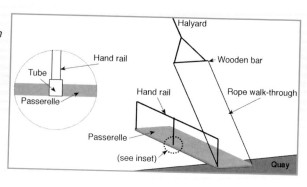

◀ A stern passerelle with a firm (but removable) rail suitable for an elderly sailor – but you don't need to be of advanced years to appreciate it.

▼ With an overhanging pulpit, the passerelle is the only boarding option but fitted like this, it is very unsafe as it will twist.

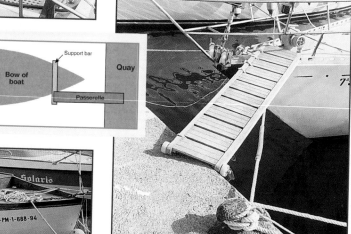

Fig 3 *A bow passerelle is much more secure if fastened to a horizontal support bar laid across the foredeck and attached to the pulpit.*

◀ A U-shaped pulpit, necessary for Mediterranean bow-to berthing so that you can climb easily ashore.

An alternative is to hang it from the gantry or on a halyard, above quay level (Fig 1).

- A permanent passerelle mustn't get in the way of boarding from the water, and needs a means of lifting right out of the way so that you don't swipe other boats with it when manoeuvring.
- Long narrow ones are difficult to balance on even when the boat's steady – if she's jerking around, it's impossible.
- A hand rail is advisable. An easy way to make one is using stanchions, joined by ropes to form the rail. Fasten short tubes or sockets on to the side of the passerelle, into which the bottoms of the stanchions can be slotted when required (Fig 1). A more secure method is stainless steel tubing bent into an extended U-shape, fastened the same way (photo opposite).

Moored bow-to

Modifying the pulpit The top of the pulpit is often outboard of the toe rail (photo opposite), giving you nowhere to stand while climbing on or off, or when leaping ashore with warps. We find it best to stand on the anchor (tied down really securely), since this extends beyond the bow roller (photo page 39). If the pulpit still gets in the way, it will need altering. Boats going to the Mediterranean normally have the front made U-shaped so it's easy to climb over (photo opposite). Jimmy removed the front of *Phæacian*'s upper rail altogether, stiffening the remainder with a curved bar at the lower level (photos page 39). It is now really easy to get aboard – whereas climbing on to some friends' boats is a nightmare.

Bow ladder Next, you need a method of reaching the bow from the pontoon. We

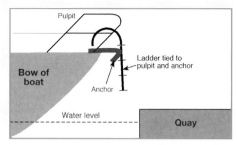

Fig 2 *Looped boarding ladder fastened to anchor and pulpit.*

use an ordinary boarding ladder with loops at the top, fastened to the anchor and pulpit (Fig 2; photos page 39). Its size depends on the height of the bow above the water, but it mustn't touch the quay and it can afford to start a good step above a pontoon. Better still, get a custom-made folding one, with a support bar holding it off the stem (photo page 43). Ladders should be all-stainless – plastic deteriorates and breaks up as a result of ultraviolet light.

Bow passerelle You may decide to have a bow passerelle as well, for when the quay *is* high enough. It must be extremely non-slip, as it will often be at a considerable angle. They are awkward to fit – since the bow is at an angle to the quay, they tend to twist (photo right, opposite). Try fastening it to a horizontal post, laid across the deck and secured firmly to the pulpit (Fig 3).

GETTING ABOARD FROM THE WATER

Most people swim a lot in the Med and it's often far more convenient to do this from the anchored yacht than going ashore, but you *must* be able to get back on board easily. We've met many people who have a real struggle to get out of the water.

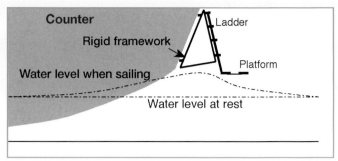

Fig 4 Stern platform and ladder on a rigid framework compensates for an overhang-ing transom; the diagram also shows how the water level rises aft when the yacht is moving fast.

Bathing platform

If your yacht has a sugar-scoop stern, then this is ideal (photo opposite). If not, either have one built on, or build a bathing plat-form. This must be as low as possible for convenience; but a platform is not stream-lined like a scoop, so it mustn't touch the water when sailing since this will add drag. A permanent one should be just above the highest water level (Fig 4); if this would be too high, consider one that folds away at sea. Make it of teak slatting in a stainless steel framework; and it must stick out well aft of the transom top if this overhangs, so you can stand upright comfortably. If you design it carefully, it should look attractive (photo page 28).

A ladder down the transom

If the transom slopes the right way (Fig 5), this is easy, and by far the best way of get-ting down to water level. Flat teak treads are far safer and more comfortable than round stainless bars. Consider making a gateway in the pushpit (photos pages 28 and 43).

If the transom slopes the wrong way (Fig 4), it's difficult to climb, so make the lower treads stick out further (photo opposite) – indeed, it's worth doing this with a vertical transom. A big overhang, or high counter stern, may require the con-struction of a rigid framework on which to build your platform and ladder.

Swimming ladder down into the water

Three important principles apply wher-ever you fit your ladder:

1 It must be a rigid one; it's incredibly dif-ficult to climb out of the water using a rope ladder that swings under the boat as soon as you put your weight on it – definitely not what you want for every-day use.

2 It mustn't overhang; and a long one should preferably slant slightly the other way to make it less tiring to climb – with a vertical ladder, your weight is out-board of the rungs, so you're literally having to haul yourself up; but with a forward-slanting ladder, your weight is taken on your feet.

3 The ladder needs a minimum of three rungs underwater, and four is far easier – have an extension put on if there is already a shorter ladder on the the boat. Stainless-steel rungs are easy and conve-nient – but, once again, teak treads are far better.

Ladder on a platform A big advantage of a bathing platform is that you can lean for-ward over it when pulling yourself up, which is a great help. Build the ladder on the platform, hinged and bent, so that it folds up out of the water against the tran-som (photo opposite; Fig 5). The treads

▲ *Phæacian*'s attractive scoop (though a bit cramped for sitting with your feet in the water) has a ladder which hinges up to stow neatly against the transom; note the gateway in the pushpit.

▲ This rather short ladder has been sensibly built on a framework because the transom was awkwardly overhanging. Note that the teak treads are the wrong way up when folded.

▲ This is a really good custom-made folding bow ladder with a support bar to hold it at the correct angle for easy climbing.

▲ A ladder over the side with a fender to hold it away from the hull. It would be better for swimming if it was longer and able to fold.

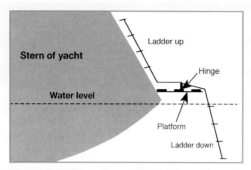

Fig 5 A hinged swimming ladder on a stern platform, bent to stow close-in to the transom when folded up out of the water.

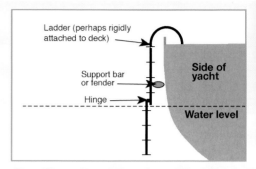

Fig 6 Where stern ladders are unsuitable, a ladder over the side (preferably folding) can be effective. It must go deep with permanent fastening points fitted to the deck.

will be the other way up when the ladder is stowed (photo page 43).

Ensure that there's room to sit on the platform with your feet in the water – the ladder may need to be to one side (unlike photo page 43). There should be a hand-hold to pull on that you can reach when you are in the water (photo page 28).

Ladder over the stern If you can't have a bathing platform, the same principles apply – but things are far more difficult. You can see that in the photo on page 107, that it will be a hard climb because the ladder has no forward slope, and there's no platform to climb on to halfway up.

Ladder over the side If a ladder over the stern is quite impossible, then try one over the side. I saw a big yacht with a super Besenzoni one (Fig 6). It clipped rigidly to permanent deck fastenings, with a support bar to hold it off the hull. When not in use, it was removed, folded and stowed away. It was very effective (I tried it!) – but, even so, it was a long climb.

Alternatively, try a normal, portable, rigid boarding ladder, tied firmly, with a fender to hold it away from the hull (photo page 43). If you can't buy a long enough

boarding ladder, get a straight piece welded or hinged onto the end of a short one.

Try to hang your ladder where the deck is low, the hull not too overhanging, and where there is something firm, preferably well inboard, to pull on (stanchions aren't firm enough). Make a proper gateway in the guard wires.

Man overboard (in harbour)

Most marinas don't have ladders, so it would be impossible to get out of the water if you fell into a marina when there was no one around to help. So tie your swimming ladder in a way that someone in the water could untie it and pull it down (this would be impossible in the photo (top left) on page 43). Alternatively you could buy a patent rope ladder (eg Sowester). These are stowed at the side of the yacht with a string hanging down – someone in the water can pull this string, which brings the ladder tumbling down.

ANCHORS AND WINDLASSES

Anchors are, perhaps, your most important pieces of equipment because the whole safety of the yacht depends on them – and

A German *Bügelanker* anchor which is said to dig in best of all; note the long, sharp point for cutting through weed.

in the eastern Mediterranean you will be lying to one or other anchor almost all the time. There are four common methods of mooring in the Mediterranean. I describe these fully in Chapter 10, but a brief summary is necessary here in order to explain the equipment you will need:

- **Free anchoring** – the kind of anchoring most people are used to.
- **Anchoring with a long line ashore** – here you anchor by the bow fairly close to the shore, to which you fasten the stern with a long warp.
- **Bow-to the quay with a stern anchor** – the method of mooring used in the many harbours where there's no marina (photo page 143). You can, of course, go stern-to and use your bow anchor, but the disadvantages of this have already been mentioned.
- **Marinas** – the use of finger pontoons is very rare. The norm is to go bow-to a quay, the stern being held off with a laid stern mooring (Fig 25, page 171).

Bow anchor

In the past we have stuck to the CQR type – having heard that a sharp point is essential for cutting through weed, and that Danforth and Fisherman types are not good for free anchoring, since the cable can catch under the flukes or stock and thus trip the anchor.

However, best of all is apparently the German *Bügelanker* (see Appendix 3) (photo above) – I believe it's called a bar anchor in English. Friends tell us that it is excellent for free anchoring, as it cuts through weed better than a CQR, and digs in when a CQR will lie on its side. Apparently you can get similar ones made cheaply in Marmaris (Turkey).

Cable for your bow anchor I recommend mostly chain, for two reasons: the boat remains much steadier at anchor (yachts on mostly rope fly around a lot), and the anchor digs in far better – when the boat is being pushed back by the wind, a lot of cable weight is needed to retain that essential horizontal pull. Also, rope along the ground can get cut by sharp rocks or debris. How much cable to have depends on the kind of anchoring you do, but as a *minimum* I suggest 40 metres of chain for normal use (preferably more), plus 15 metres of rope permanently attached to the end, for anchoring in deep water. Large yachts will probably be anchoring farther out, so will need more.

Mark your anchor cable every 5 metres (with paint or knotted cord of different colours), so you can judge when you've let out the correct amount; make sure the marks are clear enough to see as the chain flies out.

Windlass for the bow anchor As you get older, a 35-lb anchor and ⁵⁄₁₆ths chain become quite heavy enough to need a windlass of some sort; and if your yacht is 11 metres or more, you may well be hauling up a bigger one, for which you will probably need an electric windlass.

With a manual windlass, you still do the work of lifting, but it's in an easier form and far less backbreaking. An electric windlass does *all* the work for you, but sometimes annoyingly slowly – and often they won't work at all. *Phœnician's* was so unreliable that we got rid of it, and we're constantly seeing other yachts with similar problems. Four things are essential with an electric windlass:

1 Buy a reliable make.
2 It must be wired in extremely well, with suitably sized electric cable. If getting heavy cable up to the bow simply isn't possible, consider fitting an extra battery forward (*very* well fastened down, and with an independent switch) to power the windlass – then you only need smaller cable running through the cabin to charge that battery.

3 Install the windlass in a covered well to keep out the salt water, and coat the terminals with a water-repellent spray such as WD-40 to stop them corroding.
4 Run the engine when using an electric windlass, since batteries alone may not supply enough voltage.

Probably the best solution is an electric windlass with a really good manual back-up for when it breaks down (Lofrans make suitable ones, and the Simpson Lawrence Anchorman has been recommended to me); the manual back-up should be as easy as a proper manual windlass, otherwise it will be useless.

Whether your windlass is manual or electric, a two-speed one is much better than a single-speed type.

Stern anchor

This is needed every time you berth in a harbour that is not a marina – unless you are berthing stern-to, when you use your bower anchor. In France and Spain there are few such harbours left, but further east a stern anchor is absolutely essential and it must be big enough.

For this anchor I strongly recommend a Fortress. This brilliant little anchor is a Danforth type but, being made of aluminium, is about half the weight; however, it has excellent holding power (except in weed). The lightness is terribly important, since the anchor must be sufficiently powerful to hold the yacht firm even in a gale, yet you're unlikely to have the help of a windlass for hauling up. We therefore only have an inadequate 5 metres of chain, the rest being rope. The total length only needs to be about 30 metres, since harbours aren't usually very deep.

Stow your stern anchor on the pushpit ready for instant use (though tied down),

Stern anchor stowed on pushpit with chain and rope in buckets. Everything is firmly tied down so that it cannot work loose at sea. There is a pulley on the gantry for hauling up the anchor (or outboard).

with a plastic tube over the stainless rail to protect it. Then tie off the free end of the warp and, starting with that end, fake it down bit by bit, into a bucket or plastic box (also firmly tied), with the chain either on top or in another bucket (photo opposite). Then it will run out smoothly when required, whereas a rope in a neat coil will tangle when used!

Using your stern anchor and cable is actually quite simple, but the logistics are confusing, so I will describe our system in some detail in Fig 7:

1 The stowed position (A): warp in one bucket, chain in another, anchor stowed over pushpit (protected by plastic tube).

2 As the boat approaches the quay, the crew lowers the anchor and chain, leads the warp around a winch and passes it to the helmsman, who lets it out slowly as the boat advances (B).

3 When making fast, the warp is removed from the winch and led straight from the water to a cleat (C).

4 On leaving, unfasten the rope, pass it round to the stern, and haul in over the transom.

Fig 7 *Technique for using your stern anchor. The diagram shows the aft end of the deck (horizontal) and pushpit (vertical) seen from the port side with the anchor initially in the stowed position on top of the pushpit and the chain and rope in two buckets. Alternatively, you can use just one bucket with the rope at the bottom and the chain on top.*

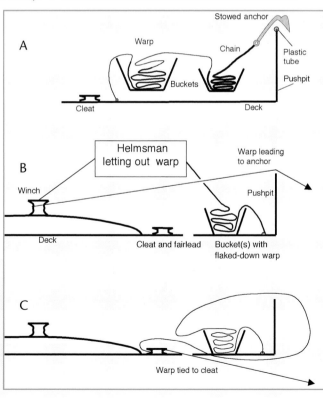

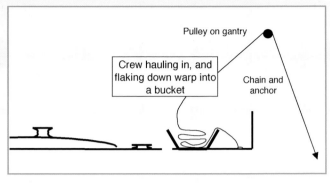

Fig 8 Using a pulley helps when hauling in your stern anchor because pulling down is much easier than pulling up.

Stern-anchor windlass Hauling the anchor up can be quite a strain, so if you intend to spend long in the eastern Mediterranean, consider installing a stern-anchor windlass. But even without one, there are things you can do to ease hauling in:

- If you have a gantry over the transom, rig a pulley on it for the anchor warp so you're hauling down rather than up – a much easier operation (photo page 47, Fig 8). The pulley should be big enough for the chain-warp joint.
- Alternatively, fit a big, open fairlead on the transom, again large enough for the

chain-warp joint, and lead the cable to a genoa winch so you can haul up using a winch handle (Fig 9.). This would enable you to handle much more powerful gear. Here, although the anchor is still stowed on the pushpit, the chain leads in through the chosen fairlead and into its bucket (A). When the anchor is required, the chain and warp can be led round the winch and the anchor lowered (B).

Whatever the system, it should be on the same side as the engine controls, since the

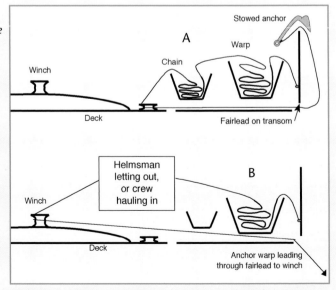

Fig 9 A special fairlead may be needed on the corner of the transom for your stern anchor warp so that you can use a winch to haul in.

helmsman has to manipulate both these and the steering while letting out the warp. (This is less difficult than it sounds – I manage in spite of my handicap.) Consider also the shape of the transom – you don't want your scoop stern to get damaged when the anchor chain is 'up and down'. The new fairlead (angled well aft) may need to be on the quarter rather than on the transom.

Storm anchors

Ocean cruisers have a really heavy third anchor for use in storm conditions. However, we haven't found this necessary for Mediterranean cruising, since one is never that far from shelter – though obviously it depends on the type of anchoring you do. Your stern anchor will double as a kedge.

One way of getting a normal anchor to hold better is by adding a 'chum-weight' to the chain, some way back from the anchor. This can be a big lead weight (or a few loops of chain), which I suggest fastening to your anchor chain with a short piece of wire and a snap shackle. When hauling in, this can easily be unclipped and fastened to the pulpit (or pushpit) while you finish weighing anchor.

DECK AND COCKPIT MODIFICATIONS

Gantry

A gantry (supporting structure) over the stern is extremely useful for:
- Various aerials.
- A wind and/or solar generator.
- The back end of the bimini or other awning.
- A pulley for hauling up the stern anchor, and/or the outboard.

- A shower-bag for showering over the stern (standing on the bathing platform), etc.

Some gantries look appalling, but not if they are well designed. They seem to look their most attractive if they mirror the shape of the transom – at the same angle to the horizontal (see Fig 10 and photo page 30). Remember, though, to take into account the height limitations of the canals.

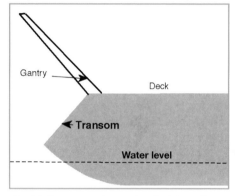

Fig 10 Stern gantries tend to look best if they mirror the transom – at the same angle to the horizontal.

Davits

Davits are ugly and you risk hitting other boats with them. The raised dinghy is also right in the way of getting ashore if moored stern-to. However, if age or infirmity is approaching, davits are extremely convenient. Try to design them as part of your gantry, preferably folding. You'll probably have to relocate your stern light, though.

Deck fittings

Fit jackstays for safety harnesses along the whole length of the deck, on both sides. They should be made of strong webbing, since this doesn't roll underfoot. Ensure there are enough U-bolts for harnesses in the cockpit.

Stern moorings provided by marinas are big, and your fairleads may be too small and wrongly shaped for heavy lines leading directly aft. Consider fitting bigger, rather open fairleads, angled well aft (as described for hauling up the stern anchor). If you moor bow-to, you may have a similar problem with bow fairleads. Cleats may also be too small.

All the above must be well secured through backing plates.

Attach the mainsheet tackle to the track with a snap shackle. It can then be easily undone so that you can use the tackle for:
- Hauling the dinghy on board.
- Man overboard.
- Moving the boom out to the guard wires, so it doesn't cover any solar panels.

Winches

Hauling in a big genoa is heavy work, so consider upgrading your genoa winches to a larger size. Two-speed or even three-speed ones will help a lot, and make them self-tailing if possible. The same applies to other winches to some extent. Where proper self-tailers cannot be fitted, an alternative is a blue plastic add-on (called The Wincher by Watski of Scandinavia), which makes a normal winch into a sort of self-tailing one.

Rigid kicker

This is far more convenient than a rope one, and acts as a topping lift as well.

Windows

Unless they are made of toughened glass, very large windows should perhaps have fitted storm boards to cover them in rough seas; these are also useful for keeping the sun out.

Try to modify your hatches to keep rain out, and also your transom windows so that deck run-off doesn't come into the stern cabin.

Cockpit table

A folding table for meals in the cockpit is essential; it must be easy to put up and down, and should preferably have folding leaves. Fiddles are a nuisance – you won't often use the table at sea, and non-slip matting is better anyway. However, you need somewhere secure for mugs (you can buy special racks for them, photo right).

Sprayhood

A good sprayhood is essential, even in the Mediterranean, and it should be big enough to cover the forward end of the cockpit. However, in hot weather it will feel like being in a greenhouse, so you must be able to remove it when necessary. Folding it down ruins the see-through panels, so we have modified ours so that we can unzip the front and fold it over the top (photo right). However, this is less effective, and it can still get damaged if we're not very careful.

Her well-cut sprayhood was one of *Phæacian's* attractions – many look dreadful. Seen from the side, the front comes down at about 45°, the top is horizontal, and these two panels are about equal in length. The whole sprayhood should be made from light-proof material, and the see-through corner panels should have removable covers against the sun – perhaps Velcroed on.

Phæacian's bimini, spray hood (front folded over the top) and rigid kicker. Unfortunately we found that this type of bimini frame has side bars which causes rainwater to collect rather than be spilled.

A folding cockpit table and mug rack on the steering console.

Winter shelter

If you intend to overwinter on board, consider extending your awning system so that it completely encloses the cockpit, with see-through panels and a doorway, to keep the wind and rain out (photo page 162). A single, large, transparent screen can be very useful against driving rain at any time of year (an awning screen makes everything too dark under these circumstances).

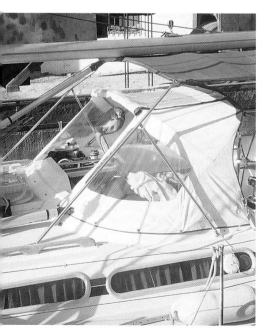

We don't bother with a complete winter cover when we go home. They keep decks cleaner, but they give more shelter to burglars and cats! Also, any cover must be very strong, and very firmly tied down or it will cause damage by flapping in gales. If you do fit one, leave gaps each end for ventilation.

KEEPING COOL

Awnings

Good awnings are essential. The sun in the Med is too hot even when low, so awnings need to come down to the guard wires; however, if you case yourself in with canvas all round, you lose the view (photo page 52) – and it's counter-productive since you cut out that vital cooling breeze. You need protection even when sailing, and your awning must be able to withstand strong winds or otherwise you'll be putting it up and down all the time.

The solution is a permanent bimini awning that can be kept up all the time see pages 54–5, and side screens that can be added when required (photo pages 26–7.) – with an over-the-boom awning for any area missed by these (see Chapter 4).

With some aft-cockpit boats the boom sticks a long way back, yet is too low for the bimini to fit underneath. So you may have to compromise, with your permanent bimini only covering part of the cockpit, and a forward extension for when you're not sailing. *Phœnician*'s was on horizontal poles, and rolled back onto the front of the bimini when not needed (photo page 173).

Opening hatches

You will probably need to fit extra hatches in order to get enough ventilation. Some (but not all) should be forward opening, to

scoop air in. Large cabins should have at least two *big* opening hatches, and all cabins at least one. Make sure each head has a proper opening hatch – a vent is definitely not enough in a hot climate (even more so if a shower is installed).

Also vital is ventilation for the galley, where you create a lot of heat. Ideally, you want a hatch above and aft of the cooker (aft facing to draw hot air out), and a bow-facing one forward of the cooker (to scoop air in and to cool the cook) – but ensure that the flames are shielded from the draught. A stern cabin also needs one hatch to scoop air in, and another to let it out. Try to make some of your coachroof windows opening ones too.

Cooling food and yourselves

Fridges A fridge is essential in a hot climate, both to store fresh food and to cool drinks. There are three different types, all of which have problems:

Electric These are convenient, but inefficient. They take a large amount of current (eg 5 amps), and a big one may need to work nearly half the time in the hottest part of the day.

Gas These create heat, and I gather they may need turning off at sea because of the flame not being gimballed. Consider also the safety aspect; the pilot light *must* have a flame-failure device.

You need to keep shaded from the sun but if your awning is too enclosed you will lose the view and the all-important cooling breeze.

running off each source of power, because this is useless – you need *one* fridge space that can be cooled by both power sources.

In particular, ensure that the air intake is as cool as possible (It mustn't get heated by the hot-air outlet, as ours was on *Phæacian*!). Read *Boatowner's Mechanical and Electrical Manual* by Nigel Calder. In a hot climate, a fridge on a boat needs much more insulation than normal, since most of the power required is used replacing coldness lost to the outside – 4 inches (10 centimetres) should be considered a minimum. It should be top opening to stop the cold air falling out, and tall enough to stow bottles upright. However, bigger fridges use more power, so you don't want a vast one – if yours is huge, adding a waterproof, insulated lining will reduce the size *and* increase the insulation. It's much better if the fridge has a drain, but the drainpipe must have a U-bend to retain the cold air.

Compressor running off the engine Apparently these are by far the most efficient type, and the holding plate will keep the fridge cool all day after only a short period running the engine. However, you have to do this every day – *even* when you have shore power.

So every type of fridge has problems, and the best solution is one that can be run off two different power sources (one of which must be batteries). Caravan accessory shops sell fridges that run on both electricity and gas. Alternatively, if your fridge uses engine alone, or 12-volt alone, consider installing the other type of unit as well. However, *don't* be tempted to install two fridges, one

Shower over the stern Consider installing a shower extension over your bathing platform – for cooling down, rinsing the salt off after swimming, and having a proper shower without causing a mess inside. However, be *very* careful regarding water usage.

Electric fans If you can afford the power, these are very useful in high summer for cooling you down in any part of the yacht that tends to overheat.

Lockers Those located immediately under the deck heat up tremendously, so if you plan to store food in these, they should be well insulated.

BIMINI AWNING

This must be:
- Horizontal to reduce windage.
- Behind or under the boom so it can be kept up while sailing.
- Rigidly constructed for security.
- And either:
    - completely solid and permanent, or
    - easy to take down in an emergency.

Under or behind the boom? On aft-cockpit yachts the bimini may fit behind the boom, and a stern gantry will conveniently form the after-end of your bimini frame. This arrangement worked well on *Phœnician* (photo page 30). We used fore-and-aft stainless poles, joined by a crossbar just aft of the boom, plus rigid poles to support the front end; but see note on rain, opposite.

With a centre cockpit, the bimini must go under the boom (photos page 51 and 26); you will need a complete, all-round frame – although the mainsheet track may need shifting.

Height? The higher the bimini, the more the sun will slant in underneath, so make it as low as possible. However, you need standing headroom for steering; and it should be higher than the sprayhood – both so that you can see over the top of the latter, and to get a cooling draught between the two (photo page 51).

Size? Your awnings need to extend beyond the cockpit in all directions because:
- You need to shade the cabins.
- The sun is never actually overhead but always at an angle.
- Nearby unshaded deck heats up and becomes a furnace, wafting heat at you.
- When it rains, the run-off must land on the sidedecks, not the cockpit.

Your bimini should overlap the sprayhood, or rain and sun will slant in between. If it extends over the sidedecks, you will have far better shade than if it just covers the cockpit. Side screens will be necessary less often, and this will improve not only the view and the draught, but also access to the cockpit. However, it may make walking along the sidedecks very difficult.

You could have:
- A big bimini, and put up with it being in the way at times.
- A small bimini, and put up with it being too small at times.
- A big one on a folding frame.
- A small one that can be extended outwards.
- A permanent frame built up from the stanchions. We know one yacht that has this, and they put up as much canvas as they need.

Make the bimini as long as possible (if very big, it may be better in two sections). It should preferably extend aft of the cockpit, and also forward of the companionway (or the sun will strike into the cabin whenever the hatch is open). It mustn't impede the folding down of the sprayhood.

Permanent or collapsible frame? We prefer a permanent framework, since the bimini will be in use all summer (indeed, we keep ours up all winter too, as protection against sun, dew and rain). However, at times a folding frame has advantages. If your boom forces the bimini awkwardly low, you'll want to fold it out of the way whenever possible. Also, if your bimini extends over the sidedecks, you could fold a collapsible one back when coming into a harbour and needing easy access along the deck. We have recently seen many charter yachts with this system, but unfortunately the hinged frame itself often blocks the

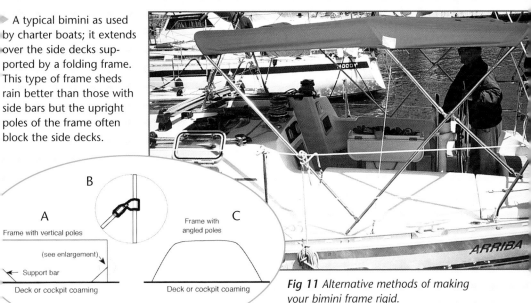

A typical bimini as used by charter boats; it extends over the side decks supported by a folding frame. This type of frame sheds rain better than those with side bars but the upright poles of the frame often block the side decks.

Fig 11 *Alternative methods of making your bimini frame rigid.*

side-decks. It should be as far outboard as possible, especially with a centre cockpit (photo above).

Building your bimini frame In general, a bimini frame should be rigid, but easy to take to pieces. The awning should be nearly horizontal (to reduce windage) and quick to remove – ours wrapped round the poles (on all four sides) and stuck back on to itself with Velcro. Whether it's a folding or permanent type, the whole thing should be as rigid as possible, both as protection against wind and because it will constantly get used as a hand rail. It must be rigid against fore-and-aft and sideways movement. If the support poles are vertical, they'll need angled bars to add rigidity (Fig 11, A), but if they themselves are angled, then this will probably suffice (C). Stainless poles can be professionally bent, and you can buy clips to fasten them together (B).

Material Your main awnings should be made from completely light-proof material. Hold a sample under something solid on a sunny day, and look at the underside of the material – if you can see a shadow of the object showing through the material, then it is not light-proof. Solid colours like blue, green or tan are best – white is also too dazzling.

Rain Remember, your bimini must protect you against rain as well as sun. Any joins should be as waterproof as possible. The frame should have slightly curved cross bars to encourage run-off and any fore-and-aft side bars must be low enough to prevent water collecting behind them – the material will stretch and sag, and rain will then dribble through into the cockpit (photos page 51 and above). Ours was poor in this respect, so we have now built a solid, slightly convex bimini-top (as motor yachts often have). The difference experienced in wet weather has been phenomenal.

ENGINE, POWER SUPPLY AND ELECTRICS

Engine

A good-sized reliable diesel engine is one of the most important pieces of equipment on your yacht, and it will be really awkward if it goes wrong. So unless you are 100 per cent happy with your engine, consider replacing it before you leave – in fact, this applies to a lot of equipment. At the very least, have it thoroughly overhauled.

Fit a rope cutter on the propeller to chew up rope, plastic, etc that would otherwise tangle up your prop.

Power supply

In our view, boat electrics are a Black Art; and when we consult the experts on this, they are either incomprehensible or disagree with one another. The following tips have been gained from hard-won experience. They refer mainly to sailing yachts with 12-volt systems.

You will need far more power than in the past – most live-aboards are constantly plagued by battery problems. You need *at least* two large-capacity (100 amp-hours or more) deep-cycle domestic batteries fitted in parallel (three or four if you have any big power users on board), as well as a dedicated engine battery (which can be a smaller cranking-type battery).

You will need a fairly complex electrical system, and very careful wiring to ensure that it works properly. This is really vital, and your whole electrical system should be thoroughly overhauled by a *competent* marine electrician. Make sure that the cables are sufficiently big to cope with the required loads without causing a voltage drop, and avoid taking wires long distances unless absolutely necessary. Try to simplify the wiring; make it easily accessible; and draw a circuit diagram for future reference.

It is essential to be able to assess the state of your batteries. Therefore install a good battery monitor. This very accurately measures all the current coming in and out of your batteries (from when they were last fully charged), and thus calculates how many amp-hours they have left in them. These monitors are quite expensive, but well worth it. They also measure battery voltage.

Without this, you haven't a hope of keeping track of what your batteries are doing. It may be preferable to have individual ammeters on your charging equipment, even with a battery monitor.

Charging the batteries

An alternator and shore-charging facilities are the bare essentials, but these will not be sufficient if:

- You do much anchoring, *or*
- You intend to go to places like Greece where there are few marinas, *or*
- You have any power-hungry equipment (eg fridge, radar, water-maker, computer, etc).

Something extra will be needed to supply power during the times when you are at anchor (or sailing); and the more the above three factors apply to you, the more generators you will need. However, regulators of different chargers can be incompatible, in which case you will either have to use only one charger at a time or have two chargers powering different battery banks.

Alternator If possible upgrade it for a more powerful one. However, check that it can be adequately fitted – they are by no means easily interchangeable because of the difficulty of lining up the pulleys and mounts. In fact, an ordinary alternator doesn't actually do a very good job of recharging batteries, so I strongly recommend getting an 'intelligent regulator' for it, such as an Adverc or TWC – these greatly increase the power output. You'll need to turn off other generators (eg solar, wind) while motoring, or they'll fool this regulator into thinking the batteries are full.

Of course, no alternator does any good unless you run the engine. Many yachts try to solve their battery problems by running it for a period every day while at anchor, but it's a lot of noise, smell and hassle (both for you and your neighbours); in addition, it's very bad for a diesel engine to be run under low load – if you ever do have to charge this way, try at least to have the engine in gear.

Shore power This is essential for live-aboard cruising, both for charging the batteries and for running mains-powered equipment (the most essential of which is a fan heater for cold spring nights). Buy a proper switch-mode charger which can recharge your batteries quickly when they are run down. (Check that your so-called charger isn't, like the one that came on Phæacian, merely designed to replace power as it is being used; these supply less than 14 volts, whereas for the rapid recharging required, the charger must be able to supply over 14½ volts when necessary.)

If you want to charge both banks of batteries (engine and domestic) at the same time, you could install a link between your two banks that can be switched over when you want to charge the engine battery as well. This enables you to start the engine with the domestic batteries in an emergency, but it adds complexity, and risks deadening the engine battery if you make a mistake. It is probably better to ensure that your charger has dual outlets for charging both banks, and to take heavy-duty jump leads for emergency use. For safety, a mains-power system should be professionally fitted.

Diesel or petrol generators A diesel or petrol generator *could* supply all your needs (and 220 volts as well), but you would need to run it for quite a while every day, which is a hassle (and antisocial). Diesel generators are generally too big, heavy and noisy for all but the biggest boats. Some petrol generators suffer from the same problem, and petrol is especially dangerous in a hot climate.

On a big yacht, a 'gen-set' may have been installed: ie a diesel generator built in like a small main engine, powering a large number of electrical goodies such as air-conditioning. While all these are wonderful when they work, such systems are very complex to maintain.

Towed generators These are not suitable for the Mediterranean, since problems are most likely to occur when at anchor.

Wind generators We chose an Aerogen 3 for *Phœnician* as it was totally silent (unlike many others), but it wasn't enough. So for *Phæacian*, we bought one of the new, bigger ones. Of these, the Air-Marine (Appendix 3) has the big advantage that it can be turned off at the touch of a switch, and has a built-in regulator so that it shorts out (and stops spinning) when the batteries are full; however, we found it to be noisy, particularly inside the yacht, and it should be fitted on a resilient mounting system in order to reduce this. The Aerogen 6 is *far* heavier, and needs a dump regulator to get rid of the excess power generated; we also thought the American 'Wind-Bug' was noisy.

Manufacturers proudly advertise how many amps their product will give in a gale (eg up to 30 amps). However, this is of little use since it happens too infrequently – our new big generator rarely gives a *sustained* output of more than 5 amps; for long periods we get nothing (or perhaps half an amp). What you need is a steady input every day, and this depends on the output in light winds – and what wind speed is required to give any at all. Manufacturers supply a power-output graph, so carefully compare the figures for these lighter winds.

Not having a cumulative ammeter, it's difficult for us to estimate how many amp-hours we get from our big generator per day, but, as a very rough guestimate, on an average day with little wind except in the afternoon, we might at most get 10 amps for 10 minutes, 5 amps for 1 hour, 2 amps for 2 hours and 1 amp for 4 hours – ie less than 15 amp-hours per day. In continu-ously windy conditions (say force 5/6), we get *far* more (5 amps for 24 hours would be 100 amp-hours a day – enough power, and to spare). But this is very rare indeed, especially in summer (when no wind at all is more common).

Wind generators need mounting on a rigid pole, high enough to clear unwary hands, and at least a metre higher than your bimini awning (as photo page 26, unlike photo page 30), since awnings slow the air flow, reducing output. It should be as far as possible from aerials (since it will interfere with their reception), and as close as possible to the batteries. If you install it on a corner of the transom, consider its vulnerability to damage.

Solar power You need a large area of panels to get a decent output, and this drops very considerably when they are not directly facing the sun, or shaded – with some, even partly shaded sections will cut out completely. Blocking diodes are normally required (to prevent the bat-teries draining themselves at night, radiating heat to the atmosphere), but see Nigel Calder's *Boatowner's Mechanical and Electrical Manual* (Adlard Coles Nautical). They may be built in – check that they work. A regulator is needed, plus a switch, so that you can turn them off when using the engine, or shore power – otherwise, when the batteries are full, they'll get boiled by the panels!

There are two main types: heavy, rigid ones that can be stuck up in the air; and light, flexible ones that can be draped over decks, etc. Some types only work if the entire panel is in the sun, so only get these if you have a suitable place. You can fix them rigidly to a pole or gantry; keep them in one place but rotate them to face the sun; or move them around to different places. One possibility is to fasten them on top of the bimini (photo page 26) – for maximum power, you may need to shift the boom to one side.

I understand that rigid panels are the cheapest and most efficient, but flexible ones are more durable and much less affected by shade. There are also 'semi-flex-ible' ones, somewhere between the two.

Solar panels are rated in watts, a mea-sure of theoretical output under perfect conditions (amps received = watts ÷ charging voltage). However, their effi-ciency is very low, so to get a real estimate of output you need to look at the manufacturer's tables of typical

Two gulets moored stern-to-quay in Göcek Club Marina, southern Turkey which has a beautiful mountain setting.

amp-hours per week in various parts of the world. We bought four 32-watt uni-solar flexi-panels from Ampair. Their estimated Mediterranean performance (when angled to face the midday sun) is 61 amp-hours per week each, so our four horizontal ones will give us much less than 240 per week allowing for losses in our electrical system, perhaps 25 amp-hours per day?

Wind versus solar A wind generator is ideal for providing power when sailing, especially at night, also in windy conditions in anchorages. However good anchorages are often sheltered from the wind, and in a gale when wind gives its best power, you may be in a marina anyway.

However, on balance, if you only intend to buy one type, solar generators are probably more suited to the Mediterranean, where for long periods in summer you get sun all day but no wind. In addition:

- They are silent *and* can be turned off (an impossible combination at present with wind generators).
- Their greatest output comes at the time of greatest need, ie on very hot days.
- You can add to them bit by bit, so that if one goes wrong you've still got the others.

However, best of all is to have both – they complement each other nicely, because sunny days are often windless, and windy days are often cloudy.

Assessing your electrical needs

Power requirement Rather than guessing how many batteries, etc you will need, it is *far* better to install ammeters or a battery monitor and work it out. We *didn't*, and as a result haven't enough batteries! However we've now tested our equipment, and I

summarise our estimated usage at anchor in the table opposite.

As expected, by far the biggest drain on the batteries is the fridge. Even on a number 3 setting (out of 7 settings), which doesn't keep it very cool, ours needed to be running for about 8 hours per day in summer (see table opposite), and this increased drastically on higher settings. All systems are different (our new Isotherm apparently uses far less power), so you should make a similar check on your fridge as soon as possible, remembering that it will be on for far longer in the Mediterranean than at home because of the high ambient temperature.

Don't forget to test all your equipment, including every light; and check that you have no hidden power losses (like a short circuit) when nothing is switched on.

Power available It's very difficult to recharge your batteries to 100 per cent, and the last 20 per cent takes an increasingly long time. In addition, it's very bad for batteries to be discharged to a low level – apparently you shouldn't go below 50 per cent on a regular basis, though down to 20 per cent is acceptable occasionally. So, realistically, you have less than 50 per cent of your quoted battery capacity actually available.

Balancing power needs In the table on page 62 I calculate how many days one could last at anchor (theoretically), using 50 amp-hours of power per day, with various combinations of wind and sun under normal *summer* conditions, and with the shortfall supplied by different numbers of 100 amp-hour batteries (each therefore with a maximum of 50 amp-hours available).

Note how the length of time one can

Measurement of power usage

	No of items used at a time	Amps used by each	No of hours used per day (guestimate)	Amp-hours per day
Cabin lights	2	1.5	2	6
Reading lights	2	0.7	2	3
Water pump	1	4.8	0.2	1
VHF: Receive	1	0.13	6	1
Transmit		6.0	0	0
Hi-fi	1	0.2	4.0	1
			Sub total	12
Plus fridge	1	5.0	8	+ 40
			Grand total	**52**

Use of fridge on board

Our (old) fridge (on number 3 setting) mid-July

Time of day	Cabin temperature °C	Percentage time running
5 am	21°	22%
8 am	24°	27%
11 am	26°	29%
2 pm	28°	33%
5 pm	30°	36%
It seems to stay on longer in the evenings	So actual average over 24 hours	**32%** **= Approx 8 hours per day**

last at anchor suddenly shoots up as your power input approaches your power requirement. Note also how adding more batteries has more initial effect than adding a generator, but can never lead to independence. All this refers to independence from the engine – if you are motoring between anchorages every few days, you could get independence from *shore power* far more easily.

If you want to spend longer at anchor, I recommend buying ice, and using that instead of electricity to cool the fridge. If we can get ice every day, our power requirements are so drastically reduced that we can last indefinitely at anchor, even with little power input. Even if we can only get it every few days, this reduces the problem very considerably.

With a better insulated (or smaller) fridge that only needed to run half as long, your situation would be vastly improved.

Your power reserves can diminish very rapidly overnight and on windless, sunless days at anchor, so ensure you have enough batteries to cope with this.

Estimated balance of power input and output when at anchor

Weather conditions	Amps from: Wind	Sun	Total daily amps input	Remaining daily amps required from batteries	1 battery 50 amp-hours	2 batteries 100 amp-hours	3 batteries 150 amp-hours
					Supplying in total:		
					Would last the following number of days		
No wind or sun	0	0	0	50	1	2	3
Some sun	0	15	15	35	1½	3	4½
Some wind and sun	15	15	30	20	2½	5	7½
Some wind/good sun	15	25	40	10	5	10	15
Good wind/good sun	25	25	50	0	**Independence!**		

Installing equipment

Electrical equipment can cause havoc with radio reception, and cause electronics to malfunction. Therefore, buy good equipment (with in-built screens), and install it carefully (using appropriate techniques to suppress interference). This is especially important as regards all charging equipment (See Nigel Calder's *Boatowner's Mechanical and Electrical Manual* for further information (Appendix 2)). We also find the Navtex interferes badly with the radio – they should be well apart.

Electric sockets

12-volt sockets (cigar-lighter type) You will probably need appropriately placed sockets to provide power for extra 12-volt equipment such as vacuum cleaner, fan and iron, and chargers for phone, razor, computer, etc.

Shore-power sockets You will need at *least* one per cabin, plus one for the galley and chart table. I recommend fitting double sockets in each place (especially the saloon), because you will gradually acquire more equipment.

If your equipment is three-pin and sockets already installed are two-pin (or vice versa) then you need to change one or the other.

Lighting

You need good lighting for the chart table and galley, positioned so that you're not blocking your own light, and good reading lights everywhere you might want them. Each cabin should also have a bright light for general use, so that you can see to eat, find things in cupboards, etc. Consider also a mains ceiling light in the saloon. An electric light for the cockpit can be very useful when sitting out during autumn evenings (especially when eating dinner).

I strongly recommend lights that can be switched to either bright or dim if you can find them – normal ones either take too much from the battery, or aren't bright enough when there *is* lots of power. Alternatively, have dim lights for at anchor, but add some extra-strong ones for when power is available. Halogen lamps are expensive, but much brighter for the same power consumption (as are fluorescent lights).

DOMESTIC SYSTEMS

Water system

Electric water pump This is very useful, but it is essential to have a hand or foot pump as well, because:

- You must be able to get at your water in the case of a power or pump failure.
- You can sometimes get water out of a nearly empty tank with a manual pump after the electric one runs dry.
- Using an electric pump adds to your battery problems.
- The electric pump is best turned off at night, so you need a hand pump in the heads.

Hot water If you install a calorifier (running off the engine), make sure that it is big enough, and very well insulated – otherwise, even after a long trip motoring, you'll only have a small amount of hot water (which will have cooled down before morning).

For hot water in a marina, you need an electric immersion heater added to the calorifier. However, since shore power in marinas occasionally can't cope with more than 1kW or so, investigate the possibility of having high power for quick heating, but being able to switch to 1kW when necessary.

Water filter Much of the water in the Mediterranean, while potable, tastes unpleasant (and even ruins tea), and a water filter will remove many of the chemicals that cause this (though our Jabsco Aqua-Filta in-line filter does not much improve either brackish or heavily chlorinated water). Nor do most filters *purify* water so we don't drink it in case of nasties in the tank. But the filter does generally enable us to use tank water for tea and coffee, which greatly reduces the amount of drinking water we have to carry.

Water makers etc A water-maker is useful in the Mediterranean, but it isn't necessary, as you are never that far from a water supply. You also need to consider whether you can afford the power to run one.

Seawater taps and rainwater collectors are both unnecessary – and, when near land, neither provides clean enough water.

Other domestic modifications

Cooking stoves A good stove with an oven, preferably gas, is essential. It should be gimballed, with a crash-bar, surrounded by non-flammable material, and *all* the burners should preferably have flame-failure devices.

Diesel heaters For general use, a small electric fan heater is far more convenient. However, a diesel heater is useful if you are at anchor in early spring; and it is essential if you want to winter somewhere without electricity. *Phœnician*'s Eberspacher was so powerful that it needed turning off after only a few minutes. But it required a lot of power to start it (we usually had to run the engine), so turning it on and off frequently wasn't easy. However, modern Eberspachers can run at varying power levels, so this problem may be avoided. Gas is another possibility (though more risky).

Bilge pumps A manually operated one is essential, in case the electrics are off (highly likely in an emergency). However, if you had to pump for hour after hour, an electric one would also be very useful.

Holding tanks If you are going to spend a lot of time in Turkey (where pumping out in harbours or anchorages is prohibited) a holding tank is necessary, though they can be installed out there. For short visits to Turkey a Porta-Potti chemical toilet (address in Appendix 3) is a convenient compromise.

A holding tank must be large enough for some days' use, since (there being no discharge facilities) you have to go to sea to pump out. It must be designed to give maximum flexibility of use, and to ensure that pumping the tank to bursting is *absolutely* impossible. It is essential to use high-quality odour-free piping, since toilet waste will constantly lie around in it. Marineforce (address in Appendix 3) do a holding tank that fits conveniently around the toilet.

Improving the companionway ladder
Many companionways are dangerously long and steep, so Jimmy usually lowers the first step to the level of the cockpit sole, and makes it bigger – more of a platform. Then he alters the angle of the remainder so that it extends further forward, thus making the steps much less steep. It may

need shifting sideways, for adequate access around it.

Hand rails Are there sufficient hand rails for safety at sea. Below? In the companionway? On deck?

STOWAGE

Stowage is always a problem on liveaboard yachts, so it's worth making a lot of effort to improve things. Have fitted stowages for as many items as possible, and move ones that are inconveniently placed. Take spare matching wood with you for future modifications, as it's difficult to get it abroad.

General
Yachts often have more bunks than are needed by a cruising couple. Could one be altered to make more cupboards? However, leave enough sea berths for use on night passages when you have extra crew. Maybe a pilot-berth could be raised, with lockers beneath?

Mattresses
Four inches of foam is not very comfortable, so consider having a thicker mattress made – perhaps a 6-inch Dunlopillo – or at any rate renewing the old foam. The mattress will need ventilation beneath or condensation will cause mould. Holes in the locker lids help, as does inserting a layer of Ventair 15 (address in Appendix 3) or plastic grid (see photo).

You need proper bedding, but Dralon-type cushion tops make bedding 'walk' when you lie on it, so that your sheets end up halfway down the bed. If your bottom sheet is fitted, it will try to do the same, pulling the mattress with it

– and it's far worse with an underblanket. So consider replacing the covers on your bed cushions with more suitable material.

▲ Inserting linings under your bunk, such as Ventair 15 (cut-away) or plastic grid (red), will help to reduce condensation.

Yachts often have many decorative shelves, which are useless for stowage because everything falls off at sea. So consider building decent fiddles, or even proper locker fronts in wood that matches the shelves – or hold things down with bungee when going to sea. Shelves in cupboards need suitable fiddles too, otherwise everything falls out if you open the windward cupboard.

Although drawers are complicated to make, and the things in them take up more room, they make access to your equipment infinitely easier.

Most women will want some sort of dressing table with a mirror and drawers for storage of toiletries. Mirrors will be needed in each of the heads. Pictures are nice, but it's fun to buy these along the way (use mirror fasteners for them).

You will also need towel hooks or rings: for hand-towel, drying-up cloth and oven-glove in the galley, and two more in each heads.

If your floorboards are fastened down, try unscrewing them to see if there's stowage space underneath. This is particularly useful for things that need to be kept cool, but build dividers to keep bilge water out. Fit proper ring-pulls – dirt falls through finger-holes.

You also need a large shoe stowage.

Bookcases You will need *plenty* of books. Try adapting open lockers for them, or turning shelves into bookcases by adding fiddles (removable when in harbour). A suitable place near the chart table for lots of pilot guides is essential.

You need enough height above books to be able to remove them when the shelf is full and the books are vertical – the height required equals the diagonal measurement of the largest book (Fig 12).

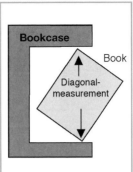

Fig 12 *Make sure that your bookcases are tall enough for you to be able to get the books out when the bookcase is full and the books are vertical.*

Lockers behind or under bunks If the cushions are large and awkward to move, get them divided into smaller pieces, ensuring each cushion neatly covers one locker entrance.

Hanging lockers These are very useful for hanging shirts, jackets, skirts, etc. But if there are too many, put shelves in one to give more vital stowage. If they are too low, try raising the rail.

You don't need a 'wet locker' – instead, fit hooks in the heads for drying things off. If you have two heads on board, one of them can be the permanent stowage for your bulky jackets.

Bedside shelf You need a shelf you can both reach in your own cabin, and preferably in the guest accommodation too. In extremis, a net-stowage is better than nothing, though no use for drinks. Marineforce do a suitable small teak 'overnight rack'.

Teak racks and boxes Obtainable from Marineforce, chandlers, etc these provide handy, attractive stowages for a variety of equipment – binoculars, hand-bearing compass, kitchen roll, spices, crockery, bottles, etc.

Phœacian's galley includes (from the top clockwise) electric fan, spice rack, curtain secured with a bottom rail, jar rack with fiddle, bottle stowage, heavy chopping board, kettle, foil and kitchen roll holders. All these items had to be added apart from the jar rack and the curtains.

Galley

Stowage for mugs and glasses These can be either a frame like a bottle-box, or holes cut in a flat shelf. Some of each are useful; they can be variously sized for mugs and jugs, and for differently shaped glasses.

Jimmy made a mug rack that lives on one half of the cooker, containing four mugs. Thus when at sea we can boil the kettle and pour drinks into *gimballed* mugs – brilliant! (photo page 83).

Plates and bowls These can be either upright on a bulkhead, or flat in a cupboard.

Jar racks Jimmy built me a lovely spice rack (photo above) – but now we find the galley is far too damp for them! It's essential to keep spices out of both light and damp, or they go off – but it's not easy to find airtight, opaque pots of the right size. Other alternatives are painting glass bottles to keep the light out; building your shelf *within* a cupboard, or in a less steamy place than the galley; or keeping the pots (labelled on the top) in an airtight box.

You need a long shelf for jars containing all the things you use frequently – coffee, jam, sugar, flour, etc. Raise the fiddle if necessary (as above). I saved up coffee jars, and now use these for everyday (take spare lids), with my main store of things being put away in a cupboard. Glass jars are usually best, as they don't retain smells. With non-slip matting on the shelf, the jars are pretty safe – or alternate them with plastic pots.

Bottle racks Also needing convenient stowage are various bigger bottles (oil, vinegar, soy sauce, etc) (see photo). Make a safe upright stowage for cleaning liquids – try under sinks, with suitable fiddles added. In addition to loose compartmentalised crates for drinks, plenty of built-in stowages for variously sized bottles are useful.

Waste bin We just use old carrier bags. These may be stowed under a hole in a worktop, in an opening cupboard, or even a small pedal-bin – a container of *some* sort is preferable, for otherwise it will smell.

4
Equipping Your Yacht

Trying to make a packing list for a short holiday is difficult enough – let alone one for six years – so I have attempted in Appendix 1 to list everything you might want. In this chapter, though, I discuss the less obvious aspects of *some* of the equipment you will need. I have italicised important safety items for quick reference.

One always has too much, so never take things just because they 'might be useful' or 'look more appropriate to boat than home' – instead, always make a planned decision that the item is required. Most people's houses are full of things that are hardly every used – so don't transfer them to the yacht! If you have two of something that is needed, then the better item should go to the yacht, since the home one can be more easily replaced.

The Marineforce (ex Cruisemart) catalogue is very useful for yacht gear, and Lakeland for domestic items; the Nauticalia catalogue also includes some useful gear (addresses in Appendix 3). Take the catalogues with you. Visit car accessory and camping/caravan shops, as well as chandlers.

SAFETY EQUIPMENT

When there are only two of you, safety becomes particularly important (read the RYA publication called *Cruising Yacht Safety*).

Man overboard

Lifebelt automatic lights are unreliable, so consider a *floating torch* to throw overboard as well. Some people wear a *personal EPIRB* when alone on deck, which sets off an alarm in the cabin if they fall overboard. But you must face the fact that if your partner does go over in a rough sea, you are very unlikely to recover them: so the absolute essential is to do everything you can to stop this happening in the first place. *Safety harnesses* are therefore far more important than lifejackets. We carry four harnesses, since we sometimes have four people on board on long passages. However, *lifejackets* are important:
- If you have to abandon ship.
- In dinghies, if you go far from shore.
- For children – on deck, in dinghies, and on pontoons.

Getting an unconscious person back on board is desperately hard, even in harbour

The horseshoe lifebuoy, an essential piece of safety kit, should be stowed within easy reach of the helmsman so that he can drop or throw it instantly.

stay, which *must* be well-tensioned – you will need a suitable (through-mounted) deck fitting.

Warning signals

White flares should be handy to the companionway, for use if a ship is about to run you down. You need a *horn* (also handy) for use in fog, and as a warning signal in emergencies (eg alerting someone that their anchor is dragging, or for attracting the attention of small boats about to ram you).

A *VHF radio* may be the only way of calling for help, so if yours isn't DSC-compatible, consider upgrading it (read the RYA's VHF booklet).

Fire-fighting

We wouldn't be without an *automatic fire extinguisher* in the engine compartment, plus *manual ones*. These should be: handy for the galley; under the spray-hood for use from outside; in each sleeping cabin so you can fight your way out (particularly vital if there is no other exit – eg if you've tied your dinghy over the hatch without a method of hoisting it clear from inside). Consider replacing them if their expiry dates are not far ahead. A *fire blanket* near the galley is absolutely essential.

Install an *electric solenoid valve*, so that from the galley you can switch the gas off at source. Also consider a *gas-leak detector*, which indicates if gas is flowing when nothing is in use (see Marineforce catalogue – address in Appendix 3), and/or a *gas detector* in the bilge.

with a bathing platform and full crew (as we know from experience), let alone at sea and singlehanded. So consider buying a *Life-Sling*, which is designed to help.

Storm equipment

Ocean-going yachts normally carry a sea anchor, but the chances of getting caught out in a storm are far less in the Mediterranean – we aim to use a *long rope* (fastened in loops to reduce the risk of it *all* being lost if it frays).

Likewise, a trysail isn't really necessary, but a *storm jib* should be carried; and if your forestay is taken up with the furling genoa, you need a means of hoisting it. A *removable inner forestay* is ideal. Otherwise have *two spare fore-halyards*, one for the sail and the other to rig as a

ABANDON SHIP!

You will need *either*:
- *A liferaft* This sounds like the obvious answer, neat, compact and foolproof – except that it isn't, because servicing in some parts of the Mediterranean is apparently unreliable.

or

- *A Tinker Tramp* (see Tinker dinghies, Appendix 3): This is an inflatable dinghy that can be turned into a liferaft by the addition of a *survival kit*. It is used as your ordinary dinghy, then set up as a liferaft before an offshore passage. You thus do your own servicing and so can be sure that everything is working. With our old Tinker, there was a lot more to it than just 'tipping it overboard and pulling the cord'; it was therefore nothing like as good as a liferaft that worked (though infinitely better than one that didn't!). Modern Tinkers, however, are much closer to a true liferaft.

   Tinkers are designed to *sail*, with a *sailing kit*, so (theoretically) you don't have to wait to be rescued, but can sail to safety. On an ordinary day-to-day basis, a Tinker with sailing kit means that you and your guests have a sailing dinghy to mess about in.

Panic box Store everything in *self-seal plastic bags* to keep dry, as the box may end up in the water. It should have a strong *lanyard* attached to it. Remember, you'll probably be wet and cold, and you may be injured. Water is essential but you shouldn't need much food.

Flares Take *lots* of *parachute flares* with you for trying to attract attention – we back up our in-date flares by keeping at least four out-of-date red parachutes as well. If some of your out-of-date flares are too old, a liferaft servicing shop may be willing to swap them for flares they've removed from a liferaft that are only *just* going out-of-date.

Extra panic bag An extra bag is useful for items you need to keep handy, eg:
- *Handheld GPS and VHF*: Useful as spares, as well as in the liferaft.
- *Personal essentials*: Passports, money, spare credit card, spare spectacles/ dentures, etc.

DECK EQUIPMENT

Mooring warps

When moored bow-to, you need two strong, shortish warps for tying the bow to the quay. I strongly recommend snubbers for them to take up the jerk in a surge – the rubber ones are quiet and handy (photo page 39) (we needed the size larger than recommended).

You need two longer warps when mooring in other ways (eg as springs), plus spare ropes (eg for use in gales), and one really long warp to use for 'anchoring with a long line ashore', as a tow rope, storm drogue, etc.

Fenders

Your fenders will take a real hammering, so make sure they're big enough – other-

Phœacian being lifted out gives a clear view of her bow fender (two sausage fenders tied firmly together) to protect the stem from damage from the quay when moored bow-to. Note that the bottom of the fenders are firmly secured.

wise it will be the yacht that gets hammered. They stow on deck or over the pushpit – I know this is bad form, but you won't have room elsewhere (see photos, pages 47 and 107). Fenders should preferably be white (or the same colour as the yacht). I recommend:

- *Two round fenders of the flattened type*: These are excellent for going between two yachts, since they don't squash like the sausage type. Place them at the beamiest part of the boat (one each side, because you'll mostly have yachts on both sides).
- *Four sausage fenders*: Place these fore-and-aft of the flat fenders. They are also needed alongside piers, as round fenders lose their position as the boat rolls.
- *A plank*: Tie outside sausage fenders, alongside piles or broken-down quays with holes that might 'swallow' fenders.
- *Two extra sausage fenders*: Tie together top *and* bottom, to fasten part-way up

the stem when moored bow-to with the wind from astern (Fig 14). This will protect the bow from crashing into the quay if the mooring or anchor drags. Don't leave it hanging loose; tie it in position (at the right height), with two long lines from the bottom, back to the stanchions (photo above).

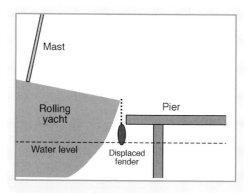

Fig 13 *Round fenders get displaced against piers if the boat rolls – long ones are better here.*

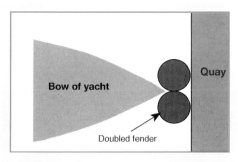

Fig 14 *Two sausage-shaped fenders, tied firmly together top and bottom, will protect the bow from damage if the yacht surges forward into the quay when moored bow-to.*

- *Two or more large balloon fenders*: These are worth their weight in gold – on either side of the bow while entering a bow-to billet; on the stern 'corners' once tied up – in case your neighbours make a mistake (highly likely if they're entering stern-first!); holding you off neighbouring yachts when rolling in a surge (or off a quay, when alongside), etc (photo opposite).

Tender

If you have a dedicated liferaft, you'll need a dinghy as well. For the Mediterranean, I don't think you can better the good old rubber-duck. It's relatively light, and easy to lift and stow; this is vital when you are shorthanded and are shifting between anchorage and harbour every few days. It won't sink (if reasonably maintained); it won't tip over as you get in or out; and it won't damage the yacht if you bump it. Have lifting-points fitted, so the mainsheet tackle can be used to hoist it on to the stern deck (or a halyard, on to the foredeck).

You may want an outboard engine. It is sad that these are so misused: people race around in them quite unnecessarily, disturbing peaceful anchorages – even children are let loose with them instead of being encouraged to row. For many years, Jimmy wouldn't have one because of the fire risk of petrol (far more dangerous than gas, especially in a hot climate). However, they are *very* useful for longer trips; and on reaching his seventies, Jimmy finally bought one.

Sails

Unless the yacht comes with a really good set of sails that will last the voyage, consider buying new ones. Choose a sailmaker who specialises in *cruising* sails. He will probably be able to sell the old ones for you.

Main If your mainsail is slab-reefing, have it full battened; this vastly improves both the way the sail sets, and its manageability. Fit lazyjacks to hold the sail together as you let it down. Or buy one of the patent fittings such as a Stak-Pak, which forms a stiff casing to house the sail.

A mainsail cover is very important, for the ultraviolet rays in the Med destroy sails much more quickly than at home. If you are having new sails, order UV-resistant cloth and stitching.

Genoa Again, this should be UV-resistant. Consider having a sacrificial strip, though they do add windage and detract from the set of the sail.

Spinnaker/cruising chute A spinnaker is more effective, but a cruising chute is easier to handle. Some cruising couples use cruising chutes quite a bit – we don't unless we have crew to do the work. If you are short of stowage space, is it worth carrying either?

Rigging, spars, etc

Bearing-out spar Even without a spinnaker, a pole can be useful for holding out the genoa when running – or two, if you

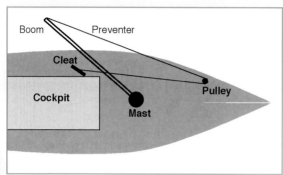

Fig 15 Rig permanent preventers to hold the boom out when running or reaching in a rough sea. This way you can control the sail and even gybe without leaving the safety of the cockpit.

have twin headsails. But you'll be handling it singlehanded, so get a lightweight one of the telescopic variety.

Boom preventers These are very necessary when running or reaching in a heavy swell, but going forward to rig them (or loosen them when hauling in) is dangerous. So rig *permanent* preventers. Snap-shackle a long rope to the end of the boom, lead the line forward outside everything to the bow, in under the guard wires and through a pulley, and back along the deck to the cockpit (Fig 15). As you let the sail out, haul in on the preventer and cleat it. When hauling in, let the preventer out.

When you've finished with it, haul the sail right in, unfasten the snap shackle, clip it on to a stanchion, and tie the free end off. Rig a similar, permanent line the other side of the boat, and they're ready whenever you need them – you can control the main perfectly, including gybing, from within the cockpit.

Climbing the mast In the Mediterranean you are unlikely to want to 'con your way into an anchorage' – you won't find any

Jimmy climbing *Phœacian's* mast ladder; this is made of webbing and is hauled up on a halyard.

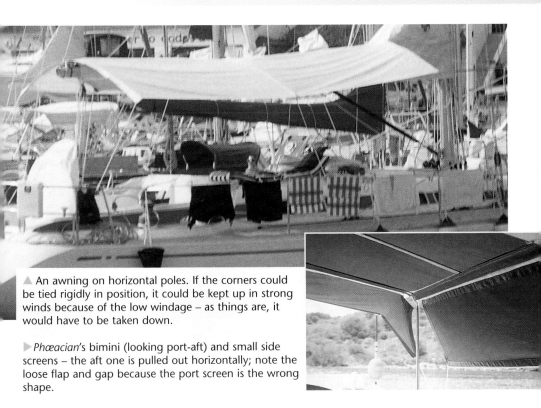

▲ An awning on horizontal poles. If the corners could be tied rigidly in position, it could be kept up in strong winds because of the low windage – as things are, it would have to be taken down.

▶ *Phœacian*'s bimini (looking port-aft) and small side screens – the aft one is pulled out horizontally; note the loose flap and gap because the port screen is the wrong shape.

uncharted coral reefs here. Therefore permanent mast steps aren't necessary. However, you have to go up the mast at times to work, so you'll need a bosun's chair. Alternatively, a mast ladder can be very useful. Ours is called Get-Up (see Appendix 3), and Jimmy is thrilled with it (photo left). Made of webbing, it's hauled up the mast slot (on a halyard) when you need it.

Whichever means you have, you will need two spare halyards, the second as a safety line.

Awnings, etc

I have already talked about building a bimini awning in Chapter 3, but other awnings/screens are needed:

Side screens The afternoon sun can be even hotter than at midday, and is much lower, so side screens on all *four* sides are vital. Ones that zip on to the edges of the bimini are easy to start with, but they deteriorate with time and use. Velcro fastenings, or ones that clip on with turn buckles, might be better. We now keep ours attached all the time, rolled up and fastened down on top of the bimini when not required. The join should be waterproof if possible.

Small side screens are best for normal use (photo above). For times when the sun is low, I suggest a continuation coming down to the guard wires. Consider making this of plastic mesh (available from sail lofts), so as not to impede the draught or the view so much. They *must* all be made with interchangeable zips – and make sure you take spare zips with you. You will also require fore-and-aft screens (these may need fitting around the

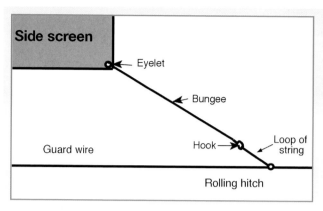

Fig 16 Fasten your side screens down to the guard wires with big, tough bungee, a loop of string and a rolling hitch.

rigid kicker or mainsheet, since it's useful if they can extend horizontally at times). Ensure the forward one *completely* shades the companionway when the sun comes from ahead.

The best method of fastening side screens is with really big, tough bungee (sold ready-prepared in car accessory shops), hooked down to the guard wires. The corners of the screens need pulling fore-and-aft as well as down-and-out, so put string loops on the guard wires to which the hooks can be fastened (Fig 16). Tie the string with a rolling hitch so that it won't slide along the wire. Fasten them to the lower guard wires so you can step over them.

'Mr Murphy' will ensure that if there is any minute gap between the screens, the boat will swing so that the sun shines through *precisely* into your eyes. So make the bottoms of the side screens bigger than the tops so that they overlap even when pulled out at an angle to the vertical; and fasten any flaps with Velcro tabs (*unlike* photo page 73). Put eyelet holes or eyelet tabs at intervals *all round* both the bimini itself and each of the side screens – it's incredible how useful they are.

Over-the-boom awning This is needed when in harbour to shade the cabins (and keep them cooler), and to shelter open hatches from rain. It should be quick and

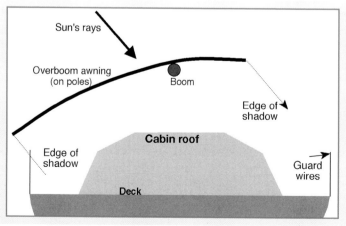

Fig 17 An over-the-boom awning on horizontal poles gives more headroom and can be slanted to face the sun, so that more of the yacht is shaded.

easy to put up, and mustn't disturb the vital flow of air (through the cabin or into the cockpit). Don't make it big and cumbersome – two smaller pieces to use independently are far better. Tent-shaped ones have a lot of windage and completely block the sidedecks, so consider building one on horizontal cross-poles (photo page 73). On calm days, slant it towards the sun and fix it lopsided – so that it covers the deck and cabin on the sunny side, but leaves the other one clear for walking (Fig 17). On windy days, if fixed horizontally and rigidly, it might not need taking down.

With a centre cockpit, you need one over the saloon and another over the aft cabin.

A new material We have just discovered *greenhouse shading*, a strange, greeny-black, see-through mesh that filters out the heat of the sun (available from hardware stores and gardening shops). If you get good quality material it's incredibly cool underneath, partly because it lets the wind through (thus even a big one won't add much windage); so it's a good material for a large awning that doesn't need to repel rain. You may be able to buy fastening clips with it.

Wind scoops In summer, your wind scoops will probably be in use day and night for months on end; and since their greatest effect is right below the hatch, you need one per cabin. Even in cooler boats, with forward-facing hatches, you need wind scoops during really hot weather (photo page 27). You can make them, but it's difficult to get them to work as efficiently as the bought ones. Fastening points on the cabin roof for the two forward corners are essential, but it's useful to have ones at all four corners.

Greenhouse shading used as an awning. This material gives good shade but lets cool air through.

Cockpit cushions

Purpose-made cushions are best, though expensive. Waterproof ones tend not to keep the water completely out, and they're horrible to sit on with bare skin, so make removable covers (of something easily washable, since they'll get soaked in sweat). Alternatively, have washable fabric ones and keep them dry (Marineforce and RYA catalogues). We prefer to have some of each type of cushion.

Garden-chair cushions are possible, but they are terribly thin and don't last well. But they can be used flat or to form a backrest, which is useful.

Other oddments

Have a long boathook, with an end that is suitable for both pushing *and* pulling, plus a patent snap-hook for picking up buoys in difficult conditions. If you have a deep cockpit locker, a short hook can also be useful for getting things out. Consider a small grapnel anchor for the dinghy, and a

FOLDING BIKES

These are tremendously useful, for both everyday activities and excursions. You really need one each. They must be very light (so you can lift them easily with one hand), and fold up to be really small. The cheap ones we bought initially were so difficult to stow, and to transport ashore, that we rarely used them. We now have Brompton's (see Appendix 3), which are super – but fairly expensive.

The bikes need baskets, because you will be using them a lot for shopping. Good locks are essential since bikes are very vulnerable to theft – the number-code type are best.

net for visiting children to fish with – both are useful for rescuing things dropped overboard!

A secure lock for the companionway hatch is essential – often all that holds a padlock are place are a few screws. We bought an excellent Stazo system (see Stazo Locks in Appendix 3) at the Boat Show, much stronger, and its fastenings are inside the yacht. You may also want a way of locking the boat from the inside.

COCKPIT LOCKER

Equipment for water, diesel and shore power

You need a shore-power lead, and a light half-inch hose. Both ours are 25 metres (80 feet), which is a good compromise. However, they're occasionally too short, and more often rather too long – so a short one of each as well (with connecting pieces for joining them) will give you more flexibility.

You can acquire end-fittings for both as you go along but:

- It's useful to make up a few short pieces of electric cable that can be plugged into your standard end-fitting: on the other ends of these, you then fit the most commonly used of the new ones – otherwise you're constantly rewiring the end.
- Take large and small universal hose-ends (rubber with a jubilee clip), plus a screw-on one; a hose-connector is useful anyway, and you may want an end-spray.

You'll need one or two 2-gallon (10-litre) diesel cans, plus *at least* two for carting and storing drinking water – try to get cans that fit into your bike baskets. Bigger ones are too heavy to carry, though may be needed for storage if your tank is small (if so, get ones with a tap). Water cans must be light-proof or they grow algae inside.

You will always be needing buckets – for cleaning, vegetable stowage, doing the laundry, etc. You need a pouring bucket (small enough to fill at the galley sink), buckets for the stern anchor cable, plus at least three others. The black rubber ones obtainable from garages are cheap, strong, and nest together. A pump-up garden spray or a black shower bag (available at chandlers) are good for showering over the stern.

Gas locker

Oil When an anchor light is necessary there may not be power for an electric one, so a hurricane lamp is useful (though Marineforce do a low-power electric light). Both are also useful for the cockpit on dark autumn evenings. (Note: paraffin is almost unobtainable in Spain.)

We did not find we used our saloon oil lamp.

Gas Calor is difficult to obtain in the Mediterranean – bottles cannot be exchanged, and can only be filled occasionally. So convert to Camping Gaz, which is easily available throughout the Med. We managed with two 2.8-kilogram (6 lb) bottles for many years, but three gives much more flexibility.

Petrol If there isn't room for the petrol can, try the anchor well – *don't* leave it in the sun.

ENGINE, SPARES AND TOOL KIT

Take the engine manual with you on the trip, plus the spares list (preferably with exploded diagrams), and the part numbers for easy identification when you need to order something. Ensure that you carry any 'special' tools you may need; some engines come with a dedicated tool kit.

It is essential to use Biocide regularly, because bugs in the diesel can completely incapacitate your engine. I also recommend a *big* diesel funnel with in-built strainer.

Take lots of old towels for cleaning the engine, plus a packet of disposable nappies for putting under it, especially when doing an oil change – they absorb spills wonderfully.

Engine spares

Get from your engine manufacturer the list of spare parts they recommend carrying – take the spares that are most likely to be needed, or that would cause most problems or be most difficult to get hold of if they went wrong. However, you aren't going 'to the end of the world', and it's not difficult to get things sent out by international courier (eg DHL; see Appendix 3). Find out who can send parts for your engine: try ASAP Supplies (take their catalogue – see Appendix 3), or ask your engine manufacturer.

It is difficult to find the right filters abroad for oil, diesel and air, and while standard engine oil can generally be obtained, take it with you if it is anything out of the ordinary.

Miscellaneous items

You will need bosun'ry: include a Speedy Stitcher (see Appendix 3) sewing awl (can be ordered from chandlers), which makes canvas repairs far easier, and also a suitable tool kit, perhaps including some power tools – possibly cordless ones with rechargeable batteries. A vice and work-bench are very useful if you can find anywhere to fit them. Also consider taking:

- Spare freshwater pump and shower pump if they are essential to the freshwater supply or drainage system – or their service kits if available.
- Heads spares: Packs are available from the manufacturers.
- Spare cooker burners: We've needed to replace the hob burners on both yachts within a few years. We found it impossible to get the first type abroad, and they'd stopped making the second.

RADIO, NAVIGATION AND ELECTRICS

Receiving weather forecasts

When preparing for a cruise to the Mediterranean, it's essential to take with you the right equipment for obtaining forecasts, but it's often extremely difficult to find out what is actually needed or where to buy it. It took us ages to sort this problem out, but we ended up being able to get forecasts when many other people could not.

SSB radio receiver The most useful piece of equipment is a suitable radio receiver, but what few of the books mentioned (until I told them!) is that the coast radio stations (who provide the best forecasts) transmit on Single Side Band (SSB). This is a different method of transmission from normal (though using the same frequencies) and requires a specialist radio to receive it. Most countries provide a forecast on their national radio stations, but generally only in their own language, whereas coast radio stations frequently give a forecast in English on SSB.

Unless you want to communicate with other yachts on the marine-band networks (such as the British Mobile Maritime Net), you don't need a sophisticated two-way radio – merely an SSB receiver, obtainable from high-street radio shops or via yachting catalogues. Sony unfortunately no longer make the wonderful 2001D (we bought ours in 1992 and are still using it!). What's available constantly changes, but the key features required (in order of importance) are:

- SSB mode.
- Complete coverage of the AM band – ordinary radios don't cover Short Wave, or have a gap between it and Medium Wave.
- 10-key (ie press-button) tuning, with a *digital* read-out to the nearest *0.1 kHz*. Check this carefully – on many radios the read-out is only to the nearest 1 kHz on the AM band (some can be tuned more finely manually, but this is no use if it isn't shown on the display).
- Good-quality radio and speakers so that you can receive and hear clearly in poor conditions – a very small or cheap radio will probably be inadequate.
- An extra, permanent, external aerial. The ordinary antenna attached to the radio will not be sufficient under poor reception conditions, so fit a dedicated backstay aerial (talk to an expert) or a big whip aerial on the pushpit. However, occasionally the small aerial is better: so rig it so you can switch between them.
- Memory keys, so you can recall the required frequencies at the press of a button.
- Timer buttons, so that you can set the radio to come on automatically at the required time and frequency: thus you will not risk missing that vital forecast. We find this feature immensely useful; we have four timer buttons, but would prefer more.

Such a radio will also be suitable for picking up the BBC World Service which, while not SSB, is Short Wave.

Navtex Navtex is the main alternative to an SSB radio, but there are still areas of the Mediterranean where forecasts are not available. We're often meeting people with Navtex who can't get one at all. However, coverage is improving, and it may well become the best method in the future. We now have a Navtex as a back-up to the radio.

Program out everything you don't need otherwise you will find that forecasts are lost in a sea of unwanted data. (See also Chapter 10, page 181.)

Weatherfax program for computers You will need a suitable SSB radio, plus suitable software and a connecting device – and much expertise!

Other electronic equipment

Built-in GPS I recommend getting one with 10-digit press buttons, since this is not only much quicker for entering positions, but makes the whole thing far more user-friendly. The so-called 'menu-driven' ones with only a few buttons are complicated to use; it's well worth paying extra for quality. Make sure Course-to-Steer, Distance-to-Go and Off-Track are written large enough to be easily readable from the cockpit.

Loran-C is not suitable for the Mediterranean, for accuracy is poor in the west and there is now no coverage in the east.

Electronic autopilot This also will be in constant use, so get a good-quality one (consider upgrading the one that comes with the boat). You will be doing a lot of motoring in light airs, so an electronic one is essential; some indicate rudder position on the display, and this is very useful when manoeuvring. A windvane type is worth considering if you want a spare, since this will presumably be in its element in the storm conditions that overpower the electronic ones.

Echo sounder This is essential for manoeuvring while anchoring, etc. It *must* have a cockpit display (or repeater) for it is here, not in the cabin, that the information is needed, since one of you will be on the helm and the other on the foredeck. Consider a 'forward-looking' type.

Log speedo This is not as necessary as it was before the advent of GPS, but it is still useful – and essential when your GPS goes kaput (and they do!). Both trailing and electronic logs do clog up with weed, but if it has a speedometer at least it's immediately obvious that this has happened.

Navigation lights If your bow light is vulnerable when you are climbing over the pulpit, consider having a permanent waterproof fitting, with the light itself being removable.

VHF radio Although this is useful for communicating with friends, it isn't very good for making initial contact with them because it's unlikely you'll be within range (especially in an anchorage surrounded by hills). However, once in contact (eg arranged by mobile phone text message), then the VHF is extremely useful – and also for picking up forecasts, and for communicating with marinas (staff often speak English). You will need an extension speaker in the cockpit (which can be turned on or off).

Radar Radar is not particularly necessary in the Mediterranean, since there is little fog (except occasionally in the early morning), and for navigation you have GPS. It would be useful down the foggy parts of the French and Portuguese coasts, but is it worth it just for this short period?

Wind instruments If you are buying wind instruments, it's fun to have ones that record maximum wind strength (installed where they can be read from the saloon as well as the cockpit).

Domestic electrical equipment
Mains-powered equipment
- *Fan heater:* This is essential, for use in marinas on cold spring evenings and nights.
- *Electric kettle:* A small electric kettle is useful. You don't need a large one which is difficult to store, though it will boil quicker. We have a 1½-pint (¾-litre) size, which only requires 1 kW.

- *Table lamp:* Screw bulbs are far easier to buy abroad than bayonet ones.
- *Microwave oven:* I'm not a 'microwave person', but if I were, and had room, I'd definitely take one for use in marinas in hot weather since they cook without creating heat.
- *Slow cooker:* If you put this outside, again it could cook your dinner without heating the cabin.
- *Television/video:* You can receive English satellite channels in the western Mediterranean if you have a 'dish', but if you want local programmes you need a multi-standard television, since different countries work on incompatible systems. Marineforce do a suitable 14-inch screen Grundig television and a video player, both of which work off either mains or 12-volt, and Nauticalia do a 10-inch (25.4 cm) screen combined unit. However, unless you have lots of spare power, television is best reserved for marinas. And do you really want it anyway?

Battery power You must decide how you intend to cope when you have no shore power. Can you restrict yourself when at anchor to equipment with internal batteries? If this is impossible, will you use cigar-lighter sockets for powering equipment? Or will you have an inverter powered by the 12-volt batteries? I understand modern ones are very efficient, and this will enable you to run 240-volt equipment when at anchor instead of being restricted to 12-volt. But having one will vastly increase your battery problems, unless you are *extremely* careful. Below are some items you may require:

- *Hi-fi radio-cassette:* You can build in a car radio that runs off 12-volt. This is convenient, but requires power that you may not have; also, you need to fit loudspeakers (these come separately). Alternatively, get a portable radio that runs off its own internal batteries. You may want a CD player – though I prefer cassettes because you can so easily duplicate all your home CDs and tapes on to them.
- *Torch:* This is needed near the companionway, ready for use on night passages or when returning to the yacht in the dark. A small one is useful to take ashore.
- *Vacuum cleaner:* Very useful. You can get 12-volt ones at car accessory shops, or Rowenta and Black & Decker make ones with internal batteries, rechargeable from the mains.

Other electrical equipment
Computers
- *Laptop computer* (plus suitable mains and 12-volt charger): If you intend to use a laptop at anchor, power will be at a premium. It needs a 'mobile processor' (ie designed for laptops not desktops – if using Windows software, right-click on 'My Computer', and check under 'Properties'), and also 'Speed-Step Technology' or equivalent: both optimise power consumption. A laptop with a modular bay may enable you to add an extra battery as one of the optional modules. You'll need a convenient place to use it, and another one (nearby) to store it safely when at sea (or build it in). It's essential to back up your work in case of computer breakdown (more likely in the adverse conditions of a yacht). A CD-rewriter is ideal for important documents that are too big for floppy disks – other alternatives are a *Zip-Drive* or *CLIK! PC Card Drive.* Various CDs are useful, such as an atlas,

dictionary and encyclopaedia (the Encarta set is good). An anti-virus program is essential of you are going to use e-mail.

- *Palmtop computer:* (see photo 76) This is good because you can work on it anywhere – at sea, in bed, while travelling, etc; and since it runs off internal batteries, it's ideal when you're short of power. Note, though, that they work on much simpler systems even than Microsoft Windows '95, so documents transferred to them will probably lose tables, pictures, some formatting, etc. They are quick and easy to start up and so are ideal for daily jobs like writing a diary. They have no hard drive, so a backup disk is essential.

- *Printer:* My Canon BJC 85 is ideal – small, convenient, and turns itself into an excellent scanner by substituting a scanner cartridge for the ink cartridge. Get the optional battery pack (rechargeable from the mains).

    Read the book *Using PCs on Board* (Rob Buttress and Tim Thornton, Adlard Coles Nautical).

Electrical oddments Standard batteries are available everywhere, but carry spares, especially unusual types. Anything with rechargeable batteries (eg mobile phone, electric razor, computer, vacuum cleaner) will need appropriate leads and regulators for recharging from the mains or 12-volt, preferably both.

OTHER NAVIGATIONAL EQUIPMENT

- *Charts*: If you're planning to head straight across Biscay, remember that weather conditions may force you to change your mind, so make sure you have enough charts and harbour information for emergency use. We use charts with scales of anything up to 1:300 000 for pottering, depending on the complexity of the coast and the detail given in the pilot guides, though up to 1:1 000 000 are OK for passage-making (with the same proviso). A few small-scale passage-planning charts are also useful – say, voyage to the Med, Western Med, and Eastern Med.

    Admiralty Charts are excellent quality but, for yachting in the Mediterranean, Imray's are perhaps better designed, with more suitable boundaries, useful insets, etc. It's worth sending for Imray's catalogue (see Appendix 3), for in addition to their own publications, they sell Admiralty charts, French canal guides, etc. You can buy excellent Croatian charts locally, but you will need a chart of some kind for your first arrival.
- *Parallel rulers*: We prefer the type called 'plotters' that have an integral protractor.
- *Pencils with an oblong rubber on the end*: These won't roll off the chart table at sea.
- *Hand-bearing compass*: Fasten its case to a bulkhead, handy to the companionway.
- *Binoculars*: Likewise, fasten their case to a bulkhead. On deck, keep them safe laid down in a padded box.
- *Sunglasses*: Very useful for keeping a lookout in bright sunlight.
- *Sextant:* Consider a sextant as a back-up in case of GPS failure, plus a dedicated calculator to do the work for you – far easier than using tables, which you probably won't have anyway, since the almanacs have stopped publishing the ephemeris.

Take spare UK-style plugs, and an adaptor for plugging Continental equipment into UK sockets (not a shaver socket); also vice versa for use ashore. If you are short of mains sockets, take some multi-socket extensions which are safer than multi-outlet adaptors. A mains extension lead is useful for tools needed outside – and consider a 12-volt extension lead.

For those who suffer from hot flushes, you can buy 'personal fans' – pocket-sized mini-fans with internal batteries. Also consider a travelling iron and a hairdryer; 12-volt irons lack power, so a small mains one would probably be better: alternatively, rely on laundries for ironing.

DOMESTICS AND GALLEY

Bedding and linen

Try to have enough linen (and clothes) aboard to last for three weeks before having to do laundry by hand – hopefully by then you will have found a launderette.

In high summer, even a sheet on top of you is often too hot, but in spring and autumn the nights get cold (especially on a boat, with little insulation or heating). Here are a few tips:

- Bed making is difficult, so a duvet is convenient; but department stores don't sell light enough ones so try specialist bedding shops. Even 4-TOG is too hot (though fibre ones are cooler than feather). Friends have a 1½ TOG and a 3-TOG that clip together which is ideal. An alternative is light, cellular blankets.
- Duvet covers: these may need fastening to the side of the yacht with Velcro to stop them sliding off – stick the Velcro to the woodwork and staple the edges down; use the sew-on type on the

material since the stick-on version comes off in the wash (don't try sewing the sticky type).

- Top and bottom sheets for both cabins. You may find fitted sheets easier. Try to find an upholsterer who makes them for a boatbuilder, since it's a complicated job and they're used to it. Fitted bottom sheets need fitted darts (and elastic) at every corner however slight, otherwise the sheet ruckles up; also, to be of any use, elastic must be fitted in a curve. Don't make the sheets too tight fitting since they will shrink over the years – pulling the mattress out of shape. Don't use ordinary poppers for holding things in place as they aren't strong enough – use hammer-in studs (available from sewing accessory shops).
- Sheets get very dirty in summer, due to sweating and suncream. Draw sheets (the shape of the mattress and Velcroed on to the fitted bottom sheet) are easy to wash. Use the soft half of the Velcro on the draw sheets, since the hooked half catches in machine washes – use this on the bottom sheets, and wash these fastened to the draw sheets. Two top, three or four draw, and two bottom sheets for your cabin are probably sufficient, plus one less of each for the guest cabin.
- Take two sleeping bags of the zipped type, the ones that you can unfold. These can then be used at sea, or by guests, or as eiderdowns on cold nights, etc.
- You'll need pillows and pillowcases. If the bed is short, it's worth making the pillows smaller.
- A light rug is useful as an extra, intermediate-weight bed covering.

Fit lee cloths for sea berths – preferably three, so all but one of a four-man crew can be off-watch on long passages. One can also be used for storage every time you go to sea.

You will need curtains for all windows (with rails top *and* bottom, see photo page 66), plus roller blinds for all hatches. Both should be light-proof.

Large and small saloon cushions add comfort (with pretty, washable covers); feather- or cotton-filled cushions and pillows are *far* cooler to lean against than man-made materials.

Shower towels should not be too large, thick or fluffy since these are dreadful to wash by hand. But have *some* larger ones for use when you do have access to a washing machine: these will double as spares for guests, and as beach towels.

Laundry

Make sure you have some storm pegs, since these don't come loose even in high winds – yellow and orange Peglock gale-proof clothes-pegs made by Hoselock, available from supermarkets and ironmongers. They work best on plastic-coated wire, so if your guard wires are plain metal, get Peg-a-Pegs (see the Lakeland catalogue) as well. Mega-Pegs (also Lakeland) are useful for hanging bedding out to air. You will also need a long, plastic-coated clothes line to tie in the rigging. In addition, one made of two pieces of elastic wound round and round each other is useful for poking small things through.

Universal sink plugs are useful ashore (sinks never have plugs).

Cookware

Ordinary cookware tends to go rusty and to need replacing. If you can find something in stainless steel, that is exactly what you want – it's well worth the extra investment.

I recommend a non-stick frying plan for ease of use (although they don't last

The galley showing gimballed cooker with custom-built mug rack, Judges kettle and other useful equipment.

long), with some kind of lid to stop vaporised fat getting all over the upholstery. Your gas kettle should be small enough to fit on the cooker *with* the frying pan; it needs a lid for easy filling (and to clean out limescale), a whistle, and a one-handed method of opening the spout and pouring. My stainless steel Judges kettle is ideal (photo above).

A pressure cooker for rapid cooking is *very* useful in hot weather, and doubles as a large pan (remember, you will be cooking for four or more at times). They're easy to use and come with clear instructions, so don't worry if you're not used to them. A steamer will enable you to cook more than one thing on a single burner.

Large, medium and small Pyrex dishes are useful, as are large and medium plastic mixing bowls (for washing-up when short of water, for preparing cooking, and for storing food). *All* these should preferably have plastic sealing lids for future storage in fridge, etc.

Get a second oven shelf from the manufacturer, and take a jam funnel for pouring things like rice and flour into more conveniently sized containers. Also, a whisk will be useful, and perhaps even a food processor (hand or electric or both – or maybe just an old-fashioned Mouligrater). Your chopping board should be deeper than the work-surface fiddle or otherwise this will get cut. I like to have a gravy skimmer (to separate fat from meat juices), and a meat thermometer is very useful for a non-thermostatic oven. Caravan accessory shops and Nauticalia both sell hob toasters (which do five pieces at a time) and portable hobs and barbecues (for cooking outside in hot weather).

Crockery and cutlery

Six of everything is to be recommended – they don't take up much extra room and you will occasionally want to entertain. We use pretty melamine tableware, but prefer glass and china for drinking. Even delicate glassware can be stored safely at sea, but may get broken when in use or being washed. We have a set of delicate wine glasses for use with guests, but use unbreakable glass for everyday purposes. It is possible to get very pretty plastic wine glasses.

Good quality tea is not easily available in the Mediterranean, and is also expensive, so most people bring it from home. But sufficient teabags for six months takes up a lot of room, so loose tea is much better. For this you will need either a teapot and strainer, or *boules-à-thé* – metal tea infusers like spherical tea strainers (available from Carwardines, Lakeland and hardware stores). You need at least two of these (they can't be used damp), plus spares. Make sure they seal perfectly.

Conversely, coffee is often excellent abroad, and making the real stuff is easy with either a filter-set (filter papers plus plastic straining funnel) or a glass *cafetière* (coffee-making jug with press-down filter). Bodum *cafetières* are usually cheaper, but Pyrex glass jugs seem stronger (they're interchangeable). Also, take a spare jug (the small size is fine), and 1 x 2 Melitta filter papers.

General galley equipment

You'll need a large draining rack for washing-up – Lakeland and Nauticalia sell folding ones, but you may find them either too heavy or too small. I was unable to find a suitable draining board, so I keep my rack on a tray. A strip of cloth leading from the tray to the sink drains the tray by suction. You will also need something to hold the crockery in place if the yacht heels .

Medium and large Klippits are invaluable for clip-sealing plastic bags of food (available from Lakeland and elsewhere).

You will need sets of airtight boxes of varying sizes – *lots* for storing dry food (eg rice), plus more for storing food in the fridge (preferably nesting, for when not in use); sandwich boxes (large and small) and biscuit boxes are also useful (Tupperware, Lakeland and hardware stores).

Non-slip table mats are really effective – far better than fiddles on the table (available from chandlers and Marineforce). A surface that is slightly tacky is better than a shiny one.

Lakeland sell open boxes that both nest and stack – ideal for compartmentalising a very deep fridge, and indeed elsewhere. Bottle boxes are useful for storing glass bottles safely. The six-bottle size are easiest to stow (plastic: from Lakeland; cardboard: from wine merchants).

Clip-on bottle stoppers are *very* useful (available from Lakeland and ironmongers) to prevent the loss of wine if the bottle tips over. Wine goes off rapidly if left open to the air, so get a pump (and seals) for pumping out air from part-used bottles. Variously sized bottles are also useful for storing small amounts of leftover wine (eg medicine bottles from chemists). Bottles of fizzy drinks need to be kept under pressure, but you need a different kind of pump for pumping these up.

Fruit and vegetables sweat in plastic bags – paper bags are far better. But in hot weather, vegetables go dry or limp very quickly: so get Stay-Fresh bags (from Lakeland).

Take an insulated butter/margarine dish (so the butter doesn't melt while in use), and a cool-bag for collecting ice and taking food on picnics. BHS sell small cool-bags for individual tins of drink.

Roasting bags will keep the oven clean, but seem to be unavailable abroad. They should be big enough for a chicken plus potatoes (Lakeland do a good size).

Food and drink

Marks & Spencer sell delicious tinned meals, ideal for when you get in late and tired and can't face cooking.

Stock up with your favourite drinks if there's any doubt about finding them – consider ordering duty-free. At sea, one needs drinks that taste nice when made just with boiling water – I find Options to be the nicest of the instant chocolate drinks made in this way. Bovril is also delicious, and you can buy sachets of instant cappuccino coffee.

I think UHT milk is horrible when you first use it, but you get used to it. Fresh milk is very difficult to obtain, and of unreliable quality. Condensed milk (though sweet) is another option.

While water is normally pretty good in the Mediterranean, it's best to take some purifying tablets. Puritabs are fine for small quantities, but for cleansing the tank, order Puritabs-Maxi from the local pharmacy or Aqua-Tabs from Marineforce.

We normally carry six 1½ litre bottles of water for drinking when tap water isn't good, then we keep the empty bottles for refilling when it is.

General domestic

Rolls of non-slip matting are *wonderful* for stopping things sliding around in rough sea (available from chandlers and Marineforce, although Lakeland is usually cheaper). (*Note*: This material is flammable.) Ensure that all freestanding objects are wide-based (eg jugs, glasses, table lamps), or fit a wooden base to them (eg on knick-knacks). Heavy duty rubber floor mats (motor accessory shops) are useful to stop *you* slipping, and try carpet or DIY shops for non-slip rugs.

Self-seal bags are convenient for storing clothes, etc, and for keeping damp out – take lots of different sizes (available from Lakeland and some stationers, and from Drix Plastics, see Appendix 3). Silica-gel drying crystals are useful for keeping stored things dry (available from pharmacies); use the Lakeland Tea-Bag Kit for storing the crystals. Alternatively, collect small sachets of silica gel from shoe shops.

Take two strong rucksacks for shopping and to use on flights home – this is by far the most comfortable way of carrying heavy loads. You should also have a small one for expeditions ashore.

Bubble-wrap is useful to protect fragile items from damage.

Toilets A Porta-Potti chemical toilet (address in Appendix 3 and available from camping and caravan accessory shops) is perfect when laying up ashore (and also if

MEDICATION

Liquids and creams are very vulnerable to heat, and such items may need replacing every year. You can easily buy everyday things abroad, but your own personal medicines or favourite brands of toiletries will be much more difficult, so take a supply.

Toiletries If you suffer from hay fever etc, being at anchor (or at sea) insulates you from the pollen, which is great. However, if you suffer from a dry, irritable skin, the heat, sweat and salt make this far worse. My salvation has been to take with me E-45 Wash, an anti-allergy washing cream that doesn't dry the skin out (also, Boots' Glycerine & Rosewater).

Medicines You can generally get to a doctor unless you are at sea, but it's not always easy and you must be able to carry out initial first aid.

After discussions with various doctors, we have compiled a list of necessary items (see Appendix 1). We have three boxes: medicines, first aid, and a serious-injury kit.

your only head gets blocked). It can be used in Turkey if you have no holding tank.

In Greece and Turkey, the sewage disposal system can't cope with toilet paper, so they provide a bin. Many yachts do the same, to avoid blocking the heads. Nappy-Sacks (from Boots) are ideal for the soiled paper.

Seasickness remedies Don't believe those who say 'there is nothing to beat' a particular remedy, since individuals react differently. However, a very commonly preferred remedy are Scopoderm behind-the-ear patches, which I strongly recommend trying. We found them incredibly effective, but unfortunately I suffered side effects. However, Kwells tablets and Boots' Travel Calm use the same chemical (hyoscine hydrobromide). (I find Kwells excellent – and without side effects!)

Some people like pressure-point wrist bands (Marineforce, chandlers and pharmacies) and Nauticalia sell an (expensive) electronic version for which they claim a 90 per cent success rate. It is also possible to get remedies in the form of suppositories to treat someone who is too sick to keep tablets down.

Insect deterrents Mosquitoes are little devils, and the only satisfactory solution is to keep them out of the yacht altogether at night by using screens. These must entirely cover every opening, however small. They should be tight fitting, but made of netting that lets the wind through easily, otherwise you'll stifle in hot weather. They can be in drop-down wooden frames, or have elasticated edges to clip round the outside of the hatch frame. The latter type should preferably be made big enough to allow the hatch to be opened without having to remove the screen.

You need something to kill off any mosquitoes that get trapped inside, and to use in the cockpit. Mosquito coils are effective, but smelly. Electric pastilles are no better, and use power. A jar of liquid killer that plugs into the mains is excellent when in a marina (available abroad).

Flies can also be a problem, so flyscreens are useful for protecting plates of prepared food.

BOOKS

If the books you want are unobtainable, contact the Out-of-Print Book-Finding Service (see Appendix 3). They will take time to get them though, and they will probably cost as much as buying new.

Reference books

Books on navigation People complain about the cost of pilot guides, but I think they are excellent value considering the vast amount of information in them, and the work involved in keeping them up to date. You could only get two or three charts for the same money. If you find inaccuracies or changes, don't just grumble! Help others by sending the correct information to the publishers (most are published by Imray, who also do translations of some of them into other languages). Don't buy further ahead than you need, since harbours change rapidly – ask Imray when their new editions are expected. Get any appropriate updates (published annually by Imray – see their website (details in Appendix 3)).

Almanacs/tide tables covering the Atlantic coast are essential; almanacs also save you from having to buy lots of pilot guides when crossing areas very quickly. The *Imray Mediterranean Almanac* (covering two years, with second-year supplement) gives details of all the larger harbours in the Med (more up to date than the pilot guides), plus lots of other information. Almanac handbooks give useful, more permanent, information.

If you intend to take a sextant, but not a dedicated calculator, you will need both an ephemeris (annual), eg *Reed's Astro Navigation Tables* and air tables (permanent); and to make appropriate sight-forms.

Books on the Mediterranean You will want books about sailing the Med, books on the area's history, and guide books to particular countries.

An atlas or touring map of the Mediterranean (or Europe) is useful, plus maps of areas you want to explore. Michelin do good ones (French is best for North Africa), and their *Red Guides to Hotels and Restaurants* are useful because they recommend good restaurants (some reasonably priced). Some caravan guides indicate where there are launderettes.

Field guides The *Complete Mediterranean Wildlife Photoguide* (Collins) covers *most* flora and fauna briefly, which is handy – but you may want some more detailed field guides. The Dorling Kindersley series seems good. Gooders's *Field Guide to the Birds of Britain and Europe* (Kingfisher) is really good at helping you identify birds, but doesn't cover Turkey or North Africa, or rare birds; the new *Collins Bird Guide* is quite good, and does cover these things. A book on sealife is also interesting – make sure it has a good section on sea mammals such as dolphins.

Dictionaries and language books You'll want an English dictionary – perhaps a small dictionary in book form and a large one on computer disk? People whose native language is not English will want a dictionary in their own language, plus one that translates that language into English, since this is the lingua franca in the Mediterranean.

In addition, you need a foreign language phrase book for each of the countries you will be visiting. Most of these also give a pronunciation guide, menu reader, mini-dictionary and mini-grammar. The *Rough Guide* series conveniently include both dictionary and phrase book in one alphabetical list (and, in Greek, manage without involving the Greek alphabet). However, they include fewer phrases. *The Yachtsman's 10 Language Dictionary* has useful sailing words and phrases.

It's vital to have a cassette giving guidance on pronunciation – it's impossible to say the words correctly without. Some phrase books have companion cassettes.

If you are staying for a long time in one country, buy a good dictionary as well. Some fail to make clear which meaning of a word is being translated (eg the word 'bar' has at least six different meanings, and obviously you must use the correct one). The *Collins Gem Dictionaries* are good.

Cookery books A small, general-purpose cookery book is advisable; and I make my own, with all my favourite recipes. Take also your pressure-cooker recipe book, and one on vegetarian meals (always useful when meat is difficult to get or store), salads (ideal in hot weather), and fish/shellfish preparation/cooking.

Other reference books A first aid book is essential, such as *First Aid at Sea*.

Foods that Harm, Foods that Heal (Reader's Digest) is an excellent guide, alphabetically listed under both 'Foods' and 'Health' headings.

Finally, make sure you have all the user manuals for your equipment, in case you have problems.

Reading books

Legends and history Before you go east of France, I particularly recommend reading all you can about the voyages of Odysseus (Latin name, Ulysses), since this is really fascinating and all the places he is thought to have visited are mentioned in Rod

Heikell's *Pilot Guides*. The most credible is Scylla and Charybdis in the Messina Strait, since the whirlpools are still there – though luckily much diminished due to earthquake activity.

Novels You'll want lots of these! There is a flourishing 'book swap' arrangement among live-aboards, so in addition to old favourites that you want to keep, take plenty of light reading material for swapping (try charity shops and second hand bookshops).

DOCUMENTS, STATIONERY, ETC

I have not found stationery easy to buy abroad, so take what you need.

Documents and money

It is essential to take the appropriate documents relating to both the yacht and yourselves. These are mostly fairly obvious, and I list them in Appendix 1. In theory you need a translation of your yacht insurance (from your insurer), especially into Italian; we have never been asked for it, but friends have.

Take a 'starter' supply of euros (and any other necessary foreign currency), plus money for your trip home from the airport. For getting money abroad, we always use our Visa debit card. However, while eurocheques remain defunct, consider some additional hard currency (or perhaps traveller's cheques) for emergencies. Also take your ordinary cheque book so that you can pay bills by post, or to give to visitors for the things they bring out.

If you wish to do any driving while abroad, you need one of the new European Driving Licences with photo. Ensure that

The pretty town of Trogir in Croatia, seen from the marina.

your passports, credit cards, etc will not expire while you are away. It is very useful to make yourselves small identity cards by getting the back page of your passports photocopied (reduced to credit-card size), and then heat-sealed in plastic.

Record books

Transfer book This is an important book in which I record all the information that I wish to transfer from yacht to home and vice versa. Mine is an A6 hardback, ring-bound book, so I can tear out sheets when I have finished with them. At the front is temporary information that can be discarded when transferred – including lists of the things to buy when next home; addresses of new friends or new addresses of old ones; jobs to do when we return; and things we need to remember to take with us. At the back is more permanently required information. The first few pages at each end are reserved for those things that are needed most frequently (a regular packing list for taking to and fro, phone numbers that might be needed en route, etc).

Address book You need your address list both at home and on board. This means either copying it into a separate book (hard work), or taking your address book or personal organiser to and fro with you (risky), or having the complete list on computer (which means keeping up-to-date printed copies in both places).

Visitors' book Ours is a treasured possession – I use a book with blank pages, and include not only written comments by all our new friends, but also photographs I take of them (preferably showing their boat as well). Most visitors' books have only a few lines per person, but everybody loves our more interesting one.

Log book I like John Mellor's *Logbook for Cruising Under Sail*, because the format is flexible and it has a column where you can copy the lat and long from the GPS. We don't fill it in every hour, so one book lasts years.

Diary and records book Unfortunately, as a record of your voyage, your logbook gives too much detail about sailing, and not enough about anything else. So in addition, in an A5-sized, lined hardback notebook, I keep a summarised record of our overall cruise. I have a couple of lines per day, stretching across a double page of the book, with columns covering the following:

- Date and mileage logged
- Harbour where we spent the night
- What we did that day (including starting and arrival times)
- Symbols indicating how we were moored, level of shelter of the harbour, and what kind of night we had as a result
- Restaurant name if we ate out, plus price and quality
- Symbols indicating whether we recharged with water, electricity, gas; did the laundry, etc
- Today's forecast (including which areas had a gale warning, to get a picture of weather in other areas for future reference)
- Today's actual wind and weather
- Barometric pressure, plus max and min temperatures

If you wish to have a more detailed record of your cruise, you must be rigorous in keeping a diary up to date as well – I find a similar book to the one for records is more flexible than a proper diary. Alternatively, keeping it on your computer enables you to add things afterwards that you'd forgotten – but print it out regularly in case of computer failure. Take a small calendar for reference.

Notebook for cruise report Writing a cruise report every year makes a wonderful record for you to keep. It can be anything from a brief, handwritten notebook to a complex, colour-printed document prepared on your computer, but the main point is to record the story of your cruise, illustrated with maps (vital) and photos. If you include enough useful information, copies will be in great demand from acquaintances following in your footsteps.

Account book If you wish to keep regular accounts, a suitable book is helpful. Collins' Cathedral Analysis Books come in all variations. Alternatively, use a computer program such as Microsoft Money. I have columns for: date; money cashed; harbour dues; meals ashore; personal expenditure; yacht expenses; drinks and fun; oddments; and food – plus columns recording who put how much into 'housekeeping'. The final column, 'Amount of Money Remaining', acts as a check.

Other notebooks Take along plenty of notebooks for general use. Weather forecasts are vital, so take a small notebook to record the frequencies (and times) on which you have successfully received one. Also useful is a Port Information Book for adding information on harbours – if you just note this in the pilot guide, you will lose it when you buy a new edition.

Other records and stationery
Photo albums If you spend most of your time on board, you'll probably want to keep photo albums there (plus sheets of negative holders). Or you may prefer to take your photos home. I tried posting my films home (developing is *far* cheaper in England), but stopped because you don't get to see the photos for months, and one film got lost in the post.

Folders The longer you spend in the Mediterranean, the more papers you acquire, so colour-coded document wallets are handy for keeping them tidy. We keep most equipment instructions in individual plastic wallets in a large ring binder.

Port forms You don't need 'Port forms in triplicate' to hand over because all anyone wants is certain information copied on to *their* form, but it is useful to have all the details of yacht and crew written out beforehand on a dual-language form (not multi-language, they find this confusing).

Stationery oddments We have not found a yacht stamp or tracing paper necessary, but visiting cards are very useful: with our names, name of yacht, mobile number, home address, e-mail address, etc.

PERSONAL GEAR

When you live in two places, with lots of travelling between the two, you must avoid carting mountains of things to and fro unnecessarily. One is normally very short of space on returning to the yacht because of the new boat gear required – and adding to this load may be the last straw. Therefore duplicate all items of clothing, leisure equipment and personal gear needed both at home and aboard, so that hardly anything is taken backwards and forwards – except for those things actually wanted on the journey.

Even if you can't afford to duplicate everything, make sure you leave enough things at home to last the first week or two on your return in order to give yourself a chance to buy more. You can buy excellent clothes from charity shops at a fraction of the new price; and while clearly you have to pick and choose, I've been staggered at the quality of what they have. Once you start buying in charity shops, paying new prices becomes really upsetting! These shops sell domestic equipment too.

Regarding clothes, most problems concern female ones, so in what follows I concentrate on these.

I find it convenient to have most of my clothes in a single mix-and-match colour scheme.

I don't use a handbag, but have a secure shoulder bag with lots of pockets for travelling, when you need to keep many things safe. A bum bag is useful ashore (easily available abroad), and clothes with zip pockets are ideal.

Clothes

Warm weather Have everything very lightweight in pale colours, since these shades deflect the sun (dark colours absorb the rays and rapidly heat up). Items should be pure cotton or nearly all-cotton – most man-made fibres are very uncomfortable because they reflect your body heat back at you. However, Rohan (see Appendix 3) trousers, shorts and shirts are ideal – the 'Bags' material is cool and light and dries really quickly; they also have wonderful pockets for hankies, money, keys, etc.

Sunhats should provide adequate protection, and be tight enough not to blow off. More than one is advisable (different types).

On board, you will probably live in swimwear in hot weather, so you need several garments. Bikinis deteriorate in the strong sun (don't leave them out unnecessarily), and often only last a year. (Make sure at least one item of swimwear is 'decent' for when passing mooring warps to men ashore!) You can get bikinis with matching saris or wrap-over skirts/sarongs – these are attractive, provide more cover than a bikini, and the saris can be stuffed in a bag to take ashore as a shawl.

Shore-going clothes for very hot weather are the most difficult to find. They should be as scanty as possible unless you suffer badly from sunburn. I like what I would call 'sun-tops' – these are much more modest than a bikini top, but still only cover the minimum, being low-cut with shoulder straps, and leaving the waist bare and cool. They can be either loose-cut or fitted, but must be very light and made of 100 per cent cotton. It may be easier to make one yourself – or get your local dressmaker to do this for you.

Cool weather Spring evenings and nights get quite cold (due to the clear skies), especially in contrast to the hot afternoons, and are certainly cool enough to make you need some warmer clothes. But again, these should not be of man-made materials that heat you up – corduroys are good. During winter you don't really need anything different, merely more warm clothing.

Take a nice, warm, fleece-lined jacket (possibly waterproof), and some clothes for cold-weather sailing. Also, have a light jacket for evenings ashore – and a bed jacket and bedroom slippers are wonderful on cold spring mornings!

Consider a towelling bathrobe for wearing when going ashore for a shower, so you don't have to get dressed in the awkward, wet conditions.

Smart clothes A smart skirt and blouse are useful for parties, but the skirt mustn't be tight. I find a long, full-cut skirt ideal – you can climb over guard wires in it, it's cosy when required to be, yet can be pulled up if you get too hot. It's a bit overdressed, but I like dressing up!

Men should have something tidy, but nothing too posh. They won't need a blazer or suit – good trousers and shirt, with a smart yacht club jumper and tie, are ideal.

Ensure you both have something that will be suitable for very hot weather.

Sailing gear and shoes Except on the voyage down, we don't find heavy oilskins are necessary. Once we get to the Med, really *light* waterproof tops and bottoms (against rain) are far more practical, though it is probably wise to keep one medium-weight oilskin jacket on board. We don't use sea boots.

You will need a number of pairs of shoes, including some you can walk in comfortably over rough ground. Swimming shoes are also useful, to avoid treading on sea urchins. In hot weather, sandals are far more comfortable than deck shoes. Everything should be non-slip and low-heeled.

Leisure items

Choices here will depend on your personal interest and hobbies, but the first essential is a good camera so that you will have a record of your voyage. Film is easy to buy, but consider a digital camera if you're taking a computer. A camera with a zoom lens is useful – you can get small automatic ones that work well so long as you protect them from knocks (I recommend a padded case).

In addition, a panoramic camera is ideal for sea views – permanent cameras that offer 'normal *or* panoramic' have not actually got a wide-angle lens, but throwaway panoramics do (get them printed on appropriately shaped paper).

Most people will want music cassettes or CDs, and to be able to listen to the radio. The BBC World Service can be received all over the Mediterranean, but get a copy of *On Air Magazine* (address in Appendix 3) from the BBC, which gives the times of the programmes (or check the internet; the *Radio Times* also gives brief details).

While the Mediterranean lacks the wonderful underwater life of the Caribbean, a mask, snorkel and flippers are still worth taking (especially for clearing the propeller!). Make sure that the mask fits perfectly so it doesn't leak. If you're short-sighted, get your mask made up with your prescription lenses (this takes time).

People often take lots of fishing gear with them, hoping to catch wonderful free meals – but for most of us this remains a rosy dream. If you're not an expert, I would suggest just towing a mackerel-spinner near rocky headlands – it's the only thing that catches us anything!

5

Leaving Home

If you plan to 'Sell up and Sail', the book of that name offers guidance. However, if you *do* want to keep a base at home, a flat is more practical than a house so long as you choose carefully. Avoid:

- Areas where vandalism is likely.
- Top floor and corner flats which often leak, and will need more heating.
- Ground floor flats which are more easily burgled, and may have a garden that needs maintenance.

Points to look for:

- A position close to family and friends.
- A garage could be useful for storage.
- Access to an international airport will be important.

LEAVING YOUR PROPERTY EMPTY

Securing your home against intruders

Join Neighbourhood Watch and invite the crime prevention officer round to advise you. Aim to put off the casual thief by making entry as difficult as possible. Consider installing lights on timers that come on randomly.

Burglar alarm

This is very important. We were advised that the best type is the one with sensors that spot any movement inside. But does anyone take any notice of an alarm bell – the burglar included? I recommend the more expensive system where you are linked to a centre by phone and they monitor your alarm. If it goes off, they immediately send the police round (or the fire brigade if it's the smoke alarm).

Use a reputable company – it should be 'NACOSS approved'. You'll need key holders to your property, one of whom will be called round if the alarm goes off in order to let the police in and turn off the alarm/reset it. Make sure that your telephone (and any valuables) are in rooms with sensors, and go ex-directory. It is best if your phone line is underground or difficult to reach, so that it can't be cut. There is also a safer but more expensive system available called Red Care. Consider outside security lights with movement-activated PIR sensors.

Caretaker

Arrange for someone to keep an eye on your home, calling in every few days to check that all is well, to remove mail from the mat, air the house, move the curtains around to make it look lived in, etc.

If you have a garden and will be away some months (especially in spring), ask someone to weed and cut the grass – otherwise you'll return to a jungle. Plant some winter-flowering shrubs if you'll be mainly living at home then.

Both caretaker and gardener must be really reliable, who can be trusted to work unsupervised. Such people aren't easy to find, so ask all your friends if they can recommend anyone; and get these systems in place early, so you can see how well they are working.

Winterising the property

If you will be away for the cold weather, you won't want to leave gas central heating on; an oil-filled electric radiator with a thermostat, left centrally downstairs, will keep your home from becoming cold and damp.

House insurance

Insurance companies aren't keen on insuring unoccupied properties, and normally you are only covered for a month while absent from home. Check with your present company as soon as possible, and if you aren't happy, ask elsewhere. I discovered that there were very few companies who would even consider insuring a property that is empty for half the year. Norwich Union Tapestry and NIG are two that will.

Phone and electricity

Look into which will be the cheapest tariffs for your situation. You'll probably need to leave the electricity on, for your caretaker and the burglar alarm, but make sure you fit circuit breakers.

LEAVING YOUR CAR

If you're away for six months or less, you'll probably keep your car. We decommission ours (see page 110) and leave it garaged, insured merely against fire and theft. On our return, we just have to recharge the battery with a trickle charger.

However, if you'll be absent a lot longer, it will be cheaper to sell the car and to hire one during your periods at home (or even use taxis). I don't know where the break-even point is, but remember to include *all* costs in your calculations (depreciation, insurance, servicing, repairs, etc).

One advantage is that hire cars are usually new and reliable. Some companies apparently rent cars specifically to ex-pats returning home, and are much cheaper – they advertise in English newspapers abroad, eg the *Weekly Telegraph*.

CATS AND DOGS

It is now possible to take your pets to and fro with you between the UK and the Mediterranean, but it is essential to keep their vaccination certificates up to date. They should always wear a collar with an identification disk otherwise they may get rounded up as strays. Cats are far more suitable than dogs for life on board – they are good at keeping rodents at bay, are able to climb ladders, and are happy to use litter trays (though apparently it *is* possible to train dogs to use them).

MEDICAL MATTERS

Health insurance

You could consider private health insurance for abroad – but this tends to be very expensive. While travelling within the European Union we don't consider it necessary, since we are entitled to the same health care as the locals, which is generally acceptable now. You must, though, complete a Form E111, obtainable from the post office. You need both the original of this and several photocopies of it, since doctors will want to see the former and keep one of the latter.

The situation is, of course, different for non-EU citizens, or for EU citizens outside Europe. Read the special report on health insurance in *Yachting World*, October 2001.

Medical check-ups

Well before leaving, visit your doctor and have a complete check-up. Explain what you're doing, and ask what inoculations you need – you may require a number of injections spaced some months apart. Get your doctor's advice about your first aid box, and ask if you can have six months' supply of your regular medications (though it may not be possible to get that quantity). Your doctor may respond to this by saying that these medications are 'easy to get abroad', but in our experience this is often not the case.

Have check-ups with any other specialists that you see regularly: optician, chiropodist, chiropractor, etc, and especially your dentist. Discuss the possibility of dental insurance to cover you abroad and, if relevant, consider getting a spare denture made to take with you.

If you wear spectacles or contact lenses, take the latest prescription with you in case you break them, and take an old pair as a spare.

FINANCE

Access to your money

This is easy in the Mediterranean, because credit cards are so widely accepted. Most Mediterranean countries now have large numbers of banks with ATMs (automatic cash dispensers), and many shops, restaurants and marinas accept credit cards too. You will save money if you use your card to pay a bill rather than using it to get money from the bank and then paying in cash, because banks charge an extra cash-handling fee. In some supermarkets, you can even get 'cash-back'. You will need identification to pay by card in supermarkets or to get money out of post offices (or from banks with no ATMs).

We prefer a debit card to a credit card – it's as widely acceptable, but actually takes the money straight out of your bank account, just like a cheque. This avoids the problem of paying your credit company while you are away. Take more than one card each (in case you lose or break one), preferably from different, major companies – don't take obscure cards.

Payment of bills

Arrange to have all regular bills paid by direct debit (eg house, car and yacht insurance, council tax, water rates, gas, electricity, telephone); where this is impossible, use standing orders (eg burglar alarm, subscriptions, caretaker, gardener).

Managing your finances

You will need to arrange that your current account always has sufficient funds, even though you won't be seeing your statements frequently. Make an appointment with your bank manager well before you leave in order to discuss your finances.

I bank with Lloyds and have two accounts: current and instant savings (which attracts interest). At the end of each month, they *used* to check the current account balance and adjust it to an agreed amount, by swapping money between the two accounts, which was brilliant; however, I now have to ring and check, and if necessary tell them to transfer extra from the savings account – so-called progress! Other possibilities are phone banking and internet banking, but I don't trust their security enough yet.

If you will only be home for short periods, you could consider becoming tax exiles, but this is a lot of hassle and you lose your entitlement to the NHS, E111 benefits, etc. Another alternative, if your income is largely from dividends, is putting your money in a tax haven like the Channel Islands or the Isle of Man. Either way, you need a good financial adviser (or ask your bank).

If you have financial matters that might need action while you're away, it's as well to give your lawyer power of attorney. You should also make a will. If you have unearned income that generates a lot of work, consider putting it all in the hands of your financial adviser or the bank – but check the security aspects carefully. We leave important documents, and all our photo negatives too, in a fireproof box – labelled and hidden in a cupboard with the key handy, in case a burglar thinks it is a safe!

LEAVING FAMILY AND FRIENDS

Elderly parents who feel that they depend on you can, perhaps unconsciously, exert a very potent emotional blackmail, but try not to let this govern your life. If you have brothers or sisters, then maybe it's time they took over your role. If this isn't possible, perhaps you can get paid help to replace you; if your parents can't afford this, social services may be able to help. If they are *emotionally* dependent on you, perhaps you could arrange for friends to drop in frequently for a chat. Going on two short cruises per year will be better than going off into the blue for six months. Also, you will find that it's the first departure that is the critical one – once that hurdle is past, and they get used to the new regime, they will probably come round to accepting the idea of you being away.

As a couple, with regard to one of you not being so keen as the other, I discussed in Chapter 1 various options of spending longer or shorter times aboard, and of possibly the two of you spending different amounts of time on the boat. Travelling to and fro alone is one disadvantage to the latter idea; also you will each be alone for part of the year. But the skipper may find friends to keep him company, perhaps to help with long passages between cruising grounds. The wife or partner can then spend time at home, perhaps with the family, joining the boat in the nicest places.

Another method of keeping close to family and friends is inviting them to stay with you on the yacht if there is room. This is super fun – though tiring! If they are sailing types, you can do mini-cruises with them; otherwise, just remain in a marina or sheltered anchorage. Alternatively, they could stay in a flat or hotel near you – there are some excellent package holidays available, or you may find somewhere privately, perhaps via the internet.

What is certain is that if leaving the family is a problem, then arranging good methods of communication will be vital for *your* happiness as well as theirs.

MOBILE COMMUNICATIONS FOR THE UNINITIATED

E-mail

By far the easiest method of communication is by e-mail – electronic mail written on computer and sent digitally by telephone through the internet to your personal e-mail address. When you want to 'collect' your mail, you simply ring the appropriate number and transfer your letters to the computer (and send the ones you've written).

There are many advantages:

- Because you are on the move, it will be impossible for people to post letters to you, but you can receive e-mails anywhere.
- You will make friends with other cruising people, and e-mail may be the only way to communicate with them.
- Sending and receiving e-mail is easy (and far cheaper than phoning) once you have set the system up.
- When you need help with something (eg equipment going wrong), you can spend a fortune just getting through to someone on the phone, whereas you can easily have a long 'conversation' with them by e-mail.

I have been staggered at how much more we've been in communication with people since we've had e-mail. There are four essential requirements: a computer, a phone, an e-mail address and access to the internet; but there are several ways of obtaining these:

No computer or phone? Go to an internet café and use their computer. They charge a few pounds an hour, so if you are a fast typist, this is probably the cheapest way; they usually have a printer. Such cafés will be connected to the internet, so all you need is an e-mail address. This can be obtained through companies such as Hotmail.

Alternatively, register with Pocket Mail, and buy their mini Organiser (costing about £100) on which you can type out short e-mails and send them using any telephone box.

If you have a computer, you can still use an internet café by typing your letters on board and taking them to the café on a floppy disk (though they occasionally won't allow this).

If not using an internet café, you must arrange access to the internet via an internet service provider (ISP) and register an e-mail address with them. Then, you can take the computer ashore, and plug it into the phone system there. You will need a special lead from your computer manufacturer (and a set of adaptors for different countries) and a place where you can use an ordinary phone and pay for the call charges afterwards – many marinas have this. You just unplug the phone and plug in your computer instead. Alternatively, if you buy an 'acoustic coupler', you can use your computer with any land phone (like Pocket Mail).

Using a mobile phone to send e-mails
You need a computer, a suitable phone, and access to the internet. All you pay for is the phone call. But it's more costly than using a land line – both because mobile phone charges are more expensive, and because they transfer information at a considerably slower rate, so transactions take longer (though faster phones are being developed). A palmtop is slower than a laptop, and is limited in the size of e-mail that it can send, but it is simpler to use.

Sending e-mails is simple with a palmtop computer which has an infrared link to a mobile phone.

Using a mobile is, however, *much* the most convenient method, and you can communicate while at sea or at anchor.

Internet service provider (ISP) You need a reliable ISP for e-mail that is suitable for use with a mobile phone. CompuServe and AOL have contact numbers within the various countries, so you are only billed for national calls, not international ones. Both these companies charge you a monthly bill, which may negate the advantage if you are on a home-based phone – the real saving here is if you are using a foreign, local SIM card, so local calls are really cheap. Alternatively, some providers (eg Virgin Net) charge no fee, and for occasional users, on a home phone, this will be cheaper in spite of the extra costs of making an international call each time.

If a member of your family has access to the internet, then you may be able to use one of their e-mail addresses – many companies allow more than one.

Hotmail offers an e-mail service that is only suitable for retrieving e-mail from internet cafés (since Hotmail themselves don't provide access to the internet).

Setting up your phone and computer

for e-mail is complicated, but the system is very simple once you've done so. With most ISPs, you instal their software on your computer to get access to them. They *must* give you a contact phone number that can be accessed from abroad. Many ISPs don't have this facility.

Phoning home

The cheapest method is to use a public phone box with a locally bought phone card. It's best to arrange one contact person, and to try to phone them at a set time each week. Then tell everyone else to contact that person, and leave a message if they want you to phone them.

However, for people to be able to phone *you*, then a mobile phone is needed. During our first eight years' cruising we experienced four emergencies at home, so we reluctantly bought a mobile phone and found that they are incredibly convenient, albeit expensive.

The mobile phone system

The question of mobile phones is a confusing and ever-changing subject. Below I have tried to explain the essentials to help the older generation who, like us, have never had one before.

When you buy a mobile phone, you are in fact buying into a system that consists of:
- A handset.
- A SIM (Subscriber Identity Module) card, which gives you a phone number and connects you to:
  (a) a network such as Vodaphone, BT's mm02, Orange or T-Mobile;
  (b) a service provider who will bill you for line rental and calls. This is often the same company as the network.

With most (but not all) mobile phones, it is possible to change the SIM card to that of another network, but to do so you may have to pay to have it 'unlocked'.

Billing Costs vary considerably between networks, yet are very difficult to compare unless you make careful tables of all the different charges. The price you pay for the handset also varies according to the 'package' that comes with it:

Pay-As-You-Talk: You buy a phone card and punch its code number into the phone, which allows you the given amount of credit. You know fairly quickly how much you have spent, but never how it has been spent.

Service contract: You pay line rental as well as call charges, but it's cheaper for frequent use. You pay a monthly bill by direct debit, and can have an itemised bill – though being abroad, you won't get it for ages.

The Virgin Tariff: Virgin Mobile is a service provider (using the T-Mobile network) that at present offers a different type of tariff, where you pay an inflated price for the phone (and any replacements), but no line rental. This works out much the same the first year, but it is far cheaper thereafter (as long as you don't drop the phone overboard).

Orange offer to match any cheaper deals from other providers, so you can request what they call the Virgin Tariff. Again upgrades are expensive, but you can get a reconditioned phone as an emergency replacement for about £50.

WAP phones WAP offers internet access from your phone without requiring a computer. However, at present it is very limited indeed, and using a mobile WAP phone for internet access could be incredibly expensive when abroad.

The pretty Greek fishing harbour of Vathi in the Savonic Gulf. There is room for a few yachts on the other side of the harbour.

Faxes by phone You can also send faxes from a mobile, which can be very useful for contacting people who have access to a fax machine but not e-mail. You may need to buy fax software for your computer, though some have it already installed. Again, all you pay for are the call charges. However, faxing is more expensive than e-mailing, since the same information is more than ten times as bulky in fax format, and therefore takes much longer to transmit.

Receiving is awkward, as you would need to keep the phone and computer set up all the time, though Orange offer a

system called Answerfax where they store up your received faxes and send you a text message to let you know. Better still, there is a company called efax, found on the internet at http://www.efax.com. You have a fax number registered with them, and they convert your faxes into e-mails which they send you. This is cheaper and simpler than having faxes sent direct to your phone.

Buying and using a mobile phone

Buying at home: It's much easier to sort out the complexities when buying your

phone in the UK and you can use it anywhere, *but* outgoing calls home are expensive when abroad, and you pay the international part of the cost of incoming calls.

At present, some UK companies won't unbar your phone for 'roaming abroad' unless you have a service contract. Even if you use cards, you'd probably run out.

Buying abroad: Local calls (abroad) are far cheaper, and this may enable you to send cheaper e-mails. Calls home may be cheaper too, and calls to cruising friends in the area on the same local network are very cheap; *but* you have a foreign language to contend with and you have to buy a new SIM card, with a new phone number, each time you change country (you won't be able to use your phone until you do).

Also, unless you have a bank account abroad, you'll have to use Pay-As-You-Talk rather than having a service contract.

A compromise? Probably the cheapest option is to buy a Pay-As-You-Talk phone in the country you are visiting, and to use this only for incoming calls and a phone box for outgoing calls. Check you will be able to change the SIM card in your next country, rather than having to get a new phone. Of course, you'll have to keep people up to date with your changing phone number.

Another option is to have two phones: one with a permanent home–country number for friends to ring you, and the other for putting foreign SIM cards in. This should be the one suitable for e-mail (preferably both in case one goes wrong).

Choosing the handset Important features are:

Dual-band: This means that the phone can use two different frequencies (900 or 1800). Vodaphone and BT's mm02 use 900, and so do most networks in Europe. However, Orange, T-Mobile and a few European networks use 1800. If you are with any of these, a dual-band handset is essential, so you can log on to the 900 networks as well. You don't need 'Tri-Band' (which supports 1900 also) since this is only used in America.

SMS: 'Short Message Service' is the facility for sending brief text messages to other mobile phones. This is *exceptionally* useful – and even abroad it is usually very cheap.

Data-compatible phone: This is essential if you want to use e-mail (or fax). The phones don't cost a lot more, but you need a software package and modem (perhaps a PC card modem) plus a special lead to connect your computer to a mobile phone.

Inbuilt modem and infrared link: Alternatively, buy a phone that comes with an inbuilt modem. If your phone and your computer both have infrared facility, this is all you need, so it's much cheaper (though the phone must be laid flat next to the computer, and this can impair reception). Otherwise, you need a lead. There's also the new Bluetooth radio link system, where the phone can be up in the cockpit with the computer in the cabin.

Where to buy the phone? You can buy your phone direct from a service provider or from an independent mobile phone shop (such as the Carphone Warehouse).

You'll need a 12-volt car charger if you have no inverter. You may want a case (perhaps a padded camera-type case) and/or a safety strap for your neck – phones are slippery and vulnerable.

Setting up your phone A number of things need to be done before you leave the UK:
1 Your service provider must 'unbar your phone for roaming abroad'.
2 The automatic answerphone service is expensive abroad, so consider getting it switched off (ring your service provider). That way, you should pay nothing for unanswered incoming calls.
3 Your service provider must 'enable your phone for fax and data calls' (for e-mail), and give you a fax number.

USEFUL SOURCES OF INFORMATION

There is no shortage of internet cafés in the Mediterranean, and they offer the easiest access to the internet when cruising (which is important since there are many sites giving valuable information, such as weather forecasts, updates on pilot guides, travel information, etc). If you've never used an internet café, get a friend to show you. You'll need to collect useful web addresses.

If you need to download something big from the internet, try to find a café that uses Broadband, and that has a CD-rewriter. Alternatively, if you have the appropriate leads and adaptors, look for a marina offering a phone-connection to your berth.

If you ever have problems with your phone or computer, you can retrieve your e-mail from internet cafés, by going to Internet Explorer, accessing http://www.mail2web.com, and entering your details. A similar facility that offers more complexities of use is available on www.compuserve.com – click on 'Classic E-mail' and register with them; then set up various options (under 'Preferences'). You have to set this up in advance as you need to reply 'OK' to a confirmatory message that they'll send you on your normal e-mail. This system lapses if you don't use it for three months.

The book *Using PCs on Board* by Rob Buttress and Tim Thornton (Adlard Coles Nautical) will give more information on more sophisticated electronic communication systems.

The Cruising Association offers much useful information to members.

Using your phone It is essential to take with you all the phone numbers you might need, both for everyday use and in emergencies (eg when trying to get equipment replaced or repaired). It's unbelievably frustrating trying to sort such problems out anyway, but it becomes a nightmare when you can't get hold of the people you need. Make sure that, for each company, you have phone (and fax) numbers that can be accessed from abroad, and that are not answered by a recorded message saying 'Someone will be with you shortly'. Also, get their e-mail address.

Before leaving home, check what time of day is the cheapest for phoning on the various foreign networks you will be using, and make your calls then. On reaching a new country, check the phone numbers of the emergency services, and enter them in your phone's memory.

Emergency number 112 is the equivalent of 999 in most EU countries (for both mobiles and land lines).

If you break your phone Retrieve the SIM card from inside (having transferred your list of phone numbers to it), then you only need to replace the handset and don't need to change your number or purchase a new contract.

DEALING WITH YOUR MAIL

Junk mail

Request a registration form from the Mailing Preference Service, and ask them to stop you being sent unsolicited mail. Put a notice outside your property saying, perhaps, 'No free papers, no circulars, and please, no charities!' Write to anybody that normally sends you papers or brochures, and ask them not to do so – consider resigning from societies (or suspending your membership).

Sorting your mail

Arrange for someone to sort your mail. A member of the family is best, or a trusted friend (solicitors are too expensive). If the person lives nearby, they can do it on the spot; otherwise you will have to get your caretaker to forward your mail to them (or, if you have no base in the UK, you will have to send everyone a change-of-address notice).

I ask the sorter to throw away anything that is clearly 'junk', and to sort the rest into:

- Personal mail.
- Papers that need dealing with.
- Papers that can be left until our return.
- Brochures etc from a given list of companies (eg Lakeland) or societies (eg the RYA).

Letters requiring action If you have a financial adviser, your sorter can contact him or her regarding financial problems. If you have a family solicitor, a phone call to them will help in some cases. If it's an unexpected bill, your sorter can either pay it and be reimbursed, or tell you about it when you're next in contact.

Forwarding personal mail

Unfortunately, not all your friends can write to you by e-mail, but other alternatives are far less satisfactory.

Posting the mail It's best to wait until you are going to be in the same place for a while, and ask your sorter to send the mail there. Be sure to get the exact postal address, including postcode. You can use a marina, or *poste restante* (though this has a poor name for reliability). You'll probably have to hang around for two or three weeks. It's best to cruise around and then come back for your letters – ring your sorter to check the situation after a few days (they'll take a while to send the letters off).

Alternatively, work out in advance where you are going to be, and have the mail sent to await your arrival. This is fraught with difficulties since you can't be sure whether those receiving it will keep it for you; or if you will ever get there; or even if it is the correct address (though post offices list postcodes for all towns and villages).

Ask your sorter to photocopy everything and only send the copies by post – then you won't lose the originals if anything goes wrong. If there's more than one packet, they should be numbered (eg number 2 of 5), so you know when it's all arrived.

Don't forget to arrange for any visitors to the boat from home to bring mail out to you – much the best way of forwarding mail.

Faxing letters This is much more satisfactory than forwarding mail, since it is immediate and the originals remain safely at home. However, sending faxes commercially is expensive, and you also pay to receive them. Marinas are the easiest places to receive them, but various shops or offices advertise fax services.

Faxing photocopied mail to a mobile phone is *far* too expensive; however, you could perhaps use efax.

6
Final Preparations

PLANNING YOUR DEPARTURE

Timing

Although it's tempting to try to set off early in the year to give yourselves as much cruising time as possible, it can be counter-productive since it's essential to try out all the things you fitted over the winter. We left on our first Mediterranean cruise in early May, and this was a mistake. First you need a final trial cruise, for a week or two – perhaps in April. So in *Phæacian*, we spent ten days on Guernsey, which taught us a lot about the equipment we had fitted (and still needed to fit); we got a lot of work done – more restfully than at home too; and we had the opportunity of shopping in a completely new set of shops, which enabled us to buy a range of things that we had been unable to find before.

Following your mini-cruise, you need to return home for another month or so to make final modifications and arrange-ments. Thus you wouldn't really be ready to leave until early June. However, this depends on the weather. If spring came early, you could launch much sooner, and bring the whole timetable forward. But don't aim to get too far south too quickly, since you won't be used to the heat – per-

haps spend the hottest months relaxing in the Rias of north-west Spain.

Be flexible about the timing of your start. Don't have a rigid leaving date – your last few weeks are enough of a panic anyway, without adding further pressure. Have a planned date for departure, of course, but be happy to extend this by up to a month, to give yourself time to get everything finished, and also to allow for possible bad weather when you *are* ready. The main problem with this approach is if you want to book crew for the Channel or Biscay crossings – it's probably safer to book them for later rather than earlier.

I originally thought it would be a good idea to live aboard for the last few weeks, but this must be impracticable since we failed to do it on both our cruises! One reason for not living aboard is that there's so much that needs to be done at home, where there are many facilities that make your preparations easier – telephone, washing machine, shops, deep-freeze, easier cooking arrangements, the post arriving, etc. However, it is certainly worth sleeping aboard the last night or two before departure (and *then* going back home), in order to acclimatise yourself to the motion. If you do live on board for the last few weeks, a car is essential; and also a phone – so you'll obviously need a mobile (make sure that everybody who might need to contact you has your number). Try to get your new system set up in time to send out your new address/phone number/e-mail address, etc, with your Christmas cards.

Studying the Pilot guides

Some months before leaving, study the pilot guides in order to plan your first year's trip in detail and to know what charts to buy. Finding your way around completely new guides is terribly confusing, so put labelled stick-out tabs on key pages to make finding them easier. Few guides have adequate cross-referencing, so add this yourself – on the main maps, put page references for coastal maps (and vice versa); on coastal maps, put page references for harbour descriptions (and vice versa), etc. This makes everything much easier.

Drawing up lists

Make lists of things to do 'urgently', during 'the last month', 'on the last day', etc. Also, draw up a list of 'last minute packing' – things you'll be using until then, but mustn't forget to take. Then there are the shopping lists, lists of people to ring, appointments to make, etc. Your mail sorter will need a list of instructions.

If there are things that you will in future have to replace from home (tea, medicines, etc), keep careful records of how much of them you use in order to know how much to take with you (both now, and for subsequent trips out in the Med).

FINISHING THE WORK

The last few months are a nightmare of hectic activity, with time rushing by, and not enough hours in the day. Everything gets delayed and life seems to conspire against you. You will have literally dozens of phone calls to make, letters to write, and appointments to keep.

Keep hassling those people who haven't finished work for you. People under pressure do the work that seems most urgent first – so make sure this is *your* job!

Label valuable equipment (at home and on board) with an ultraviolet security marker (in case of theft).

Jobs at home

There'll be lots of cooking, washing, mending, etc to do, so try to find someone (perhaps your cleaner/caretaker) who can help you with this. Get this person to clean the fridge and wash your home bedding after you've left. Wash the yacht bedding, etc while you have the chance.

Those holding your house keys need a chance to become familiar with the burglar alarm, and the jobs they have to do. Ensure that letters on the mat can't be seen from outside. Photocopy important documents, and keep copies safe in a fireproof box.

Things to do on the yacht

- Work out the best way of using the heads, and write out instructions for visitors while you still have the opportunity to get them heat-sealed in plastic. This obviously applies also to instructions for other pieces of equipment, too.
- Get the cooker burners cleaned – they work much better afterwards.
- Check your steering compass for error

(on different points of sailing and motoring) and make a 'deviation card'.

- Some equipment (eg Autohelm 7000) requires a complex setting-up procedure, so get this sorted out before you leave. The same applies to e-mail.
- Practise using *all* new equipment to make sure it's working properly and that you understand it (eg GPS, SSB radio, pressure cooker). If possible, try out both the mobile phone and e-mail from abroad prior to your actual departure date.
- Your cruiser will inevitably float lower in the water with so much gear on board, so when you antifoul, repaint the waterline 2 inches (5 centimetres) or so higher.

STOWING YOUR GEAR

It is unbelievable how many car-loads of gear you will need to take. A lot of it you will have been using the previous year, but I don't recommend leaving things on board during an English winter (especially in wet areas) because everything tends to go mouldy. If you *do* leave things on board, wrap them in self-seal plastic bags to keep the damp out. It's worth keeping the bags on items for the trip down, but once you reach the Mediterranean they won't generally be needed, since the climate is far drier, even in winter. However, the bags are still useful – simply as a means of keeping things neatly stored.

Dry the boat out regularly with an electric fan heater or use Humidity Killers from Nauticalia.

Stowage plan

Draw a careful plan of the yacht on a triple sheet of A4, make some photocopies, and write in each locker what you are putting there. You will inevitably change things round, and the plan/list will enable you to keep track of where things are. Plan the stowage of the most essential items first, ensuring that things you will use most often, or might need in a tearing panic, have the most accessible stowages.

Medicines and toiletries need to be stored in the coolest place aboard (probably the bilge but protected from sea water). Some items will need to be stored in the fridge in summer (eg contraceptive pessaries which melt).

Most yachts have a slight list, so try to design your stowage so that heavy items go on the other side, to compensate.

The following items will probably need stowing on deck:

- Stern anchor, chain and warp; outboard; fenders – on the pushpit (photo below).
- Passerelle/ladder/plank; spinnaker boom/ bearing-out spar – on the cabin roof? Along the guard wires? Permanent installation?

Fenders need to be stowed tidily and safely. Incidentally, it would be quite a long, hard climb up on this ladder.

- Boathook; mop/scrubber; dinghy oars – on the cabin roof.
- Sailboard – along the guard wires.
- Cockpit cushions – under the sprayhood.
- Dinghy and/or liferaft.

Non-slip matting

Cut up your rolls of matting and put pieces wherever needed to stop things sliding around. It works incredibly well (I'm into my fifth roll!) I put it in cupboards, on tables, along shelves, under the sprayhood, and under things that I want to leave out at sea – like the chopping board and draining rack. It's also useful on the chart table (though solid matting is better here, since you'll be writing on it). Consider sticking it to the bottom of things you want to leave out on shelves, eg knick-knacks.

Heavy-duty, black-rubber mats can go on the cockpit sole, on sloping bits of cabin sole, at the bottom of the companionway, etc; and they are very useful on the companionway steps themselves so long as you fasten them down. They aren't as non-slip as the rolls of matting, so put linings of this underneath.

Lockers

Large lockers If you're lucky enough to have plenty of stowage space, this may be in cavernous lockers where everything loses itself. On *Phœnician*, our solution was to fill the spaces with suitably sized plastic boxes (try getting old ones from shops or fruit and vegetable farms). You'll probably have to move one box to reach another, so stow things you'll want least often at the back or bottom, and make rope handles for boxes that will need lifting out.

Ice cream boxes When empty, these are exceptionally useful for stowing all smaller items, so save them up regularly as you eat the ice cream, and get your friends to do the same – you simple can't have too many. Label the boxes on the side *and* top in felt-tipped pen (water-soluble so that you can alter them). Then stow wherever convenient – in drawers, under the floor, in lockers. Where one box is on top of another, put the things you'll need least often in the lower box, and make sure this has a concave lid that will hold the upper box in place – failing this, stick non-slip matting to the base of the upper box.

Lockers under bunks It's awkward lifting first the cushion, then the locker lid, then getting out what you want, and then putting it all back. It's much easier if there's only one thing to lift. For this reason, we remove the locker lids where we're not going to be sitting on the seats – either by sliding them out of the way or stowing them somewhere completely different. Where this is impossible, try Velcro-ing the locker lid to the cushion so they move as one.

Stowing for sea

The rule is 'A place for everything, and everything in its place' – but unless every single thing *has* a set place, then you can't put everything in its place! In fact, many things will need two set places – one for in harbour, and a safer one for at sea. Take special care to make a secure stowage for anything delicate – thin glass is particularly vulnerable. Make sure heavy things can't crash around and break other items. Wedge glass bottles so they can't move, and put padding where they touch (or alternate glass with plastic).

In a rough sea, things tend to get thrown not only sideways but also upwards and forwards, so plan stowages with this in mind. Tacky non-slip matting will help to stop things being 'lifted'.

Washing-up liquid comes in a poorly fastened bottle so we tip ours into a plastic one that has a screw lid.

GETTING OFF AND AWAY!

Much of this section will be needed *every* time you leave home. So if you are taking this book with you, photocopy these lists and keep them at home and also the lists in Chapter 9 of things which need doing on visits home (pages 159 and 160).

Leaving home
In addition to all the preparations you would make for a short holiday, you need to:

- Cancel your television licence and car tax (you can get rebates).
- Reduce car insurance cover to fire and theft only.
- Ring your household insurer to let them know your leaving date and approximate return date.
- Leave out a note to remind yourself to reinstate all these things as soon as you get back.
- Make lists of jobs to do on your return.
- Dry-clean or wash woollens, and stow in self-seal bags to protect against moths.
- Make sure you have filled in your tax return.

Put out of sight from windows anything a burglar might think was valuable (even if it isn't), or that might make him think there were valuables inside the property. We got burgled because we'd left an old wireless (that didn't work) and a jewellery box (containing only costume jewellery, but of sentimental value) in sight, and these were the only things taken – the thief hadn't much time since the police arrived within a few minutes (due to our sophisticated burglar alarm!). Leave nothing out (and easy to grab) that you particularly don't want to have stolen – hide away all keys and any important items, and put any valuable jewellery in the bank for safe-keeping.

Regardless of how long you'll be away, make sure you leave things ready for when you come back. You will obviously expect to buy fresh food on your return, but it's disconcerting to open the cupboards and find them bare of tinned and dried food, as we did once. So, before you leave, make a list of all the things you must buy on your return.

Preparing for the journey
Either get friends to help you prepare food for the journey; or buy convenience items; or cook it yourself months in advance and freeze it – you won't have time at the last minute. Supermarket frozen meals are ideal for the last few days at home and the first night or two on board. Prepare labelled bags of food for each day of the long trips. Marks & Spencer's tinned meals are very useful for this purpose.

Do final preparations in a marina; everything is so much easier than on a mooring.

Last-minute jobs
- Turn off water, gas and central heating system, and perhaps fridge, freezer and electricity.
- Drain radiators and, if appropriate, turn on the electric heater.
- Unplug other electrics.

Southern Turkey has many lovely, unspoilt anchorages.

- Seal up with sticky tape those tins with food (eg flour) in them.
- Leave a notebook in which your caretaker can record important events, and money for him/her to buy anything required.
- Leave a note asking your caretaker to keep the water (and electricity?) turned off except when they're there.

- Decommission the car – ie disconnect the battery, pump up tyres fairly hard, leave the handbrake off, and chock wheels against movement.
- Post off car tax disc and television licence, with the forms requesting the rebates.
- Sit down and have a good think before finally leaving!

7

The Voyage to the Mediterranean

THE ATLANTIC ROUTE

This route has been described briefly in Chapter 1 (see Map 1), but only as an outline route – no details were given about the cruising grounds along the way.

West Brittany

This attractive, well-indented coast offers good cruising, but is difficult because of rocks, tides and fog – and it has surprisingly few well-sheltered anchorages. The best are in the two inland seas (the Rade de Brest and the Morbihan) and up some of the rivers. There are many marinas, and some of these have a strong tide running through; if so, wait for slack water before entering or leaving. Prices vary considerably – it's worth buying the French almanac *Votre Livre de Bord* just for the sake of the price list given in it.

For crossing Biscay, the French forecasts are more helpful than the BBC Shipping Forecast, since they divide the region into smaller areas and give an outlook for a second 24-hour period. French harbourmasters can usually get you a five-day forecast – request the forecast for *au large* (the open sea) and not *cotière* (the coastal one), and don't take it for gospel!

I strongly recommend getting one of the extremely useful annual booklets (available free from French marinas) called *Le Guide Marine de Météo-France* (see Appendix 3), which gives up-to-date details of all available forecast times and frequencies (for both the Atlantic *and* Mediterranean coasts).

The north Spanish coast

This coast is interesting, though (once again) not easy. There are no particular navigational hazards and tidal streams are weak: it is mooring that is the problem. There is little yachting and thus few marinas or facilities, and rivers are silting up, thus making anchoring difficult. Mostly you have to tie to fish quays: you need long spring warps (running *along* the quay) so you don't have to tend them all night as the tide rises and falls; big balloon fenders (to protect you against broken-down quays, and wash from fishing boats); and perhaps a ladder for climbing quay walls. Finding a place on the quay that the fisherman won't want to enter or leave at 4 am can be a problem. But people are friendly and helpful (even if they speak little English), and the scenery is lovely (photo page 113) – the weather is warm but damp, so the mountainous land is green and fertile. Crew changing is easy: regular coaches run from the ferry ports of Santander and Bilbao to most of the harbours.

The Rias of north-west Spain

Rias are bays of varying size and complexity, forming large areas of semi-sheltered water. There are islands, long sandy beaches, and dozens of anchorages; and while few of these have all-round shelter, many are open only across the bay, and thus sheltered from any swell that enters the Ria (like anchorage B in Fig 19, page 127). Fishing harbours usually have huge, sheltering breakwaters to anchor behind, and there are a growing number of marinas. Except in fog (sadly not uncommon), navigation is generally fairly simple; though some of the Rias have a number of rocks and reefs, nowhere is it as difficult as in Brittany.

Summer weather is delightful, lacking the blistering heat of the Mediterranean (which we feel compensates for the fog), and the area is still completely unspoilt. Crew changes are nearly as easy as in north Spain – either by coach (from La Coruña) and ferry; or by air from that beautiful, interesting city, Santiago de Compostela.

The beautiful fishing harbour of Ribadesella (Biscay, Spain) on its winding river, with the Picos de Europa behind.

Portugal, the Algarve and south-west Spain

The coast of western Portugal is foggy, and beaten by a continuous heavy swell; northerly winds prevail. There are few natural anchorages, just man-made harbours every 40 miles or so, and the occasional river. You can anchor in some of these, and marinas are also being built. Some ports can only be entered at high water if the swell is big because of a dangerous bar.

But as you round the striking Cape St Vincent and turn east for Gibraltar, the swell disappears, with the sea becoming blue and inviting. Harbours and marinas are attractive and close together. The weather is very hot in high summer (well over 30ºC on many afternoons). At Lagos, go on a 'Grotto Trip' – an exciting visit by small boat in and out of caves in beautiful, golden-limestone cliffs. (Don't go in your own dinghy, the tripper boats make it far too dangerous.) Further east are tidal lagoons and interesting rivers to explore (with huge white storks and other exotic birds).

Then you find yourself back in Spain, in Flamenco country. A visit to one of the shows (if you can find a good one) may be the highlight of your cruise, with exciting Spanish music, sensual dancing and brightly coloured costumes. For some, a bullfight makes an unforgettable spectacle. The rules of the game are totally different in Spain, Portugal and the south of France – and you may find one more to your liking than the others. The Spanish *corrida* is admittedly gory, but is very exciting and full of wonderful colour and pageantry.

Then there are the beautiful cities of Seville (up the River Guadalquivir) and Cadiz (visit the fascinating Camera Obscura in the Torre Tavira), while Jerez (pronounced 'her*e*th') is the home of the Andalusian School of Equestrian Art (the origin of the famous Spanish Riding School of Vienna) and they do superb displays.

Gibraltar

Gibraltar offers excellent shopping, and it's advisable to restock really thoroughly –

diesel is exceptionally cheap. There are three good marinas (also cheap), or you can anchor near the airport runway (though the boat gets very dirty).

Take the cable car to the top of the Rock to see the view. Those who are interested in birds should come at migration season, and watch the steady progress of huge birds (eagles, vultures, storks, etc) flying overhead. There are experts on hand (on one of the terraces at the top of the cable car) to help you identify them. If you walk down, you can see the Barbary apes, and the Cave of St Michael with its stalagmites and stalactites. There are also many fortifications for those interested in military history.

FRENCH CANALS – GENERAL INFORMATION

The alternative way of reaching the Mediterranean is through the French canals (see Map 1), although you have to buy a licence or *vignette* (obtainable from the VNF Offices (see Appendix 3) in various towns) to use them. There are three types:

- When we returned home via the Midi in 1997, our *vignette* cost £90 (£140 if your boat was over 40 square metres, length x beam), and allowed us 30 *non-consecutive* travel days.
- Also available was a fortnight's permit at about one-third of the price.
- You can also get one for the *calendar* year for just over 1½ times as much.

You can't avoid this *vignette* since lock-keepers sometimes ask to see it, and you will require the appropriate qualification in boat handling (see page 18).

All masthead fittings (including lights) should be removed when going through the French canals, since these always seem to get broken. We noted it was generally the *bow* of the boat being ground into the quay by the surge in the locks, so it would perhaps be wise to have all the overhang at the stern (where, in addition, the shape of the boat adds protection), leaving the anchor to take the knocks at the bow.

However, if you have a long mast (or awkward boat), consider sending the mast by road to avoid the hassle of coping with it in the locks. We used Port Napoléon at Port-St-Louis-du-Rhône (paying £300 for the Midi route), but other firms offer this service at both ends of the canals.

(See Canal-du-Midi on page 120 for a list of useful equipment, though there are differences between various canal routes.)

THE MAIN FRENCH CANALS

We have not cruised these canals, but other books give details. The canal system is quite complex and you need a large number of canal guides. In addition, there is a useful book covering the trip up the Seine to Paris, called *Paris by Boat* (Adlard Coles Nautical). See also the details of going down the River Garonne (page 125 in this chapter) for information about tidal rivers. You will need a VHF with which to communicate with the lock-keepers; and there are some very long, unlit tunnels, so you need a powerful spotlight to light your way.

There are many different kinds of locks, but luckily these tend to go in groups of similar types. Normally they are an easy shape (though a few are oval, or have awkward, sloping walls), and they always have ladders when these are needed to reach the top of the quay. There

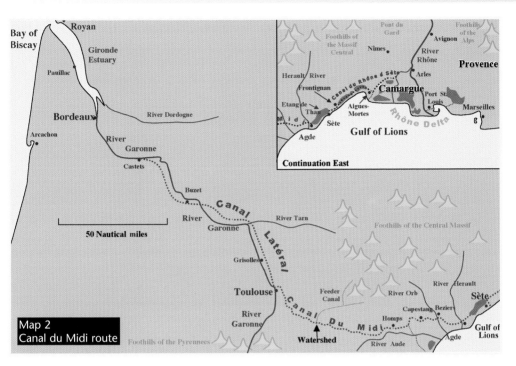

Map 2
Canal du Midi route

are many commercial barges, and these can cause a surge if you are tied up in a lock behind one that keeps its propeller turning. These barges are also a pain in the canals themselves, since you can't overtake them, and if you meet one it won't give way, so you are driven into the shallows. Even in summer, certain routes can be closed – unbeknownst to anyone, it seems – so you may have to backtrack and find a different way round.

If heading south, then having negotiated the canals you will embark down the Rhône. Here the locks are huge, but floating bollards make tying up easy. Just before Arles (see Map 2), you have a choice – either continue down the Grand Rhône to Port-St-Louis-du-Rhône (where you have to enter the Canal-St-Louis to reach the Mediterranean, the mouth of the Rhône, being unnavigable); or branch off to the right, into the Petit Rhône, which leads to the Canal-du-Rhône-à-Sète and the Camargue. From there you can reach the

sea at a number of places, including Aigues-Mortes and Sète.

The River Rhône flows strongly and, if going north in the spring, you might have problems with flood water. Don't be fooled by the laziness of the current at Port-St-Louis – at one point part-way to Arles the current strengthens for a few miles by at *least* a couple of knots: so allow for this when assessing whether to start.

THE CAMARGUE AND THE CANAL-DU-RHÔNE-À-SÈTE

Who has not heard of the Camargue – that marshy wilderness where white horses and black bulls gallop in wild freedom, and the famous pink flamingos feed in the salt lagoons? In some parts rice is grown, and other areas are devoted to producing salt. But elsewhere it remains desolate and marshy, one of the most important nature reserves in Europe.

The Canal-du-Rhône-à-Sète winds westward through the Camargue from the Petit Rhône to Aigues-Mortes, then through shallow coastal lagoons to Sète, where it disgorges into the 10-mile-long navigable lake called the Etang de Thau. At the other end of this lies the Canal-du-Midi. Apart from entering/leaving the Rhône, there are no locks; and the maximum dimensions are good (1.8 metres draught; 5 metres air height).

East of Aigues-Mortes is by far the best part – mooring is easy along the deep, muddy canal banks and the wildlife is superb. We saw many large rare birds such as purple heron; swimming heads we thought were otters turned out to be coypu; and, just west of Aigues-Mortes, colonies of bee-eaters were nesting in the banks of the canal – we passed hundreds of these beautiful little birds, flashing a myriad rainbow colours, a sight we will never forget. But, thereafter, surroundings were dull, and for miles (until we reached Frontignan) we found nowhere safe to stop.

The best time to visit this area is spring: the birds are better, and you avoid the mosquitoes (these are ferocious in summer and autumn, but we saw very few in early May).

Places of interest The Camargue is at the western end of Provence, an area full of fascinating history and with some beautiful old stone towns such as Arles and Nîmes (with their huge Roman amphitheatres), Avignon and Aigues-Mortes. The Pont du Gard is a superb Roman aqueduct. (Note: Nîmes and Pont du Gard are both inaccessible by boat.)

Visit a *course camarguaise*, which is totally different from a Spanish-style *corrida*. The bulls are not hurt in the former – the aim is for the men to try to grab pompoms that have been tied between the bull's horns. There is less colour and pageantry, but it's still very exciting.

THE CANAL-DU-MIDI ROUTE

I will describe the Canal-du-Midi as a route home, because that is our experience of it – and because it is as this that I really recommend it. You can enter from a number of ports such as Sète or Agde.

The Canal-du-Midi only runs about one-third of the way from the Mediterranean to the Bay of Biscay, climbing to the watershed, and dropping briefly to Toulouse (see Map 2). Here boats join the Canal-Latéral-à-la-Garonne, then the River Garonne itself, before reaching the Gironde estuary and the sea.

The Canal-du-Midi

The Canal-du-Midi has a fascinating history, being the earliest canal of its size and type in the world. Built in the reign of Louis XIV, the 'Sun King', it was an enormous feat of engineering, breaking new ground all the way. It is a beautiful canal, with arched, stone bridges, and small, oval locks. It is lined throughout with lovely old plane trees, a haven for red squirrels and birds (in the lower reaches we frequently saw exotic rarities such as golden orioles).

Though the Midi route is much shorter than the main canal route, it seems to have more problems – yet, in spite of all our efforts, we failed to find out in advance what these were and how to overcome them. So I am covering this section in detail, in the hope that other people will find things easier than we did.

The maximum air height is 3 metres,

An oval Midi lock. The man on the quay is holding this keel-less penichette really easily; Jimmy would have struggled to hold *Phoenician* in the surge.

much the lowest bridge being at Capestang (see Chapter 1 for more details. The draught limit was then 1.6 metres (our draught), but:

- Depths are very variable.
- It is being allowed to silt up.
- The banks are shallower still.

So, though there was plenty of water, we were constantly lurching our way sickeningly over mud banks. Getting into the sides to tie up was always difficult, often impossible; and occasionally, in the morning, the water was up to a foot lower than normal, leaving us hard aground until it rose again. Friends apparently went in bow-first, holding the stern off with a large bamboo lashed to the pushpit; then, if they got stuck, they could sometimes reverse

out into deep water. The upper reaches are the most shallow.

It is vital to clean the water filters frequently; but a worse problem was that dead leaves stirred up by our passage would block the inaccessible engine-water inlet, with dire results. We eventually discovered that pumping air back through the system with the dinghy pump cleared the inlet beautifully. Thereafter, we did this routinely every day or so, which cured the problem.

The Midi locks These are very difficult, because:

- Instead of remaining the same width as the entrance, they widen out into an oval shape (photo above), which is awkward for manoeuvring.

- They have an overflow culvert around the side, which occasionally sends a sideways current right across the lock entrance, making steering into the lock terribly difficult. Luckily there are only a few like this (mostly around Homps), and I learned the technique of taking such entrances fast, since this is the only way to maintain control. However, this takes a lot of nerve!
- The water is let in with incredible violence (photo opposite), throwing keeled yachts around terribly.
- Except for three very deep locks (at Béziers and Toulouse), there are no floating bollards, so you have to tie to bollards at the top of the quay, and shorten in the warps as the water rises. But shortening in is incredibly difficult, pulling against the violent surge. Some form of mechanical help is badly needed with a big, heavy yacht. If at all possible, lead the line through a pulley to a genoa winch and haul in with a winch handle – but it is essential to find a strong enough point to fasten the pulley as the stresses are greatly magnified because of the angel the rope goes up.
- Locks are only a few metres deep, but generally have no ladders: so usually someone has to be put ashore first, to take the warps. Just before the lock, we would nose into the bank (if it was deep enough, that is!), so Jimmy could jump ashore with the boathook. Then I manoeuvred *Phœnician* into the lock, and he would lean down with the hook and pick up the warps (which we would leave with a bight hanging ready over the guard wires). Have a single line bow and stern, each with a loop tied in the end to the hook over the bollards – preferably ones immediately ahead and

astern of the yacht, so they hold her both in-to-the-quay and fore-and-aft.

There is no doubt that it is hard going in the locks if:
- You have a big, heavy yacht – smaller, lighter yachts have far fewer difficulties *or*
- Your yacht has a big keel (amazingly, the surge just seems to skid underneath the keel-less *penichettes* without troubling them, photo page 117) *or*
- You are weak and elderly, or short-handed.

Everything is *far* easier when there are four people to share the work, and to be available for fending off – indeed, it would be fun instead of a hassle. So I recommend getting friends to come and join you (which is easy, since the Bordeaux–Sète railway conveniently follows roughly the same route as the canal).

Many locks are still hand-operated, and here one is expected to help; but this is easy – and there is less surge than in electrified locks. There were no automatic locks in the Canal-du-Midi. Our canal guide implied that lock-keepers would take your warps, but this was nonsense.

Many locks are grouped into small staircases – but these doubles and trebles are far easier to negotiate than the same number divided up into singles, because it's getting into the first one that's difficult; thereafter, Jimmy just 'walked' the bow line round from basin to basin, while I steered. Interestingly, the big, six-lock staircase above Béziers had been bypassed by a water-slope (where a whole basin of water

The typical violent surge as the water enters a lock – in this case the lower half of a double lock.

Phœnician well fendered for battle in the locks.

plus barge were pushed hydraulically up and down an inclined plane). But this is often out of order, and no barges now use the Canal-du-Midi. Whichever system is in use, you go through in convoy at set times.

Facilities Provisioning and water are no problem. Electricity, diesel and the occasional shower can be bought from hire-boat firms; these are fairly common, and some have deep-water basins where you can tie up. The hire boats or *penichettes* can apparently be a real pain in summer, but they were no problem in May.

Equipment needed

Fenders It is *essential* to have the sides of the boat exceptionally well protected (photo above). Ring the sides with old car tyres (wrapped in dustbin liners). We found we had to go out and search for tyres (try a garage). A dozen is not too many, one from each stanchion, plus one either side of the pulpit and pushpit. Big balloon fenders are also exceptionally useful.

Some fenders are needed hung at water level, since occasionally locks fill to within a few inches of the top of the quay.

Planks Tie a plank outside the fenders just forward of the beam, since this gives protection *between* fenders – very necessary if the side current sweeps you into the cornerstones of the lock entrance, as it did to me on a couple of terrifying occasions. (Though, fortunately, it hit a tyre each time!)

Both deep- and bilge-keeled yachts will often find it hard to get in close to the bank, so a light plank is also necessary for getting ashore.

Warps Have four good, strong warps ready and waiting on both sides – long enough to go up, over the bollards, and down again (since when going *downhill*, you must be able to release them from deck level on leaving the lock, (photo right). The bollards may be some distance away, and a few locks in the Latéral are up to 5 metres in height.

Boathook This is vital for picking up the warps from the top of a high quay when going up the Midi where there are no ladders. Our 1.3-metre one wasn't long enough, even with our high topsides.

Depth marker pole A long bamboo pole marked off in feet or half-metres would have been useful to poke ahead of the yacht when coming into a bank, to avoid going aground.

Stakes These are useful for driving into the ground to take mooring lines, though there were usually trees (or tree roots) to tie to in the Midi route. We used our stake more in the Canal-du-Rhône-à-Sète.

Trestles If you have the mast with you, that is.

Books We used the French *Guides Navicarte* (No 11, Canaux-du-Midi), but we weren't particularly impressed as it didn't give as much information as we wanted (eg it gave the heights of the locks, but not whether there were ladders or floating bollards, nor the depths in basins). *Guides Vagnon* also do one (No 7, Canaux-du-Midi). Both are multilingual, but they are surprisingly difficult to get hold of locally, so buy one on your last visit home.

Costs France is an expensive cruising ground, and though mooring is free on the canal banks, you have to add on the cost of extra diesel (we used two or three times as much as normal for that number of miles motoring). Then there was also our canal

You will need long warps for going down locks so that you can release them from deck level (some locks on the Canal Latéral are 4 or 5 metres deep).

permit (£90), demasting at Port-St-Louis (£11), and remasting at Royan (£40). We also tipped the lock-keepers, hoping for better service, but this was a waste of money.

Times and distances The entire trip 'from sea to sea' *can* be done in ten days, but this means a hard slog for probably 11 hours a day (averaging nearly 20 locks per day). This may be acceptable for youngsters, but it certainly isn't for retired couples. We took 39 days and, with our big yacht, found even that was very tiring – anyway, the canal is so attractive that it deserves savouring.

The speed limit is 8 kilometres an hour, or about 4½ knots – but it's difficult to manage even that. About 4 knots is a good average (going up, against the slight current). Locks takes about ten minutes each, but much more if you have to wait for them to open – say an average of 15 minutes per lock. So a good rule of thumb when going up is:

> Distance (in nautical miles),
> plus number of locks,
>
> all divided by 4 = number of hours
>
> (Going down is faster – divided by 4½)

Don't try to do too much in the first few days, which are likely to be hectic as you learn the ropes. We hurried over the early stages, which was a mistake, since the lower reaches were the best – and later we found ourselves doing more locks than we wanted per day, just because there was nowhere deep enough to tie up.

In the table given below, I offer a suggested timetable for the uphill section. Taken together with the downhill section (see the table opposite), this gives a total of 42 days, which can be expanded or contracted according to your timetable. Overall, this means *averaging* about 2½ hours of travel per day – plus mooring times, and unforeseen extras such as getting stuck in the mud. You will probably manage three locks a day at first, rising to four as you become accustomed to them. In fact, once we were into the swing of things, we found it best to do all we could in one morning, and then take the whole of the next day off. This was much more restful than pushing on every day, and it halved the number of times we had to struggle to find a deep-water mooring. Lighter yachts, with fewer problems and stronger crews, would be able to do far more per day, for the same level of tiredness.

The hours indicated in the tables are the actual number of travel hours we took (excluding all extras), but they match up reasonably with the times given in a hire-boat brochure. I count each lock basin as one lock (so a staircase counts as two or three), but our *Guide Navicarte* counted each staircase as one lock – so their numbers differ from mine. The Long Pound is a very attractive stretch of canal with no locks, just above the lock staircase at Béziers.

Locks uphill – from Sète to the summit of the Midi

	Etang de Thau	Midi up	Long Pound	Midi up	Total up
Locks	0	13	0	59	72
Nautical miles*	10	20	28	53	111
Hours	2	8	7	28	45
Suggested number of days	←——— 4 ———→		3	15	22

[* Number of nautical miles = number of kilometres divided by 1.85.]

Locks downhill – from the summit to Biscay

	Midi down	Canal-Latéral	River Garonne and Gironde Estuary			Total down
			Castets to Bordeaux	Bordeaux to Pauillac	Pauillac to Royan	
Locks	18	51	2 locks into river	0	0	71
Nautical miles	28	104	33	23	30	218
Hours	10	32	4½*	2½*	4*	53 plus
Suggested number of days	3½	13½	1	1	1	20

(* We went down with springs ebb; more time is needed at neaps or when going up – ask advice).

From the Summit of the Midi, down to Biscay

Our first 'down' lock was a revelation, it was so quiet and easy. Gone was the terrible surge, the fighting to keep the yacht under control – she simply dropped, as in a lift. It was unbelievable! However, this did not mean that our problems were at an end.

The descent to Biscay divides into three sections:

1 The Canal-du-Midi down to Toulouse.
2 The Canal-Latéral-à-la-Garonne.
3 The River Garonne and the Gironde Estuary.

The Canal-du-Midi down to Toulouse Locks are often very full when you enter, so low fenders must be in order. There is a current from astern to allow for – tie your aft line first. Put long lines up and over the bollards and make sure they are long enough for the 'drop' (photo page 121). In the deeper locks, get back aboard before it's too late.

The Canal-Latéral-à-la-Garonne The Canal-Latéral is much less meandering than the Midi, with higher bridges, greater depths, and long, narrow, straight-sided locks *with* ladders.

Fig 18 As you approach an automatic lock, there is a pole hanging above the canal that you have to twist. This sets the system going.

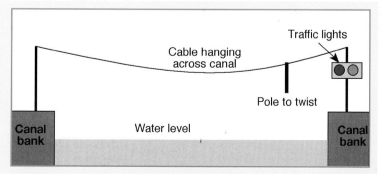

Many of the locks are automatic, and these are quick and easy. When the traffic lights are 'red and green', you signal your presence by twisting the plastic pole that hangs above the canal just before the lock (Fig 18). Then, when all the lights go green (and *not before*), you enter and tie up.

The locks on the upper reaches are fully automatic: a single press of a button; you step back aboard; and it all happens in sequence. In the lower locks, however, you turn a lever to signal each operation, so someone must remain ashore until the gates open. However, there's a platform at the lower end of each lock, so getting back aboard is fairly easy. Equally, when going *up*, the platform makes it easy to put someone ashore, in order to take the warps and operate the controls.

The side surge from the culverts never seems to cause much of a problem when going down, but there are a few that might when going up – especially when putting someone ashore on the platform at the entrance.

The upper reaches: These are horrid – ugly and noisy; and since the edges here are often so shallow that dogs paddle, we could find nowhere deep enough to tie up for miles (until we reached the old barge quay at Grisolles).

The middle section: This is better from all these points of view, but has become infested with terrible weed – the boat has to swim through a jungle of great, long tentacles as thick as your finger. We thanked our lucky stars for our rope cutter!

Gliding through a sea of weed in the Canal Latéral; thankfully we had a rope cutter on the prop.

snakes, more coypu, and the area offers some interesting trips:

* There was a working example of a water slope near Montech; this is worth a look, if the one at Béziers is out of action (check times with the lock-keeper).
* At the Halte Nautique de Buzet, a horse-drawn carriage took people up to the Chateau Matelot each evening for wine-tasting – great fun!

The River Garonne and the Gironde Estuary At Castets you join the river. This is generally broad and lazy in itself, but extremely tidal (we had 5½ knots with us below Bordeaux!) It's best to leave Castets at high water – check with the lock-keeper.

Our canal guide said that Royan up to Castets could be done in two days, stopping at Bordeaux. But we were warned by the Cruising Club of Bordeaux that when going down, *three* days (or tides) are necessary (at any rate, at springs), and we were advised to stop at Pauillac. The problem is that HW Bordeaux is two hours later than HW Royan, which only leaves four hours of ebb to get down to Royan before LW, when the flood starts against you; and this is not possible since it is a 6–8 hour trip even with the tide. You can't make Castets to Pauillac in one tide either, for the same reason. (Possibly at neaps you could make it by stemming some of the flood, as is possible in other rivers, though the tide flows quite strongly until shortly before changing.) In contrast, when going up, the two hours work in your favour, and you get *eight* hours of flood.

The only difficult bit of the river is the Pont-de-Pierre at Bordeaux – a wide, low-

The lower reaches: These, in complete contrast, are delightful (photo above). Depths are good, since this section is still used by a few commercial barges; the countryside is pretty; and many *Haltes Nautiques* have been built, some with deep-water pontoons. At two or three pounds a night (plus water, electricity or showers), charges were extremely reasonable.

There were fewer exotic birds than in the Midi, but we saw a number of water

Racing with the tide through the Pont de Pierre at Bordeaux.

arched stone bridge, with the tide simply *roaring* through it, and the water level actually dropping by nearly a metre (photo above). However, we passed through without problems (though we understand it's impossible to get through if there's *any* tide against you). The two white-painted arches in the centre are the navigable ones, but check with the book and the signs on the arches. Take care when manoeuvring in the strong tide at Bordeaux and Pauillac marinas.

The channel down the Gironde Estuary is well buoyed, though care is needed at the Royan end. A sea chart of the estuary is recommended: certainly the maps in the canal guides are useless here, but you could probably manage with the chartlet in the French almanac *Votre Livre de Bord* (Channel/Biscay edition). Normal marina prices are charged. Re-masting is possible at both Bordeaux and Pauillac – although it's difficult with the tide. Facilities are much better at Royan, and there is no current there to contend with.

Conclusions

In spite of all the problems, we enjoyed the canal immensely (at any rate, in retrospect!) The history was fascinating; the canal itself both beautiful and peaceful; the wines and food excellent. There were many interesting places to visit and exotic birds to watch; and the whole experience was so utterly different from normal cruising that we wouldn't have missed it for anything. We just wished we'd done it in a smaller, lighter boat.

8

Mediterranean Cruising Grounds

GENERAL INFORMATION

Open anchorages

In our early years of cruising we suffered a lot from poor anchorages. We'd heard much about the wonderful *calas* in the Balearic Islands, and had a hard time learning our lesson: that *calas* are fair-weather anchorages, hopeless if there's any swell around. The problem is if you can see out to sea, then the sea can get in to you. *Calas* are almost invariably open to the sea in one direction (anchorage O, Fig 19 is a typical *cala*); and even when wind and swell are coming from the reverse direction, any bay that is open to the sea may be uncomfortable – since swell is perfectly capable of curling round corners and into the anchorage (eg W). Conversely, anchorages open only to a

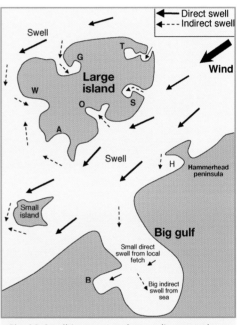

Fig 19 *Swell is very good at curling round, even into those anchorages that are sheltered from the wind.*

Key to Fig. 19

Total shelter:	(T)	Could withstand even an onshore gale
Good shelter:	(G)	Could withstand anything except an onshore gale
Semi-sheltered:	(S)	Can't properly see out to sea, but any swell would work its way in
Open:	(O)	Good deep bay, but completely open to the sea in one direction
Wide open:	(W)	Good anchorage, but open to the sea for about 90º

NB To assess the shelter of an anchorage, picture it from the outside, looking in from the direction of the swell

large gulf (anchorage B) will not suffer from this *indirect* swell, only from any smaller, directly wind-generated swell, from the fetch across the bay.

In 1994–5 we only anchored in open anchorages twelve times, but regretted it on nine of the twelve – bitterly so on four occasions, when we were nearly driven on the rocks (once) or forced to leave in the middle of the night. Not a good average! We learned to categorise anchorages as best we could (see the key to the anchorages in Fig 19).

With even a little more shelter, the proportion of good nights shot up from 3 out of 12 ('open' and 'wide open') to 15 out of 20 ('semi-sheltered') – a staggering difference. So we avoid open anchorages now, and as a result our cruising is much less stressful. You may well have better luck than us, or you may not dislike rolling as much as we do. Certainly many of our friends anchor happily in places that we wouldn't dream of. You'll just have to discover what works for you.

Another factor that affects shelter is depth of water. *Calas* tend to be cut out of cliffs, with deep water close to the sides and nothing to dissipate the swell. An anchorage where the entrance is partly masked by shallow water, reefs and islets will have much more actual shelter. In addition, vertical underwater sides reflect the swell back and forth – harbours with solid quays all round have an awful motion, whereas those with internal edges made of piled rocks are much quieter because swell and wash are absorbed. Similarly, the swell is reflected off cliffs at the entrance to many *calas* and into the anchorage behind: whereas if the sides of the entrance were sandy beaches, again the swell would be absorbed and so the anchorage be far better.

Also, swell does not curl round sharply, so there will be shelter *close* under the lee of a long, thin point or breakwater. A good example is Pollensa Bay, Mallorca (Fig 20). In strong north-easterlies the town anchorage is extremely uncomfortable, while under Punta Avenzada it is totally calm.

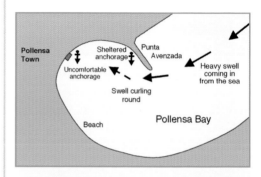

Fig 20 *Swell curls round gently, leaving shelter close under a sharp point or a breakwater.*

Again, if the lee side of an island is big enough and doesn't have rounded corners that will 'pull' the swell around, the anchorages under its lee will be sheltered (A as opposed to W in Fig 19). Conversely, a solitary, small round island will probably offer no shelter.

In addition, if there is a big swell running *along* the coast, a bay facing the opposite way will have good shelter even though open (eg one side of a hammerhead peninsula, anchorage H, Fig 19). But remember, things can change rapidly!

Navigation

Navigation is easy in the Mediterranean, since there is little fog and only occasional offlying dangers. Depths are generally considerable, except very close in; and when the sky is blue and the sea calm, shallow water can often be spotted from a distance by the change in colour: dark blue changing to light turquoise over sand and pale rock, and to dark brown over weed or mud. The water is often wonderfully clear, so in calm weather the bottom can be seen at 5 metres or more. This can be very helpful – though daunting at first.

Cruising weather

The typical daily weather pattern in the Med is for there to be little wind early in the day, but for it to get up quite strongly in the afternoons before dying away after dusk. This tends to happen regardless of the wind direction. The weather is far more difficult to forecast from a synoptic chart than at home. But we find that gales are still generally accompanied by a noticeable drop in pressure, despite having being told the contrary. A characteristic of the Mediterranean is that any strong wind rapidly creates a very rough, short, steep sea, which is difficult to make progress against. You have to be prepared to turn back under these circumstances.

Summer July and August normally have lovely sunny weather, but the result is that it becomes *excessively* hot, so doing anything at all becomes a pain rather than a pleasure. There is often very little wind (except in the Aegean) and no rain, other than during the occasional thunderstorm.

Spring Spring weather, in contrast, is usually very pleasant indeed. Often there are cold nights, but mainly glorious afternoons (similar to a good English summer day), and generally it is cool enough to go shopping, and for walks and excursions, in comfort, without getting hot and exhausted. However, the weather is much more variable in spring, with periods of poor, unsettled conditions as well, and a higher risk of gales or rain (especially during early

spring) – but there is usually quite enough sun to make us glad of our awning.

Autumn Autumn is similar to spring: with much more variable weather than summer, but often really good. The water is much warmer for swimming than in the spring, but the days are far shorter.

Variations The sections above give the general pattern, but there are big variations in different areas – and indeed in different years. For example, sometimes the weather breaks at the end of August and you get a long, unsettled autumn; in other years (or places), summer continues right on until October. The worst weather, all year round, is in the Gulf of Lions (southern France), where you get a lot of gales.

Temperatures

- The further south you go, the hotter it gets.
- Water is much cooler than land in summer, and has a cooling effect on the air temperature – so it's cooler afloat than ashore, and on the coast rather than inland; islands are cooler than the mainland; and an onshore breeze is cooler than an offshore one. But the reverse applies in the winter.
- Any wind that is cooler than blood temperature will carry away the air around you that your body has heated up, and replace it with cool air. So a windy area is cooler than a calm area.
- Evaporation causes cooling: therefore if your skin is wet, evaporation from it will cool you down (this is the basis of sweating causing cooling). Any breeze adds greatly to this effect.

Summer afternoon temperatures in many places can be up to blood heat (37ºC) and

Average temperatures in the Med

	Typical minimum temperatures (ºC)	Typical maximum temperatures (ºC)
	Summer	
S Italy and Ionian	22–25	31–36
Croatia	24–25	27–36
Balearics	21–23	29–32
NW Spain	14–17	22–27
	Winter	
Tunisia	8–12	22–28
SE Spain	6–10	17–20

even beyond – which means that unless your skin is wet, breezes are no longer cooling, but instead like a blast from a hot oven. Further south, even summer nights are too hot – and the mornings also until the cooling breeze develops (the only fresh time of day being around dawn). At the humidity levels of the Mediterranean, above 32ºC or so (90ºF), we can do *nothing* except try to keep cool; and to go shopping or sightseeing, the temperature should be well below 30ºC. Late evening and early morning are the best times (it's worth following the Continental habit of a long siesta in the hottest part of the afternoons).

In 1994 I started recording minimum nightly temperatures and maximum afternoon temperatures (in the shade), and averaging them (very roughly) over fortnightly periods (see table).

The difference between the minimum and maximum temperatures was usually very roughly 10ºC. Therefore, if you read in a book about *average* temperatures, you can guess that typical maximum and minimum temperatures will probably be that, plus or minus 5ºC (±9ºF).

Thunderstorms

You can get thunderstorms at any time of year, though the frequency varies with the area and the time of year. Croatia is prone to them; we averaged one a fortnight during summer in Greece and southern Italy, though we had far fewer in the Balearics. They are usually brief but quite severe.

Places of interest

There are a vast number in the Mediterranean, so in the following sections I will mention just our favourites (those marked ** being an absolute must). OAPs often get a discount on entrance fees, and the same sometimes applies to all EU citizens in EU countries: so take your passports/identity cards.

Information from other people

Other yachtsmen can give you lots of useful information about places you are going to, but take it with a pinch of salt because they can be wrong, and also their attitudes may differ from yours – it's a good idea to ask them about places you already know first, to see if your impressions agree.

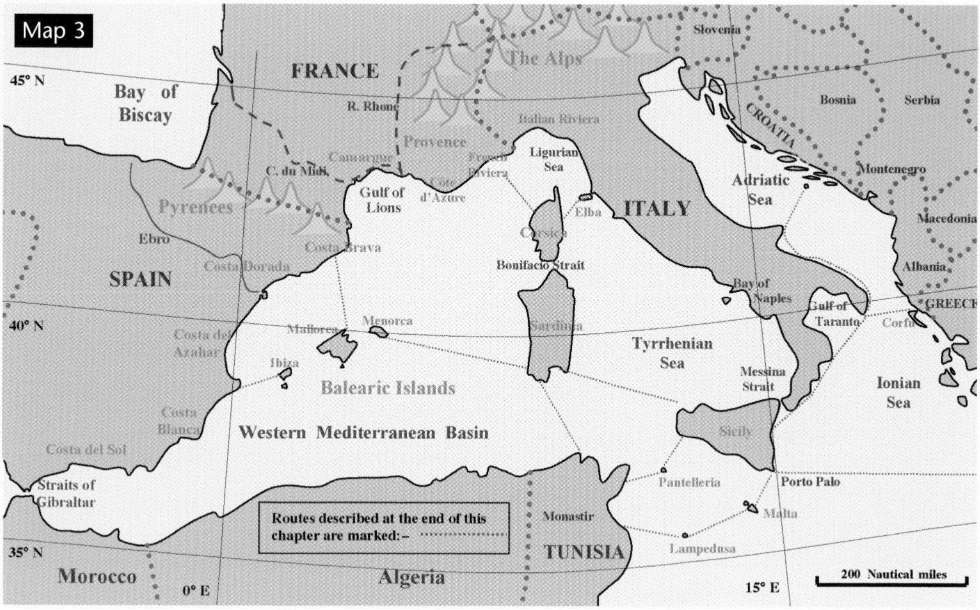

Map 3

THE MAINLAND COAST OF THE WESTERN MEDITERRANEAN BASIN

This coast, from Gib to the Messina Straits, is singularly lacking in natural anchorages, and almost all the sheltered ones are in commercial harbours. However, there are a great many marinas. Prices vary, so check in advance if possible. In Spain, there is a Spanish/ English newspaper called *El Mercado Nautico/The Boat Market*, freely available in yacht clubs, and this often gives a list of marina prices. The French almanac *Votre Livre de Bord* (Med edition) gives prices for French marinas.

The west coast of the basin

The Costa del Sol This coast has very few anchorages indeed (other than off the open beach). It is marina country, and one must just accept it. A range of mountains lies just back from the coast (attractive, though dry and barren), but the coast itself suffers badly from concrete jungle.

However, many of the marinas are very pretty and they are *far* less expensive than those farther east and north. The climate is super in spring and autumn, but desperately hot in high summer (up to blood temperature and above on many August afternoons).

Places of interest
The Alhambra ** This is an exceptionally beautiful Moorish palace in Granada (photo page 5); there are organised tours from coastal resorts.

Costa Blanca The mountains here come right down to the sea in places, so the coast is more attractive, with less concrete and more anchorages. It is still not very sheltered though, except in the Inland Sea, the Mar Menor. Rugged peninsulas alternate with wide valleys and sandy beaches.

Places of interest
Guadalest A striking, preserved fortified village in the mountains near Altea.

Calpe Port This is set right under a huge, Gibraltar-like rock; you can easily climb the slope to the bottom of the cliff, and the view is superb. The slope is a feast of small birds.

Santa Pola The saltpans west of the town (and indeed elsewhere along this coast) contain interesting wading birds in winter and spring, eg flamingos and avocets.

Costa del Azahar and Costa Dorada

These areas resemble the Costa del Sol, with mountains in the background and the coast being very built up. There are fewer purpose-built marinas, but more industry – and therefore more commercial and fishing harbours. One can anchor in some of these, and also in a couple of lagoons around the Ebro Delta.

Costa Brava

In Spanish *brava* means 'wild', and it is indeed a wild and rugged coast, located where the Pyrenees run down into the Mediterranean. This is the most attractive of the Costas, with sandy coves and mountainous peninsulas; and, there being a lot more rainfall, everything is greener. It has the best anchorages too, many in rocky inlets like *calas* (see page 137). However, again there are none with *total* shelter, and bad weather often comes down from the Gulf of Lions.

There are a number of expensive marinas, and the coast is crowded with inconsiderate motorboats in the summer and these cause a dreadful wash. Take care with navigation, since there are many more dangers than on the other Costas.

Places of interest

Barcelona We hate cities, but still felt we had to visit Barcelona to see the extraordinary (and very variable) architecture of Antonio Gaudi.

Blanes On the cliffs above the harbour lie the beautiful Botanical Gardens of Marimurtra (photo opposite).

The north coast of the basin

Languedoc-Roussillon and the Gulf of Lions The first few miles are beautiful (a continuation of the Costa Brava), but soon after Port Vendres (photo page 134) the mountains stop, and the coastline becomes flat and marshy, lined with saltwater lagoons. There are one or two pretty old towns, but most harbours are vast, unattractive marina complexes, which are moderately expensive. The coast is shallow, and dangerous in heavy onshore weather. In order to reach deeper water, the marinas usually have long entrance channels, in which one can occasionally anchor.

The weather tends to be stormy because depressions sliding down into the Mediterranean get squeezed between the Alps and the Pyrenees, causing a very violent northerly wind called the *Mistral*. Though the frequency of this is greatest in winter and least in summer, you can get *Mistrals* at any time of year. The weather is much cooler than farther south.

Places of interest

Banyuls, *Collioure* and *Port Vendres* These are all beautiful.

Sète and *Martigues* Both these places have picturesque old canals.

Provence and the *Camargue* Provence is a beautiful area with many superb Roman remains. In addition, the marshes of the Camargue are a must for bird-watchers – although they are interesting for anyone (see Chapter 7). It is worth hiring a car for

These botanical gardens on the cliffs above Blanes, on the Costa Brava, are well worth a visit.

a few days to tour this area. Alternatively, taking your mast down is cheap, and you then have the entry by boat to the Rhône, the Canal-du-Rhône-à-Sète and the Camargue, though not everything can be visited in this way.

The Côte d'Azure

We don't know this coast well, but it is beautiful, with a number of islands, and also limestone hills that in places form *calanques* which are similar to the *calas*. As usual, few of the anchorages are very shel-tered, but there are several quite good ones, though they become crowded in summer. Because this area (and the Rivièra too) has always been patronised by the rich and famous, the coast has not been spoilt. Marinas are plentiful, and are variable in price. The weather is much less windy than farther west.

The French and Italian Rivièras This beautiful, mountainous coast is not one we have visited by boat, but looking through the pilot guide suggests that there are anchorages, almost all of which are open or wide open. The best appear to be in the Gulf of Naples.

Problems Cruising northern and western Italy out of season is apparently fine, but in our experience it is an area to avoid like the plague in summer, because:

- The many marinas are often phenomenally expensive: the cheaper ones cost as much as expensive ones elsewhere.
- Alternatives to the marinas are the old harbours, in which one traditionally moors bow-to with a stern anchor. However, these ports, being much cheaper than the marinas, tend to be very crowded. In the event, most of the old harbours that we tried in 1994 had been filled with mini-marinas, and we could rarely find space to tie to the quay.
- The few anchorages are desperately overcrowded, especially at weekends.
- Italians individually are lovely people, but behind the wheel of any vehicle they can go crazy! Sometimes they will anchor right on top of you in the most antisocial way, and while you are worriedly eyeing one yacht that's anchored too close, another will come and anchor *in between* you! Often young men in motorboats will whizz round in noisy circles all afternoon, with the crisscrossing wakes turning a peaceful anchorage into a maelstrom (though, admittedly, this latter problem is becoming common everywhere in summer).
- It's very hot at this time of year for traipsing round the monuments etc, which are what most people visit Italy to see.

The south Tyrrhenian and Ionian coasts of Italy South from Naples, Italy is totally different, being traditionally the 'poor

Fishing boats berthed in the picturesque harbour of Port Vendres in the Gulf of Lions, southern France.

about half-a-dozen reasonable anchorages, with degrees of shelter ranging from 'good' to 'wide open'. Marinas are plentiful – they are probably expensive in the summer, though apparently not so in the spring.

The east coast of the basin

The North Tyrrhenian Sea From Elba, south-east towards Naples, the coast is flatter and duller. Groups of small islands off the coast form mini-cruising grounds, but their anchorages are rarely even semi-sheltered. The mainland coast has few

relation'. The few marinas are reasonably priced, containing small motorboats rather than yachts. The Amalfi coast is beautiful; and a little farther south we found some very pretty old harbours which were (then) still available for mooring bow-to. But from there south and east, one is simply passage-making, with ports of any kind few and far between (see page 145).

Messina Strait This is one of the few places in the Mediterranean where you get an appreciable tidal flow. Since it can be up to 4 knots, it is important not to have it against you. Rod Heikell tells you how to calculate it in his *Italian Waters Pilot* (Imray) but you need the time of Gibraltar high water.

The south coast of the basin

Tunisia The coast is typical of the western Mediterranean mainland, with few good anchorages. However, there are more old-style fishing harbours, with a space set aside for yachts (often alongside). There are also some good marinas. The northern section of Tunisia (between the north and east coasts) is varied in scenery – the desert is well to the south. Judging by autumn temperatures, Tunisia must be unbearably hot in summer.

Places of interest

Go on a *desert safari* – ask the nearest hotel or travel agent for details.

THE ISLANDS OF THE WESTERN MEDITERRANEAN

These are totally different from the mainland, being quite well indented and with a large number of anchorages. Only a few have total, all-round shelter, but there are plenty of marinas to go to in bad weather. All the islands are attractive, and form excellent cruising grounds. While summer is normally hot and sunny, temperatures are much more pleasant than the baking heat of the mainland, and the scenery is often spectacular. In general, navigation is easy, though some parts do have many rocks and shoals. There are international airports on all the major islands.

If you visit Tunisia, you must go on a desert safari to the Sahara – there is so much of interest to see.
Photo: Karin Peters.

The spectacular ravine at Sa Calobra, Mallorca.

The Balearic Islands

One of these islands' chief charms is the astounding variety of scenery. The northwest coasts of Mallorca and Ibiza offer savage coastlines under magnificent mountains (photo above); elsewhere are rolling hills loosely covered in bright-green pine trees. There are also areas of sand dunes, sandy coves and rocky islets; and, finally, the famous *calas*, where low limestone cliffs have been eaten away, forming long, finger-shaped openings (often ending in a beach). These may be small or large, single- or many-fingered, beautiful or forbidding, wild or built up. In calm weather, they offer hundreds of delightful anchorages. However, most suffer a surge if there is any swell around – it seems to curl in whatever direction it's coming from.

Luckily there are other anchorages with more protection, and marinas abound. Summer prices can be expensive, but are very variable, so check in advance; confusingly, some are the same price all year. An increasing number of larger harbours are also developing public quays: these are often less attractive and with poorer facilities (eg stern mooring lines, but no showers) – but half the price.

The Islands get their fair share of gales, particularly Menorca, which lies closest to the path of the *Mistral* as it whistles across from the Gulf of Lions to Corsica. In summer, one is generally on the edge of the bad weather, which brings cooler, cloudier conditions, with higher winds but only rarely up to gale force. However, keep an eye on the forecast, especially if there are storms up north – there is always a chance they will spread south, and they invariably send down a heavy swell.

Cabrera The Balearics are very crowded in the summer and it is difficult to get away from the disturbance of jet skis and fast motorboats. The only 'anchorage' that doesn't suffer seems to be the nature reserve island of Cabrera (photo page 3). You need a permit to visit it, but this is free, and easy to obtain – marinas in Mallorca can arrange it. From October to May you can get a permit for a whole week.

Other places of interest
All the islands have trips available on glass-bottomed boats.

Mallorca
The Caves of Drach** at Porto Cristo are really spectacular.
A narrow-gauge railway runs over the mountains from Palma to Soller.
The Albufera marshes Located four miles south of Alcudia, these marshes have hides for bird-watching.

Corsica
This French island is beautiful – a granite mountain range sticking up out of the sea, covered with trees and maquis scrub. The west coast is more interesting than the east, being much indented, with many anchorages (though these tend to be full in summer, and virtually none have total shelter). There are many rocks in places, so careful navigation is necessary. Corsica is in the path of the *mistral*, so winds can be vicious, especially around Cap Corse and the Bouches de Bonifacio. However, if you get good weather and can avoid the crowds, it is a very attractive cruising ground. There are a dozen or so quite expensive marinas.

The Madalena Islands
In the Bouches de Bonifacio lies the Italian Madalena archipelago, a delightful group of small, low-lying islands that together with the adjacent corners of Corsica and Sardinia make an excellent cruising ground and offer some well-sheltered anchorages. Take great care with the navigation, since the area is strewn with rocks and shoals – you *must* have a large-scale chart of the archipelago.

Sardinia
The Italian island of Sardinia is another attractive island of mountains and hills. Some of the coast is fairly indented and forms pleasant anchorages, though they mostly lack all-round shelter; however, like Corsica, the east coast has few (apart from the north-east corner). Harbours vary tremendously: from posh expensive marinas (Porto Cervo being astronomical!) to a small pontoon at the local yacht club, and from a part of a quay in a commercial harbour to anchoring-off in a fishing harbour.

Sicily
This is rather different, with fewer anchorages (none with total shelter), and more old-style fishing harbours where you fit in as and where you can. Some harbours are rather unsheltered, and others are crowded out with fishing boats. However, there is a great deal of variety, and some new marinas are being built, though these tend to be expensive. The scenery is splendid – often mountainous, but green with trees (see photo opposite, foot of page); and at intervals on the north coast, big headlands are formed by vast, volcanic plugs of rock (photo opposite, top), often 1000 feet high.

Places of interest
Mount Etna This should be visited.
The Aeolian Islands These also boast a couple of active volcanoes. A night passage past the continuously flaming north-west side of Stromboli would be a sight never to be forgotten.

▲ The town of Cefalu, northern Sicily, nestles at the foot of a volcanic mountain.

▼ Taormina Roads on Sicily's east coast, must be one of the most beautiful anchorages we have seen – though it is not very sheltered.

THE EASTERN MEDITERRANEAN

It's a long, hard trip to the eastern Mediterranean, but when you get there it offers the best cruising of all. Much of the coast is very indented, both mainland and islands; and there are literally thousands of anchorages (of *all* degrees of shelter). Cruising is therefore cheap, because you are not obliged to use marinas. There are many ordinary harbours where you can tie up as convenient, bow-to the quay (or stern-to); there may be designated areas for yachts and fishing boats. Italian yachts pour into Croatia and the Ionian in the summer.

One thing should perhaps be noted: while being at anchor is highly enjoyable, and far cooler and prettier than being in a marina, it is also more stressful because unless conditions are very settled, you cannot totally relax – even at night. You have to keep a constant watch on the weather, your check-bearings, and other yachts; and if the wind gets up there is constant, niggling tension. This is true even in harbours in the eastern Mediterranean because you will be secured by your stern anchor. So, although the rewards of anchoring are great, you pay for this to some extent. At such times, a few days of total relaxation in a marina are very welcome.

Both Greece and Turkey are simply littered with ancient ruins, many of which are well worth visiting.

Countryside Much of the eastern Mediterranean is mountainous and rather barren; however, it is attractive – broken, rocky hillsides, with maquis scrub growing among the boulders, and populated by delightfully belled sheep and goats.

Walking in such areas can be impossible, however, unless there is a path. Winters tend to be cold and summers hot and dry, so little grows in summer except in the rare river valleys (though the Ionian islands and Croatia are lusher because they are much wetter).

Apparently most of the countryside used to be covered with indigenous forest, but this was systematically felled from classical Greek times onwards. The effect was as devastating as is the felling of the tropical rainforests today: loss of the trees caused climatic change; loss of the tree roots caused erosion; and loss of the soil destroyed the land's ability to retain water – the result being that a fertile countryside becomes a desert. However, even now, wild flowers in the spring are a delight, and you can't go for a walk without tripping over tortoises or seeing the flicker of escaping lizards.

The Eastern Adriatic

Croatia Croatia was one of the first of the new states to secede from the Federal Republic of Yugoslavia, and though it suffered some bombing initially, at the time of writing it has been completely stable for many years.

Most of the Adriatic coastline between Italy in the north and Albania in the south belongs to Croatia (see Map 3). It is very indented and, in addition, there are a vast number of islands that are close together and close to the shore. This creates large areas of semi-sheltered waters and thousands of anchorages. Distances are short, and the inner waters often calm, so one can do more actual sailing. Navigation tends to be of the 'turn right at the next gap' variety. Anchoring is normally free, but you have to pay in certain designated National Park anchorages.

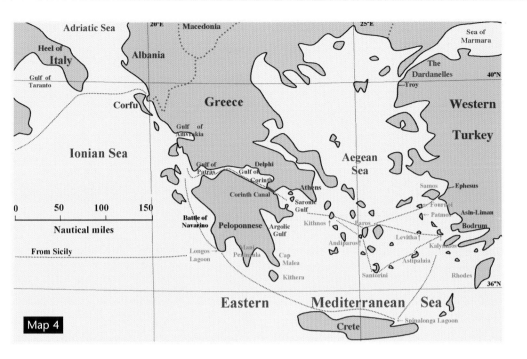

There are many excellent marinas as well as ordinary harbours – and vast numbers of charter yachts and flotillas. Marinas tend to be quite expensive (typically £20 for under 12 metres, 2002). The scenery is attractive, though lacking the variety of, say, the Balearics – bare, silvery mountain ranges along the coast, with wooded lower slopes and islands (except the Kornati group, which are strange and stark). There are many beautiful old stone towns and villages (photo page 35).

I do not recommend cruising Croatia in high summer because:

- It's much hotter in summer than we expected from its northern latitude.
- It's very crowded (particularly with charter yachts), and you will find that many helmsmen are totally inexperienced .

Slovenia and Montenegro These are the two other 'Yugoslav' states along this coast. Slovenia (with a short coastline to the north of Croatia) also seceded from the Federal Republic of Yugoslavia early on, and has been peaceful ever since. Montenegro, to the south, still (with Serbia) belongs to the Federation, and may be less politically stable. Their coasts are generally less indented, with few islands.

Albania Cruising Albania is now possible, though best done in company since it is an extremely poor country and great precautions are needed against theft. The scenery is spectacular but there are very few facilities or good anchorages.

Greece

Harbours and anchorages Outside Athens (see Map 4) there are hardly any marinas – some are being developed, but few seem to get completed! However, there are hundreds of anchorages, including many with excellent shelter. There are also plenty of ordinary harbours (photo below), but in strange contrast these are often worryingly open: they are sometimes merely a piece of quay built along the coast of a bay, open to a fetch of two or three miles (sometimes considerably more). Any ground swell (or passing boat) will leave the yachts pitching uncomfortably (with the constant danger of being thrown on to the quay if the anchor drags by so much as a yard), while strong onshore winds must surely make them untenable. Yet many such quays are home to large charter fleets.

Our usual habit was to visit such places just for an hour or two in the calm of the morning, to shop and fill the tanks, then return to a sheltered anchorage before the afternoon wind got up. With so many good anchorages this was easy, and we rarely spent the night in harbour.

We haven't visited southern Greece, nor the Aegean north of Athens, but I will describe below the areas we do know.

Ionian Greece Much of the coast of western Greece is rugged mountains, and the Peloponnese coast is particularly wild. However, from the Gulf of Patras north to the Adriatic the character of the area is changed by the presence of the Ionian islands immediately offshore. Bare mountaintops are tempered with beautifully wooden lower slopes, and the coasts are much indented, offering many sheltered anchorages. When people think of the Ionian, the picture conjured up is often of the islands of Corfu, Paxos and Ithaca etc – with their delightful sandy coves; the resinous scent of pine trees; dozens of yachts anchored in every sparkling bay; quays and harbours stuffed with charter boats; and tourists crowding streets that are lined with a

variety of shops and restaurants for their delectation.

But there is another side to the Ionian, one that we often prefer: the mainland coast, only a little of which is like the vision above. Generally this consists of barren mountains running down to low, scrubby hills. In places it is deeply indented, forming some of the most sheltered anchorages that we know of. Surroundings are austere rather than beautiful, but they have their own charm, especially in spring, when flowers push their way out of

the stony soil and the bright-pink blossoms of the Judas trees add vivid patches of colour. These anchorages are remote and lonely, with no shops or restaurants. They are ideal places to get way from the crowds.

Gulfs of Patras and Corinth These two gulfs, together with the Corinth Canal, turn the Peloponnese into an island. They are mainly used as a short-cut between the Ionian and Aegean, but the north side of the gulf of Corinth makes a pleasant mini-

cruising ground, having a number of good anchorages and attractive harbours.

Places of interest
Delphi** (the home of the Delphic Oracle). This is superb, and lies in spectacular, mountainous surroundings.

Saronic and Argolic Gulfs The northern shore of the Saronic around Athens is a disaster of industry and pollution, but the rest of the area is delightful – with the rolling, tree-covered hills being a pleasant

The charming little harbour of Vathi in the Saronic Gulf. Few Greek harbours are as well-sheltered as this one.

contrast to the harsher Aegean islands; and the lighter winds also. There are plenty of anchorages but, due to the proximity of Athens, it gets very crowded in summer with both yachts and ferries (the latter causing a horrendous wash).

Places of interest
Athens** Athens, of course, has many fascinating sites and museums (there are frequent ferries from other ports).

The Aegean
Summer weather in the Aegean is dominated by the *Meltemi*: a strong northerly wind that starts blowing fitfully in June, reaches full strength in July and August, and dies away during September. It may blow anything from force 5 to force 8, and it may die overnight or last a week at full strength. Cruising plans should be to go with it or across it, but not against it.

This wind is so strong and regular here that in the pilot guides anchorages are graded according to how much shelter they have from the *meltemi*. During the summer, an anchorage that is wide open south is considered safe, since neither wind nor swell will come from that direction. We had our doubts, but in fact found that though the swell *did* work its way in, it didn't do so badly as long as the anchorage was well and truly sheltered from the wind direction.

Places of interest
Santorini** This is a most striking village and ancient site, on a volcanic island-ring.

Turkey
Harbours and anchorages The Turkish coast is deeply indented and well supplied with sheltered anchorages. In high season when anchorages are crowded, it will frequently be necessary to anchor with a long line ashore (photos pages 153 and 169); this can be a problem for yachts with much windage. There are an adequate number of excellent marinas dotted up the Turkish coast, and in addition many small harbours of varying degrees of shelter and facilities. The south-west corner where we cruised (from Fethiye to just north of Bodrum) was super (photo page 110).

Winds and weather The weather in spring and autumn is very pleasant indeed – like an English summer. However, we avoided Turkey in July and August since

Ephesus in western Turkey has been magnificently restored and should not be missed if you visit this area.

we understood it to be excessively hot, particularly along the south coast (over 40°C, on some August afternoons); and in the Aegean there was the *meltemi* to contend with.

Places of interest

*Ephesus*** This has been magnificently restored and is superb, but very crowded. Visit it from Kuşadası – either by expensive tour from the marina, or cheaply on a local bus (photo below).

Iassus (at Asin Liman, in the gulf north of Bodrum). This is the reverse of Ephesus – overgrown, tranquil and deserted. Get a map from the attendant, and find the mosaic floor on the far side of the hill: take a soft brush to sweep away the sand and reveal the treasures beneath.

MOVING BETWEEN CRUISING GROUNDS

Crossing from the western Mediterranean mainland to the islands

Reaching the Balearics is easy coming from south-east Spain (see Map 3), since Ibiza is only 50-odd miles from the nearest corner of the Costa Blanca. Coming from the north is less convenient, the shortest passage being just over 100 miles (from, say, Barcelona).

Crossing from France to Corsica, the shortest passage is over 100 miles, but from Italy it's easy, going in day-hops via Elba. Sardinia is within easy reach from southern Corsica, but it's a long way from anywhere else.

Tunisia is 130 miles from Sardinia and 100 miles from Sicily, but the latter can be split into two day-trips via Pantelleria. Malta is also a day-sail from Sicily; from there to Tunisia (via Lampedusa) is two passages of 90 miles each.

Heading east from the Balearics

The Balearics to Sardinia and on to Sicily comprise the longest trips you'll need to do in the Mediterranean: two passages of nearly 200 miles. These can only be avoided by going right round the mainland coast (which is an awful long way, though very interesting).

'The Boot' of Italy and crossing the Adriatic

The main problem with the wonderful cruising grounds of the eastern Mediterranean is that you have to get there. This means crossing 'The Boot', and here:

- There are no natural anchorages.
- Harbours are a long way apart (often 60-

plus miles), with some getting a nasty surge in onshore or southerly winds.

- The weather is poor; and in our experience, forecasts are usually contradictory and often completely wrong.

Most yachtsmen dread this trip and, if going to Greece, many prefer a long sea passage straight across avoiding this part of the coast altogether – if they can find long enough windows in the weather, that is! However, it can be done in long day-sails; as can the trip to Croatia, by continuing up eastern Italy to Vieste, whence the Adriatic crossing is only 60 miles.

Crossing from the Ionian to the Aegean

The shorter route is via the Gulf of Corinth (see Map 4), passing through the Corinth Canal – which is striking but costly (we paid nearly £100 in 1995). The only nearby harbour on the west side is Corinth itself, which was small and awkward. But don't try to spend the night in the canal entrance – we were turned out at dusk by the pilot boat.

The alternative route is round the Peloponnese. This coast looked spectacular, though rather inhospitable, with no totally sheltered anchorages, though it does have some safe harbours.

Crossing the Aegean from Greece to Turkey

One problem in crossing the Aegean from the Corinth Canal to south-west Turkey is that while the western half of the Aegean here is relatively full of islands, there is a large gap farther east. We avoided the night passage in each direction, but it was difficult.

The shortest distance between moderate anchorages or harbours was over 60

Mainland Ionian Greece has a number of really sheltered anchorages. This is the entrance to Pagania showing the typical Mediterranean maquis-type countryside with beautiful Judas trees in flower.

miles, and between good ones a lot more – and you can't afford to be delayed by headwinds because most anchorages are unlit. My conclusion, therefore, is that we probably made the wrong decision – and that a night passage between two good anchorages is actually far better than a long day passage with poor anchorages at either end.

Our routes across this 90-mile gap were:

1 Naoussa (Paros Island) east to Kalymnos Harbour. We avoided the night passage by using Levitha, which is well sheltered; however, it is narrow and rocky, so you really need to anchor fore-and-aft or with a line ashore.

2 Pythagorian (Samos Island), west back to Paros. You can reduce the long passage by calling in at either Patmos (there are some reasonable anchorages on the east side), or the desolate Fournoi Islands – the best we could find was the one right on the southern tip of Fournoi Island itself (and even that was open south).

Another way of avoiding the night passage would be a big curve down south, eg:

Fikiadha (Kithnos Island) to Ormos Dhespotico (Andiparos Island)	45 miles
Andiparos to the new harbour on Santorini	47 miles
Santorini to Vathi (Astipalaia)	45 miles
Astipalaia to Kalymnos	40 miles
Total	177 miles

9

Life in the Mediterranean

FORMALITIES, FACILITIES AND FOOD

There is a big difference between countries belonging to the European Union and those that don't. In general, shopping is good within the EU, formalities are negligible, and sending equipment to the yacht is easy. Outside the EU, things are more complicated.

Formalities

These are almost non-existent for EU yachts in France, Spain and Italy; and so long as you behave yourself, the only people who are interested are those who want money from you, eg marinas. At the time of writing, Portugal and Greece require more formalities.

Outside the EU you have to fly the Q flag and complete entry formalities, but this is normally easy. You are then given visas and some kind of cruising permit, which thereafter (in Croatia and Tunisia) will be wanted by harbourmasters, etc instead of your registration documents.

Facilities

There are excellent marinas throughout the Mediterranean, although some suffer a surge in gales from certain directions. They vary greatly in price, but usually have good facilities, often including a restaurant, food shop, chandlers, etc. Diesel is available in most harbours and/or marinas.

Water normally has to be paid for. This usually works out at a few pounds to fill the tanks – unless you're in a marina, when it is often included in the price. In our experience, tap water is safe everywhere in the Mediterranean. However, it doesn't always taste nice, and is sometimes not fit to drink, being slightly salty. It is then usually labelled 'non-potable'. If it tastes OK we fill all our cans and bottles: these will then hopefully last until the next place that has good water. If we run out, we have to cart bottled water on to the boat (which is heavy!).

Unfortunately, self-service launderettes are extremely rare, and proper laundries expensive, but marinas occasionally provide a washing machine, or some kind of laundry service.

Shopping

Even with the phrase book, explaining to a shopkeeper what you want can be terribly difficult, and it's infinitely easier just to show them an example. If you can't try drawing it!

Chandlers tend to be expensive, and stocks may be poor (though you can usually order things).

Food shopping varies considerably throughout different parts of the Mediterranean. The following foods are likely to be difficult to find in areas where shopping facilities are poor:

- Marmite, Bovril, etc.
- Tinned or frozen ready-meals (eg bolognese, lasagne, chilli con carne).
- Tins of meat (suitable for turning into stew, curry, lasagne, etc).
- Tinned salmon and soups.
- Breakfast cereals.
- Tinned puddings other than fruit (eg rice pudding, treacle pudding).
- Particular varieties of things (eg cheeses, hot drinks). Good tea is expensive when available.
- Items normally available in good delicatessens, and also vacuum-packed food.
- Cashew nuts.
- Brown sugar.
- Tomato purée in tubes.
- Bread that keeps.

So before leaving a good shopping area, stock up with these things, making sure they have long shelf-life dates. Also, when changing from one country to another stock up well to give yourself a breathing space to aclimatise to the differences.

Chicken, pork and lamb are generally excellent throughout the Med, though products derived from pork are very difficult to get in Muslim countries. Full-grown beef is very scarce in Spain, due to the lack of summer pasture; and meat derived from younger animals (eg veal) is rather tasteless. So take beef stock cubes with you to pep up stews.

Cooking apples appear to be completely unknown in the area, but you can cook with acid eating apples. Marmalade is known as orange jam – *mermelada* usually just means jam.

Spit-roast chickens are often available as take-aways and are delicious hot or cold – likewise with pizzas in Italianate countries.

All over the Mediterranean you can get dry-cured ham – called variously Parma ham (Italy), Serrano ham (Spain), or Pršut (Croatia). It keeps much longer than cooked ham, and is delicious so long as it's cut *wafer* thin. The same applies to *lomo embuchado* (cured pork loin) in Spain.

Cooking

On board, one wants simple, tasty recipes, made from readily available ingredients that keep well, so whenever I find a suitable recipe I write it down (and in future editions of this book I hope to have room to include some of these recipes). Particularly useful are ones that can be created from ingredients that you usually keep in the normal ship's stores, for use when you are far from shops. Vegetarian recipes are very good in this respect, because nuts, beans, lentils, cheese, eggs, etc are much easier to store than meat – and some of the recipes are really tasty.

Salads are tremendously convenient because they are cool to prepare and eat in summer, and make things easier when trying to cook meals on a two-burner hob. Lettuce and carrots are often unobtainable in the hottest weather, but one learns to cook and make salad with the traditional Mediterranean vegetables: tomatoes, cucumbers, aubergines, peppers, onions, olives, etc. Buy *unripe* tomatoes and keep them in the fridge. When available, lettuce should be stored cool and dry, sealed in a plastic bag or box. Remove any bad bits *every* day, to make the rest last.

We found that fish from Croatian waters tasted particularly good – these lobsters certainly did!

It's frustrating to be forced back to civilisation simply to buy bread, and in the eastern Mediterranean it can be difficult to find bread that keeps for more than a day. You can easily make your own, though, using the quick recipe given on the Allinson's Easy-Bake Yeast packets – make a flat, oval loaf, cooked on a greased baking tray.

Eating out

In parts of the Mediterranean, restaurants tend to open far later than in the UK (often not until 8pm, or occasionally 9pm, in Spain). Many restaurants have a 'fixed-price meal' and this will be much better value than ordering *à la carte*. In south European languages, the word *menu* (if it is used at all) means this fixed-price meal, and they have a different word entirely for the full range of food available. The house wine is likely to be good quality and excellent value – and cheap merely because it has been bought in bulk.

Of course, there is no way of judging the quality of the chef from the menu, the prices or the décor. The only way of ensuring a good meal is to get a recommendation – either from the *Michèlin Guides,* a magazine, another yachtsman, the harbourmaster, or even a passer-by in the street.

On the subject of fish, Mediterranean fish are generally not nearly as tasty as cold-water Atlantic fish.

GENERAL POINTS ABOUT MEDITERRANEAN COUNTRIES

In all the countries we've been to (given below with the dates of our last visit), quite a few people speak some English in tourist areas, but hardly anyone does elsewhere.

Gibraltar (1998)

There is excellent shopping here, but it is not part of the EU.

Spain and the Balearic islands (2000)

Nowadays shopping is excellent on the 'Costas'. You can get pretty well anything, though you may have to search – smaller, local shops with an English clientele sometimes have a better range than the big supermarkets. North-west Spain is not nearly as good in this respect.

You really need to pick and choose to find good restaurants. Fixed-price menus are often only available at lunchtime.

An increasing number of marinas now have washing machines.

There is a continuous classical music programme (Radio Classica) on various FM frequencies.

Southern France (1997)

This area offers excellent shopping, though it tends to be expensive. Camping Gaz costs three or four times as much as elsewhere in the Mediterranean. However, there are plenty of good, large supermarkets within easy reach of the ports.

Self-service launderettes exist in most towns.

The French language here sounds much more lilting than in northern France, since the silent Es at the ends of words *are* pronounced.

Italy and the Italian islands (2002)

The Italians (ashore!) are charming people, always ready to go out of their way to be helpful. When tying to a quay, you often have to pay for both mooring and water, though water is sometimes free on the fuel quay.

Restaurants are excellent but expensive, and they frequently have no price list – so this makes things *very* difficult. One can usually get a good meal at a reasonable price at a pizzeria (many serve other dishes as well); these often open earlier than restaurants.

There seem to be fewer large supermarkets in Italy than in France or Spain.

Malta (2003)

Like Gibraltar, Malta offers excellent shopping, but again it is not part of the EU. There is a Marks and Spencer's food store, Boots the Chemist, and a Dunlopillo shop. British three-pin electric plugs are available. *Most* people speak some English as well as their native Maltese.

Croatia and the Dalmatian islands (2002)

The people here are friendly and helpful, and the younger generation usually speak some English. German is widely spoken in the north. No visas are required for EU citizens, but yachts must enter the country at a port of entry and obtain a cruising permit. These cost well over £100, but do last 12 months. Local currency is only obtainable *within* the country; there are no banks in the outer islands, but people there will accept hard currency – so take lots with you.

Shopping is fairly good in the larger mainland towns, but is expensive and very limited on the more remote islands (they especially lack meat and vegetables).

There are excellent restaurants, with some of them (catering for yachtsmen), even in lonely anchorages; these often serve *superb* fish. Ask flotilla leaders for recommendations.

Laundry services are often provided by the marinas.

Greece (1996)

Facilities Yachts need to be self-sufficient regarding electricity in Greece, because of the lack of marinas. This causes huge problems running an electric fridge if you don't have good supplementary sources of power.

In ordinary harbours, water is available from a 'water man' who has to be found and paid. Diesel is often available in a similar manner (from a bowser on the quay).

Laundry is mainly 'do it yourself', since laundries tend to be very expensive.

Formalities and costs Port police usually want forms filling in, but details of formalities seem to be changing constantly. Harbour dues used to be minimal, but are gradually increasing. However, we spent so little time in port in Greece that charges were fairly irrelevant. The lack of marinas makes Greece a very cheap cruising ground.

Food Eating out we found disappointing. The best choice is usually the 'dish of the day'. This is often not mentioned on the menu, but is on view in the kitchen, so go and have a look – this is accepted practice.

Shopping is not as good as in France and Spain, but far better than in some non-EU countries. They do some quite nice wines in 1½-litre bottles. The milder retsina wines (flavoured with resin) are actually quite pleasant.

Turkey (1995)
First impressions A number of things about Turkey are particularly striking as soon as you enter any of the old harbours such as Bodrum – the deep wailing cries of the *muezzin* arise from minarets all over town, calling the people to prayer; spices, exotic jewellery and Turkish carpets are for sale in the streets – there are even camels in places; and in the big harbours there will be scores of *gulets* lining the quay. These are beautiful, traditional wooden ketches, built now for the tourist trade.

We found the Turkish people to be charming, friendly and honest.

A Turkish gulet anchored with a long line ashore, in the sheltered bay of Değirmen Bükü. Her shore line does not show but the huge passerelle at the stern would cut a swathe of destruction as she swung if she were free-anchored.

Formalities A three-month transit log costs about £20, but getting it is a lengthy procedure, involving filling in long forms, then traipsing around five different offices to get them stamped (some marinas will do this for you, for a fee). You also have to pay £10 each (in English currency) for visas. To renew your visas and log, you have to leave the country formally for one day (the same process in

reverse) and then return, and do it all over again.

Facilities and costs Most of the ordinary harbours have water available, and the odd one has an electricity point.

There are strict laws in Turkey against polluting harbours and anchorages, and you can be fined hundreds of pounds for doing so (though this is unusual).

Therefore you will need a holding tank or a chemical toilet.

When we visited in 1995, shopping was very poor – though I gather that it has now improved. Goods and services provided for the locals are very cheap (eg food, Camping Gaz, public transport, ordinary harbour dues), but those aimed specifically at tourists will be priced accordingly (eg tourist restaurants, souvenirs, marinas).

There are so many good anchorages to be found that one is rarely *obliged* to use a marina.

Eating out Restaurants vary wildly in both quality and price (and with no particular relationship between the two). Even in isolated anchorages, there will often be a primitive outdoor restaurant that serves simple meals. In less remote areas there will be a chilled cabinet with a mouth-watering display of cold starters, and the fish, steaks, meat balls, kebabs, etc that you will be offered as a main course – plus, possibly, a hot cabinet with oven-cooked dishes on display. As in Greece, it is usual (and sensible) to go and look to make your choice, even where there *is* a written menu.

No wine used to be available in restaurants, as the majority of Turks are Muslims – but we didn't find that to be the case anywhere that yachtsmen could be expected!

Inflation The economy is in chaos at present. Previously, inflation was *extremely* high – yet this seemed to cause no problems; bills were quoted in hard currency and converted to Turkish lira at 'today's rate' when you paid.

Tunisia (2001)

Though geographically totally different from Turkey, in other ways Tunisia is rather similar: being Muslim, non-European, and with an Eastern atmosphere. There is the same wailing of the *muezzin*, the exotic street stalls, and lots of camels. It is full of contrasts – mule carts alongside smart cars, and old women in yashmaks mingling among girls in trouser-suits, etc.

Women are advised to dress modestly, not wander round on their own, nor look at a local man unless they need to speak to him. However, while these rules may well apply to places off the beaten track, it seemed that people in tourist resorts behaved much as normal.

The local language is Arabic, but enough people speak French to make things easy if you are familiar with that language. But in tourist areas quite a few people speak some English and/or German as well.

Ramadan is the holy month where Muslims have to fast between sunrise and sunset. It is a short month and therefore the timing comes forward by one month each year. It has little effect on visitors, except that opening times of shops, restaurants and offices will change.

Formalities Tunisia is similar to Turkey in this respect, although getting initial paperwork done is much easier since they come to you. Visas only last for three months, but new ones can be obtained locally. Port police usually insist on keeping your papers until the very moment of your departure (but they do remain open all night).

Shopping There is good fresh produce in the markets, but the supermarkets are very poor indeed. You will find a fair range of yoghurts and cheeses, but very little else in the way of delicatessen items (ie no cold meats). They do not have pork, bacon, ham, etc, nor frozen food. Only a few foreign manufacturers have entered the Tunisian market (eg the ubiquitous Kellogg's, Nescafé, and Uncle Ben's). However, there are some very pleasant local wines and beer. Most of the 'difficult to obtain' items on page 149 are completely unavailable – plus low-fat products, stuffed (or even stoned) olives, and salt-roasted nuts.

A lot of Tunisian food is very spiced (with hot chillies), making it almost inedible for us. Beware the difference between sweet peppers (*poivrons*) and chilli peppers (*pimentes*), which can look very similar (the former are broader).

Take egg boxes with you as eggs are supplied loose.

Other facilities There are good restaurants, but many bad ones too, and they vary considerably in price. Many of the smaller ones, or those catering for locals, are unlicensed, so serve only soft drinks.

Food is generally cheap, as are moorings – even in most marinas. These marinas sometimes run a reasonably priced laundry service. Diesel is very cheap indeed.

Flying home is expensive, since if you enter by yacht you can only fly out on a scheduled flight. However, if the boat is booked in for six months, you are entitled to a much reduced 'residents' fare, though only certain travel agents can arrange this.

LEARNING LANGUAGES

Why bother?

Abroad, we all have to face the question, 'Do we struggle to learn the new language, or do we rely on the people there speaking English?' Many Brits choose the latter course, but I feel this is the wrong decision, because away from tourist resorts people often speak no English; and even when they can, it creates resentment if you *expect* them to speak your language in their country. Also, it lets the side down – we British are the laughing-stock of Europe with regards to languages.

How to set about it

Actually, we find this fun, although we have no special flair for languages. But if you put in the effort, the rewards are considerable and very satisfying. As for how much effort this involves, the answer is really as much or as little as you like, so long as you set about it in the right way. It's *vital* to do a little work every single day – a few minutes daily is far better than an hour once a week, because each day's work reinforces what you learned the day before; whereas newly learned information will have been forgotten again in a week's time if you do no revision in between. Do five minutes a day, *however* little you feel like it – preferably at a set time of day (eg over breakfast).

Normally, a vast amount of time is wasted learning words and phrases you rarely use. So another absolute essential is to choose what to learn with the greatest possible care. You can get by pretty well with a few hundred words and phrases, *so long as they are the right ones*. These are the ones you need to know by heart, as opposed to those things you can look up in the dictionary when you want them.

Using what you have learned

After the hard work comes the fun – that is, when you arrive you can actually communicate, albeit very simply. Don't feel shy about trying out the language and don't worry if it doesn't seem to work immediately – learning to *use* what you know takes time, as does getting used to the local pronunciation.

You must resign yourself to not understanding people's replies to your questions – they will invariably speak too fast and use too many words that you *don't* know! So phrase your questions so that they elicit a one-word answer or a pointing response.

LANGUAGE LEARNING TECHNIQUE

Copy each important word or phrase on to a card – English on one side, the foreign language on the other – and use the cards for the actual learning. Study the pronunciation until you feel familiar with it, adding guidelines to your word cards. Then pick out those foreign words that feel most familiar – these will be the easiest ones to learn.

Choose about a dozen and go through the cards, saying the words, and seeing which ones which you can successfully translate into English. Check every time; and those you get wrong, do again until you get them right. Next day, go through them again. When you can get them all right first time round, add a few new words. Keep the cards in labelled piles according to how well you know them. Make sure you never have many in the 'don't know' pile, since this is confusing. Learn individual words first, then add phrases that incorporate the words that you know – the more ways you use a word, the easier it becomes. Anything you have difficulty getting your tongue round, practise slowly about a dozen times.

For those words you feel confident about, turn over the cards and start learning them the other way round (English into the foreign language) in exactly the same way. Once a week, say Monday, put aside the pile you know well, and don't look at it for a couple of days (ie until Wednesday); those you still know then can be left three days (ie until Saturday). After this, look at the cards after four days (Wednesday); then after another week (Wednesday), then 10 days later (Saturday), then after two weeks (Saturday), etc. If you keep not-quite-doubling the time like this, your brain will remember the words pretty well. Thus you don't have too big a pile to look at every day, which is terribly important. If you do have time, it's extremely helpful to go through your piles of cards a second time, for extra practice. Occasionally check all the cards the other way round as well.

If you get really confused between two words or phases, leave one until you know the other thoroughly; conversely, if you know the difference between two words or phases, when you think about it, but muddle them when you're not careful, then keep them together in a pile marked 'pairs', so you can practise differentiating between them.

The great advantage of this method is that it reduces to a minimum the amount of time required each day, while at the same time maximising the length of time you'll remember the words. However, it takes time to learn the required number of words, so try to get started many months before you need the language. Carefully regulate the number of new words you add each week. The fewer you add, the shorter the time you will need to spend each day – but the longer it will take to learn the required number of words. If you'll be passing through several countries rapidly, it's much easier if you learn one language each, rather than both struggling with two.

VISITS HOME

Where to leave the yacht

The security of your boat Are you going to leave your boat afloat or ashore? There may be problems with either; however, in Jimmy's opinion, out-of-the-water is usually by far the safest. Also, drying out glassfibre yachts ashore for a few months every year greatly reduces the chances of their getting osmosis. Check, though, that the boatyard/marina has adequate security against thieves and vandals.

Ashore: A number of boatyards have travel hoists, and you may prefer this, rather than one with only a crane, or some kind of trolley.

The major danger ashore is the possibility of the yacht blowing over, so it is absolutely essential to ensure that she is well chocked up. Many yards have cradles. The method of balancing the yacht on upright posts is also quite common, but it is not very secure because they can shake loose and fall down – the posts should at any rate be fastened securely together. If you are unhappy with the way she is chocked up, a pair of home-made 'legs' firmly fastened to the yacht will greatly increase security (or you can buy telescopic ones). The danger of blowing over is much reduced if the mast is taken down, since there will be much less windage. It is also worth trying to choose a yard that doesn't suffer overmuch from strong winds.

Afloat: Wooden hulls are best kept damp or the planks will dry out, shrink and warp. On the other hand, when the yacht is afloat there are far more dangers to consider. These include:

- Storm damage.
- A through-hull fitting failing, so the boat sinks.
- Other boats hitting your vessel.
- The marina moving your yacht, and making a mess of it.
- Someone stealing her.

Choose a harbour that doesn't suffer from much surge. Use extra warps, and all your fenders (tied on securely) in case of storms. Shut all hull valves securely.

Costs Prices are incredibly variable, so keep your ear to the ground for where the cheapest places currently are. It is sometimes possible to negotiate a price, and it's usually cheaper if you pay for several months in advance. Check whether VAT has been included; remember that electricity and water may be additional while you are living on board.

Closeness to an airport This is important if you are flying home.

When the boat is ashore

Living on board while the boat is ashore is horrible, and some people rent a flat or go to a hotel. The problems are threefold:

- You have to climb up and down a ladder to go 'ashore'.
- You have no *useable* toilet on board – a Porta-Potti is a tremendous help at night.
- All waste water from sinks runs underneath the boat – so you will need to stick a short hose in each sink outlet with a bucket underneath.

Agua-Fuerte removes crustaceans from the propeller (but don't leave it on long); and coating the propeller and log impeller with Vaseline at the start of the season helps to reduce fouling.

Travelling home

What we dislike most about this way of life is the hassle of flying to and from home. It should be easy, but often it's a nightmare. There are two major problems:

- obtaining your air tickets
- getting to and from airports.

Buying plane tickets When we first started cruising, we naively assumed that it was merely a question of going into the nearest travel agent and booking our flights. Perhaps this is the case with expensive scheduled flights, but charter flights are very difficult because no one seems to have access to everything that's available. To explain the problem, I need to go back to first principles.

Holiday charter companies charter blocks of seats within a plane from an airline; so the seats on one plane can be divided up between many different charterers. For people just wanting flights, travel agents have to check with *each* charter company to see what seats they have available on any *individual* day between two *specified* airports. It seems impossible just to call up a complete list of what's available, so you can then choose the most appropriate option. (Note that you generally have to buy your ticket in the country you're flying from.)

One travel agent may tell you there are no seats left on a particular flight, simply because he forgot to check with the only charter company that *did* still have seats left in the block they had bought. Or he may sell you a high-priced ticket, not realising that another company has them much cheaper because *they* still have lots of seats to sell and the departure date is getting close.

Charterers don't release tickets for general sale until they're sure they won't need them for their own holiday customers –

sometimes, for flights home, this is not until one week before the flight. Then, of course, there's a rush by all the travel agents to grab the available tickets for *their* customers – and you may fail to get one.

All in all, it's a bit of a minefield, and we have sometimes found it easier to ring the charter companies direct – they advertise in local papers. Other methods of getting cheap tickets are the internet, Teletext, etc.

Finally, if you're desperate for a really cheap or immediate flight, go to the nearest big airport with your luggage and wait until a cancellation becomes available.

Getting to and from the airport The ideal is to lay up in a marina close to an airport that flies to somewhere near your home, but things aren't usually that convenient. Normally we have a difficult journey at one or other end of the trip.

If you can't avoid this problem, ensure that at least the foreign part of the journey is easy – it's bad enough coping with travelling at home, without adding a foreign language to your difficulties. Also, you will build up more and more experience of getting to and from the main airports at home, so this becomes easier.

Try to leave your boat only a taxi ride from the airport in the Mediterranean, and get a flight *home* in the morning, but *out to the yacht* in the afternoon. That way, you've got half a day available for travelling at the home end.

Before you leave your boat

Much of the Mediterranean is fairly dry in winter, so precautions against damp will not usually be needed. Leave the yacht prepared for the likely conditions when you return (eg heater and suitable bedding ready). In addition to all the normal laying-up jobs, the following are also necessary:

Contacts Make sure the marina/boatyard knows when you're going and coming back, *and* when you want to launch – and also has a means of contacting you if necessary. Take with you addresses, phone and fax numbers, etc of the marina and any new friends that you've made.

Ring home to let people know when you are arriving, and perhaps ask someone to leave some food in the house. Consider contacting your car insurers to ask them to upgrade your insurance again, and to *send* your new certificate to your home, so that you will be able to tax the car when you get back.

Security We never employ anyone to look after the boat while we're away, since they often don't do it properly; and we don't want to leave the keys with anyone in case of misuse. However, we do ask a friend or neighbour just to keep an eye on her.

Secrete all valuables away in a hidden locker, just in case – a professional thief would probably find them anyway, but hopefully not a casual burglar. Secure the yacht very thoroughly, but leave air vents open (screened against insects). All food should be left in airtight boxes (or doubled, sealed plastic bags). Put down cockroach traps and ant powder. Clean the fridge, and any lockers that might have particles of food in them.

If you'll be away for some time, the batteries will need top-up charging – a small solar panel or wind generator (with regulator) is ideal.

Packing Make a list in your Transfer Book of regular items that you will need to bring back from home each year; and keep a record of how much of them you use (especially medicines). In addition, throughout the year make a note of everything else that you think of that needs to be brought back out after your next trip home. Then, before you leave the boat, check through your stocks of all these things. See if you can't buy some of these items locally, then compile a shopping list for home.

Take a document from the marina showing that you are laid up there. If the yacht is in a non-EU country, you just might find such a document useful on your return. Also, when we visited the Earl's Court Boat Show, we found that by registering on entry as 'overseas visitors' we could get a pass that enabled us to re-enter, free, on future days.

Wear home clothes that will be suitable for the conditions when you arrive – preferably ones you no longer want on board (to save space on the return journey).

While you are home

There is a lot to do on visits home, especially if it's winter. The following are matters that will probably need immediate attention:

- Get the car serviced, MOT'd, insured and taxed.
- Reorganise all the other things you cancelled or altered on leaving, eg:
  – house insurance;
  – television licence;
  – phone and electricity tariffs.
- Consider getting flu jabs (remember, you are used to a hot climate now).

In addition to buying equipment for the boat, seeing your family, and possibly organising Christmas, you may need to do some of the following:

- Get the chimney swept and the boiler serviced.
- Do any necessary home maintenance jobs.

- Update insurances (yacht, house and personal) and VHF licence.
- Check whether your passports, credit cards and driving licences need renewing; and get any necessary visas for next year.
- See your doctor, dentist, or optician, etc; get any required inoculations, stock up with medicines, and renew your E111.
- Get any necessary foreign currency.
- See your bank manager and/or financial adviser; complete your tax return; and update any standing orders, etc.
- Buy your return air tickets.
- Update your lists of addresses, Christmas card list, etc, and add new entries to your Transfer Book.

Equipment If you have too heavy a load to carry with you, have some of your purchases sent directly to the yacht, or send a parcel of books. DHL Worldwide Express (see Appendix 3) is a fast courier service, though the ordinary postal service is much cheaper. Swift Air is good. When the boat is in an EU country, there are few problems bringing or sending equipment out.

When your boat is outside the EU, things are not quite so easy because of Customs. The big advantage is that you can buy things without having to pay VAT:

- If you bring goods out of the UK with you, explain what you are doing at the time of purchase and get the vendor to fill in a VAT Reclaim Form. This you show (with the *unused* equipment) to the customs officer at the VAT Reclaim Desk immediately you've passed through the security check at your departure airport: he stamps the form, which you post (in the box provided) back to the vendor, who credits you with the VAT.
- If you have things *sent* out, they may get

stuck at customs until you go and clear them; this latter procedure can be complicated, and it's easier to pay an agent to do this for you. You sometimes have to pay some import duty, though having 'yacht in transit' written on the parcel may avoid this. In Turkey (and maybe elsewhere), it is essential to ensure that they are sent straight to an airport that is close to your boat, because you (or the agent) have to go to the airport where the goods enter the country, in order to clear them.

We've had things sent successfully by post to Spain, the Balearics, Tunisia, Greece and Croatia; and by courier to Gibraltar, Spain, Tunisia and Malta. Our only problem was during a strike among customs officials in Portugal.

Things to do before returning to your boat

- Fax the boatyard to confirm when you want to launch.
- Update your instructions for your care-taker, mail-sorter and gardener.
- Set up all the same arrangements as when you left originally (see page 109) – you will need new packing and action lists.

VISITORS

Friends and family coming out to visit you will find booking return tickets for a week or two in the Med, much easier than how it is described above. However, it can still be difficult, and they should try every travel agent available to get the best choice. Advise them on suitable clothing to bring, and whether or not they need towels, sleeping bags, etc.

You yourselves should allow plenty of time to reach your rendezvous point, to avoid the worry of bad weather delaying your arrival. When planning where to take visitors, remember that they will be unused to both the heat and the motion, so don't overdo it. Cost-wise, allow for more use of marinas, restaurants, etc while you have guests.

If you want grandchildren to visit you, it can be arranged, on scheduled flights, for unaccompanied minors to be supervised by flight attendants for the journey.

OVERWINTERING

The winter is a time when one tends to stop cruising and to lay up the yacht. It is also likely to be your only opportunity for maintenance, so leave time for this. Your choice of where to winter will depend on whether you intend to go home or not. Important points if you are going home have already been covered, but if you're staying on board, there are other factors:

Choice of harbour

Surroundings Shelter from wind and sea is even more important if you will be living aboard. If you like tranquillity, check for traffic noise and discos. Are the surroundings attractive?

Shopping It is essential to have a good supermarket within easy reach. Make absolutely sure that it (and the other facilities you want) will be staying open throughout the winter. Other useful shops are a butcher and baker; places that sell stamps, stationery, films and computer equipment; a chandler and hardware store; and somewhere that develops films.

Other facilities Water is essential; and, for most people, mains power also. If you are considering wintering without electricity, then good alternative methods of heating the yacht and powering the batteries will be necessary; and remember that you will be unable to use the immersion heater, printer, power tools, etc.

Good showers and toilets, and a launderette, are a great boon. If you like eating out, check that there are good restaurants locally, plus haul-out and repair facilities if needed. Access to a town is very important for those who like shopping, nightlife, cinemas, libraries, etc. Do you want to ride, ski or play golf? Check what facilities will be available, in a language you can understand.

Social life This is really important, since it so much enhances the quality of your life. Obviously, a large live-aboard community gives you more choice of friends than a small one. Where live-aboards congregate for the winter, they usually arrange a variety of social events, which may include a Sunday barbecue, a weekly club night, quizzes, a series of talks, classes in yoga or languages, etc. Another very useful facility is a 'book-swap'.

Weather

The winter weather everywhere is warmer and drier than back home, but varies considerably from area to area. In the better places it is often good enough to go sailing, with lovely warm sunny days even though the nights are cold. The three most important factors are temperature, wind and rain. If you plan to winter anywhere that suffers badly from any of them, I would strongly recommend building a see-through, winter cockpit cover (photo overleaf).

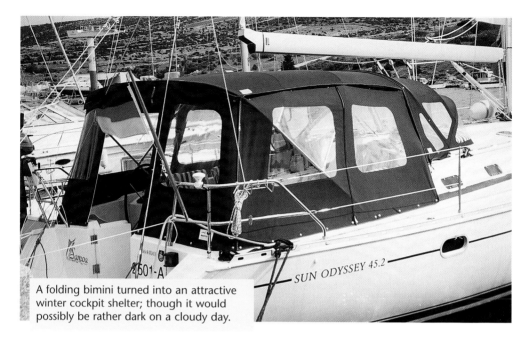

A folding bimini turned into an attractive winter cockpit shelter; though it would possibly be rather dark on a cloudy day.

Study the weather tables in the *Admiralty Sailing Directions* (and Rod Heikell's *Mediterranean Cruising Handbook*).

Temperature The northern Mediterranean is colder than the south, and the mainland is colder in winter than the islands, especially near high mountains that may have snow on them. Temperatures rarely get down to freezing, but wind will introduce an extra chill factor.

Wind The Gulf of Lions is particularly stormy in winter, and any straits are likely to suffer from wind. So too are major headlands. One doesn't mind the odd gale, but continually windy conditions are very trying. Mountainous areas tend to be gusty.

Rain This is perhaps the worst of the lot, and west-facing coasts seem to be the wettest.

Summary of places to overwinter

Our experiences (and comments from others) lead us to believe the following:

South-east Spain This has excellent winter weather; it is fairly warm and dry until you get close to Gibraltar, which is much wetter and windier. There are some excellent, cheap marinas for over-wintering, with plenty of live-aboards. Apparently, marinas are now filling up by the end of September or earlier, and some have no room at all.

Balearics We've heard adverse comments on the winter weather here, and many marinas are expensive – even in the winter (though admittedly not all of them).

Southern France This is cold and windy west of the Rhône, though we've heard good comments about wintering in the Canal-du-Rhône-à-Sète. There is said to be an excellent winter climate along the Côte d'Azure and the Riviera – *if* you can find anywhere cheap enough (Toulon has been recommended, and apparently has an excellent train service).

Croatia The weather is cold, wet and windy at times in winter. It's very difficult to find anywhere to lay up *ashore* for the winter, since most of the boatyards seem to be full, especially those with travel-lifts.

Malta (Valletta) This is a beautiful city and an interesting island. It has quite a good winter climate. Msida Marina is excellent, though it has little room except in winter (and the alternative, Lazarretto Creek, gets a bad surge in north-easterlies). We've heard though, you won't get into the boatyard unless you book in advance.

Tunisia There is pretty good winter weather (rather like an English summer) in Monastir, which has a good marina and is the place most people go to. You will find plenty of live-aboards, though fewer English and more French than elsewhere. Tunisia is cheaper than anywhere else we've been. The marina, though, is full by the end of October.

Greece The Ionian can be very wet and windy in the winter (though still better than England) but apparently the weather varies a lot and some winters are fine. There are fewer places to get electricity than elsewhere. Greek Cyprus is said to be good for living aboard, but you will need to book in advance.

Turkey This is said to be excellent for living aboard, but we've also heard adverse comments about the weather. It seems, like the Ionian, that the weather is variable from year to year.

Drvenik, on the island of the same name in Croatia, is particularly beautiful in the evening light.

10

Living on Board

ANCHORING AND MOORING

In the Mediterranean, one has to learn a number of new techniques and to improve some old ones.

Free anchoring

Choosing your spot Clearly, this needs some thought.

Neighbours: Choose your neighbours carefully. Some large yachts have very antisocial spikes sticking out (eg passerelles), and these can swathe a path of destruction as they swing. Do any of the boats have dogs, jet-skis, or crowds of youngsters on board who might be noisy? Conversely, are *you* the one who might be antisocial? If you have any of the above, want to swim or sunbathe in the nude, or play loud music, then pick a secluded spot – and if you want to zoom around in a motor-dinghy, then choose an empty bay where you won't disturb anyone.

Swinging room: Don't anchor so close to the shore, a rock or another boat that you would have to move if the wind got up or came from a different direction (which it often does). Overnight, all-round swinging

room is essential: so if in a very small bay, drop your anchor in the centre of it. On the other hand, if anchoring among other boats, having reached the spot in the centre of them where you want to end up, remember that you then have to continue forward a sufficient distance upwind before laying the anchor, so that you will *drop back* to the correct place. A good spot to lay the anchor is just astern of the boat upwind of you – or, if there are two boats, in between their sterns. But if there's no wind, remember that boats can be lying anywhere in relation to their anchors. If there is plenty of room don't anchor too close to other boats.

Depths: You don't want to anchor in 10 metres (30 ft) or more because of the heavy chain you'll have to haul up again – the work involved goes up by the square of the depth. If you can see the bottom, then try to drop your anchor on sand or mud; these usually have good holding, though it takes time to dig into hard sand.

Motor quietly around considering the above points. Then, having chosen your spot, check the depth there and decide how much chain you'll need. The usual rule of three times the depth isn't nearly enough in very shallow water, as there simply won't be enough weight of chain – drop a minimum of 15 metres (45 ft). You also always need to put out far more in strong winds, or in a swell, or if your cable is mostly rope.

Dropping the anchor If you need to use a trip line, adjust the length of line on your anchor buoy. Then approach your chosen spot, upwind, with the anchor all ready. Go into reverse to stop the boat; and as she stops, lower the anchor – not all in a rush, yet not so slowly that the boat blows out of position before the anchor reaches the bottom. Continue in reverse until the boat starts moving backwards, then take her out of gear and let the wind do the rest (if you don't move backwards, the chain will pile up on top of the anchor so the latter has no chance of digging in). Then pay the chain out at the speed the boat drifts back, until you have the required amount down.

Digging in the anchor There is an accepted practice of 'digging in the anchor with the engine'. Our recommendation is, 'Don't!' In order to succeed in digging the anchor in, a horizontal pull is essential – and if you charge back under engine, you will straighten out the chain and apply a pull that is angled upwards. This is more likely to pull the anchor out of the ground than dig it in. We see many yachts dragging their anchors all round the anchorage, again and again (picking up weed on the way) when the holding is perfectly good – simply through a misguided application of this rule.

A much better technique is to motor very gently back, stopping every few moments and waiting until the boat starts to move forwards again, before going on back. In this way, the chain on the seabed is straightened out and the anchor dug in, without ever completely straightening out the catenary, thus keeping the pull horizontal. Don't make a final test under high power until you are sure it is holding well under low power – indeed, we prefer to wait some hours to give the gentle tugs of the wind a chance to dig the anchor in really deep. Also, never reverse back hard (simulating high winds) with only enough chain out for light winds – again, you will probably drag.

Dragging anchor One indication is if the boat remains 'on one tack' to the wind, instead of swinging first one way and then the other. Once she starts, she will probably move quite fast. So get the engine going rapidly to stop her blowing backwards. Make sure you take the anchor right up and remove any weed before re-anchoring – it will never dig in if cluttered up with weed.

Trip lines The pilot guide will generally indicate whether a trip line on the anchor is necessary; or you may see, in clear water, that one would be advisable. We always have one ready, but prefer not to use it unless there is a special reason to do so, because:

- They are very awkward, and add further hassle to the already tiring job of anchoring and weighing anchor.
- They can tangle with the anchor chain, thus making themselves useless.
- They are designed to trip your anchor, and will sometimes do just that by mistake.

In our opinion, the certainty of problems if you *do* use a trip line greatly outweighs the slight chance of it turning out to have been necessary in the general run of anchorages.

Also, do you use an anchor buoy on the trip line or not? If not, it negates part of the usefulness of having it (showing yourselves and other people where your anchor is). But if you do:

- It makes the whole thing even more awkward.
- It can get chopped off by someone's propeller.
- It has been known for other yachts to use them as mooring buoys.

It is essential to get the length of the line right with a buoy, since:

- If the line is too short, the buoyancy of the buoy may trip the anchor.
- If the line is too long, it may get around *your* propeller.
- In either case, it will fail to show where the anchor is.

So feed the end of the line through a ring underneath the buoy, with a weight on the end; this hangs down, making the length self-adjusting.

Anchoring with a long line ashore

This method is particularly common in Turkey, but is also used in Greece and Croatia, and occasionally elsewhere. If the seabed is steeply shelving, the anchor has no chance to bite if you are free anchored in an offshore wind, but just drags down into deeper and deeper water. To counteract this, it is common to take a long line ashore as well (Fig 21 and photo page 168). The method is also often used in crowded anchorages, since boats can line themselves up along the shore by the dozen.

You reverse in towards your chosen space, dropping the bow anchor on the way; then the crew rows desperately for the shore, towing a long warp that they tie to a tree or a rock. The difficulties in doing this with a shorthanded crew and/or a strong breeze are considerable, the usual problem being that the yacht blows off sideways so that the crew is trying first to tow the yacht upwind, and then to tie a rope that is being pulled out of their hands.

The first essential is that everything should be completely ready before starting. If the wind is directly *onshore*, then there's no problem. If the wind is directly *offshore*, I suggest tying the rope ashore before anchoring, with a fender attached to the end so that it will float. You can then pick this up after laying the anchor (though beware of catching it around the prop).

With a beam wind, if there are boats downwind of you, then fender-up well. If not, then:

1 Attach a long length of fairly thin line to the stern of the yacht, and fake it down into a bucket in the cockpit (tied end first). Your long warp should be flaked out in the dinghy, its free end tied to the free end of the light line (and the other end easy to get at).

2 Tie the dinghy painter to the warp, near the outer end (so that the dinghy won't blow away as you leap hurriedly ashore).

3 Anchor and dig in, reversing back towards the shore but aiming considerably upwind to allow for drift.

4 While the helmsman finishes this (again, carefully avoiding catching the rope in the propeller), the crew should jump quickly into the dinghy and row ashore to tie the rope.

The advantages of this method are:

- When you row ashore, you will be towing only a light line – much easier.
- You will still have enough line to tie on, however far away the boat blows.

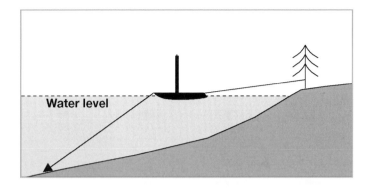

Fig 21 *Anchoring with a long line ashore is common in the eastern Mediterranean.*

Water level

- The excess can then be *winched* back on board, thus hauling the stern of the yacht into position.

Alternatively, some people prefer to drop a stern anchor first of all, to hold the stern in position while they deal with the bow anchor and shore line.

A second stern line, at a good angle to the first, can be laid later if there is the likelihood of much wind. The main disadvantage of anchoring in this way (apart from the sheer difficulty) is that when the wind blows on the beam, the strain on the anchor is greatly magnified. In a high-sided yacht, with a lot of windage, it becomes almost impossible without dragging. Important factors to note in order to avoid dragging are:

- Use your heaviest anchor and chain, and let out a long scope.
- Don't anchor too close in otherwise, if you drag, you will be aground before you can take avoiding action (the anchor drags towards the boat, not in the direction of the wind).
- Don't succumb to the temptation to tighten your lines in hard (Fig 22). The yacht must be able to drift downwind of the anchor a little, since it is only this that enables it to combat a force on the beam – an anchor has no power against a force that is at right angles to the chain. The more you can reduce this critical angle the better.

If you *do* drag, the quickest way of stopping this is to release the stern line and let the boat lie head-to-wind, thus reducing

Fig 22 *An anchor will tend to drag if the wind is on the beam, partly because the windage is so much greater, but also because the wind is at right angles to the chain.*

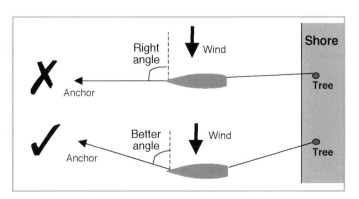

the strain on the anchor. Either let go completely (and rescue the rope later) or take the stern line to the bow (Fig 23). This will give you time to work out a more permanent strategy.

If there isn't room to do this, cast off all lines, motor rapidly forwards out of your slot, and re-anchor; however, if there are other yachts upwind, you are much less likely to drag.

A good alternative if there is room, and if a prevailing beam wind makes dragging likely, is to anchor fore-and-aft, head-to-wind, with one shore line to hold the boat in position.

Mooring in harbours

Always have your warps and fenders ready before approaching the quay. Fenders should be well spaced, with big ones right forward where they will protect against bumping other boats on the way in (you can rearrange them afterwards). Get the heights appropriate for whatever will be alongside you.

Warps should be laid out on deck, with the inner end looped out over the guard wires, in under the pulpit, through the fairlead and fastened to the cleat; the other end should poke out forward, over the guard wires, ready to be grabbed by someone ashore (Fig 24).

Phœnician anchored with a long line ashore in a narrow creek at Yedi Adalari in Turkey. There wasn't sufficient swinging room to free-anchor; our anchor was laid well over on the other side. Even so we dragged when the wind came on the beam and ended up anchored fore-and-aft.

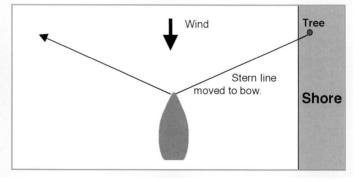

Fig 23 If the anchor drags when you are anchored with a long line ashore, try quickly moving the stern line to the bow, if there is room, so she can lie head-to-wind.

Wind

Tree

Stern line moved to bow.

Shore

Fig 24 Approach a bow-to berth with the bow lines ready to be grabbed by someone ashore.

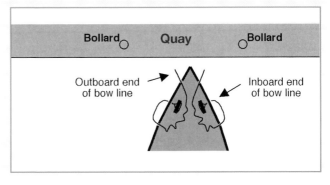

Bow-to with a stern anchor The normal method of tying up in harbour (theoretically over the whole Mediterranean, but in practice no longer used much, west of Italy) is to go bow-to the quay, laying a stern anchor to hold you off (photo page 143).

Keep the anchor stowed permanently on the pushpit, tied on; and carefully fake the warp and chain down into a bucket each time you haul them in (otherwise the rope will inevitably tangle next time you pay it out). Our method is simple: I control the boat (steering and engine), lining us up carefully between the anchor chains of the other boats; Jimmy drops the anchor, passes the warp round a winch, and hands it to me to pay out while he rushes forward to deal with bow lines, fending off, etc. I steer forward, keeping her slightly upwind of the chosen slot until the last minute to allow for leeway. Then, when we are a few yards from the quay (or from the other boats, if the gap is narrow) I stop the yacht, using the engine and, if necessary, the anchor (though I try not to put too much weight on the anchor until it has had time to settle in the mud and dig in). Finally, we work her in those last few yards by hand, tie up, and haul the anchor chain in tight.

Try to choose a billet with another boat immediately downwind of you that you can 'lean against' (only do fender up well), since this will prevent you blowing off sideways; and try to find one where your mast won't be in line with those of the neighbouring boats – you don't want the masts clashing if the yachts roll.

If someone else lays their anchor chain over yours, getting the anchor up can be a real problem. In the last resort you may have to wait for the other boat to leave. However, if you are good at diving, you may be able to slip the offending chain over your anchor, thus freeing the latter.

Stern-to with a bow anchor Many yachts prefer to go stern-to so that they can use their main bower anchor, but this offers infinite scope for problems on the way in. If you do go stern-to, choose a wide gap; and remember, 'He who hesitates is lost!' – the wind will immediately take charge. Either go for it, or give up and start again. In a cross-wind, I have been told that 'steering' can be improved by the following technique (starting well upwind):

- If you want the stern to head more up into the wind, then let out more chain so the bow blows off.
- Conversely, if you want the stern to head more downwind, tightening the chain will hold the bow in position so the stern blows off.

Going alongside Going alongside a quay as your overnight billet (and rafting up if necessary) is much less common than at home, because of the twin dangers involved: vermin coming aboard, and damage to the vulnerable side of the yacht if hit by wash or swell (in Greece, in particular, harbours tend to suffer from these latter problems). However, you will frequently have to go alongside a fuel quay or waiting pontoon, and since these are quite likely to be in windy situations, you can have a problem if the wind is blowing *off* the quay.

The easiest solution is to fasten a warp amidships – if the crew can get this tied ashore, then neither end of the boat can blow far.

Mooring in marinas

In marinas you go bow-to the quay or pontoon, but instead of your having to drop an anchor, the stern is held off with a

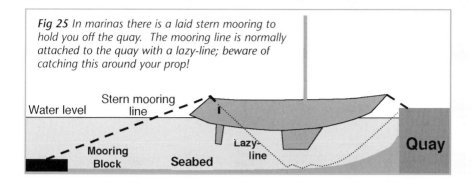

Fig 25 *In marinas there is a laid stern mooring to hold you off the quay. The mooring line is normally attached to the quay with a lazy-line; beware of catching this around your prop!*

laid stern mooring; this is usually attached to the quay by a lazy-line that you pick up as you go in and tighten in behind you (Fig 25, photo page 27).

This is much more secure, and theoretically it should be easier; but in fact, unless the wind is blowing straight off the quay, it is actually more difficult than laying your anchor, because:

- If the wind is coming from astern, you need to hold the boat off the quay with the engine until the crew has hauled the stern line tight – yet you daren't do so for fear of getting the lazy-line round the propeller.
- If the wind is from one side, unless you can find a space with another boat downwind of you that you can lean against, you will inevitably get blown sideways before you have a hope of securing both bow and stern.

Luckily there is usually a *marinero* there to help. His job is to show you your berth, pass the lazy-line, and then fend off the bow and hold it while the crew hauls in the stern line (first a boathook, and then heavy gloves, are useful for this). If there is no *marinero*, hang around a little, or call the marina on VHF (try channel 9) and ask for someone to come and help – they'll probably speak some English. If still no joy (eg at siesta time), either go alongside the 'waiting quay', or try to find an upwind berth, or one which has another yacht to leeward.

Some marinas prefer you to go alongside the waiting quay first anyway, and go to the office with your documents. They allocate you a berth that a *marinero* will then show you.

Going stern-to is terribly difficult unless the yacht steers really well in reverse. Learn what your boat likes to do (probably reverse round into the wind) and always plan to go along with this. If everything goes wrong when you are within reach of the other boats, it's far safer to *stop using your engine* and pull her in by hand.

When leaving, give the stern line time to sink before using the engine. If stern-to, a dinghy tied to the bow will make turning sharply into the wind almost impossible.

Other methods of mooring

You will occasionally come across marinas that use other methods of mooring:

Lazy-line tailed to a buoy This may be easier, since you pick up the stern line earlier.

Stern mooring buoys This is often the most difficult, since the crew may have to lie on deck trying to feed a line through the ring at the top of the buoy – meanwhile, the boat blows everywhere.

Stern mooring posts These are difficult with a shorthanded crew. You pass between two posts as you enter the billet, and tie your stern warps to the posts, one each side. The idea is that crew members flick a rope round each post as you pass in – but, of course, with only one crew member it's only possible to do one. You often can't lean on another boat because they are too far apart; however, there is occasionally a taut rope between post and quay that you can lean on.

Have two *long* warps ready, one for the windward post (fastened to the quarter, and with a long loop tied in the end), and one fastened to the windward bow, ready to pass ashore. Pass close to the windward post and the crew must ensure that he gets that stern line looped over the post and passed to the helmsman to let out. The crew should then rush forward and get the bow line tied ashore. You are then safe, and can slowly work the boat back until you can reach the other post.

Getting out can be equally difficult if there is a wind, because the bow will blow off as soon as you let go. Rig a temporary bow line looped around something that is well upwind.

Pontoon fingers In southern France the marinas often provide pontoon fingers, and you go bow- or stern-to the main pontoon, and alongside the finger – the same as in the south coast of England and northern France.

LIFE AT ANCHOR

Saving power

When you have no mains electricity coming in, it is extremely important to do everything you can to save as much power as possible – especially if you have an electric fridge. The rules below should start being followed as soon as you plan to leave somewhere with shore power – don't wait until you have a problem.

General The following are all important things to remember:
- Recharge any necessary batteries before you leave (eg shaver, mobile phone, computer).
- Always turn off everything that you are not using, including lights.
- Whenever you have a choice, use hand-operated equipment (eg water pump), or things that run off their own batteries (eg radio, fan, VHF), rather than power-operated items.
- Don't use things that need a lot of power (eg television, computer) – or at least, not unless you're running the engine.

The fridge There are a number of things you can do to reduce its power usage:
- Is it bigger than you need? If so, fill up the excess space with insulating material.
- The day before you leave, fill the fridge with all the things you'll be needing over the next few days, and cool everything right down while you still have electricity; however, be wary of leaving the fridge on high overnight if you intend to leave early, in case of a power failure.
- Just before you leave, buy a bag or a block of ice and stow it in the fridge (two or three, if there's room). One 2-kilogram bag of ice cubes would cool

Phœnician moored bow-to at Carlo Forte, Sardinia. You can see her gantry, scoop, wind generator, bimini awning and extension awning over the boom.

our small fridge in *Phœnician* for 24 hours, thus making a huge saving on power. So buy more ice at every opportunity, and then the batteries will only have to cope when you are away from shops for days on end. Put the ice in an upright container, though, because the bags aren't waterproof.

- If your fridge is small, store pre-cooled drinks in a *well*-insulated cool bag, along with some ice.
- Anything added to the fridge just before you leave, or after future shopping expeditions, should – where possible – be bought pre-cooled. When you need to restock the fridge with more drinks from your store cupboard, do it first thing in the morning when the tins, etc are at their coolest.
- When you take something from the fridge that you are only going to use partially, take what you want and put it straight back in the fridge.

- Finally, as soon as you unplug from mains electricity, turn the fridge down low (it uses *far* less power).

Saving water

However much or little water they have, live-aboards can *never* afford to be careless with it. Even if you have a water-maker, you'll probably lack the power to run it. So develop the following habits, and apply them according to your needs:

- Avoid using the electric pump unless you want a lot of water – use a manual pump, so you can dribble out small amounts.
- Don't use the shower, since these use more water than anything else. Have a strip wash instead, or swim every day.
- If you need to rinse off after swimming, use a jug or a shower bag.
- Save the water that your ice from the fridge melts into, and keep it for washing.

- Wash up in a bowl of water, not the sink – and save the rinse water.
- Wipe very dirty dishes clean with paper, and/or give them a quick pre-wash with a cupful of hot soapy water before doing the washing-up.
- If you need water from the hot tank, save the cold water that comes out of the pipe first.
- Wash and rinse your hands in the small amount of water that hasn't drained away in the bottom of the basin, then just turn the tap on briefly for a final rinse.
- Never throw any water away if you can possibly use if for something else.
- Don't do the washing until you have a water supply again. If you run out of clean things, just soak and rub them in warm water with no soap – it gets a surprising amount of dirt out. This latter tip also applies to hair.
- Collect a can of water from a tap every time you go ashore.

If you have no gauge on your water tank, you'll need to keep careful records of your water usage so that you can gradually work out how much you use per day. The occasional marina that meters the water supply is very helpful here. You will end up by being able to judge roughly how much there is left in the tank. We found that we could get our usage down to 5 gallons a day when being *particularly* careful – this included drinking water from the cans, but not anything exceptional such as laundry or showers. If you have an electric gauge, it's worth keeping the same records, because it will probably go wrong.

If you are obliged to do a proper wash, reduce the rinse water needed as follows:

- Don't use too much soap.
- Use three or four rinse buckets, and put the clothes in first one, then the next, etc, until they finally come clean out of the last bucket.
- Wring out the clothes to the maximum each time.
- When the first rinse water is too soapy, wash the cockpit with it; rinse the bucket, and refill with fresh water; this becomes the new last-rinse bucket.

Rinsing clothes many times in small quantities of water is much harder work than doing them fewer times in a large quantity, but it uses less water.

All these precautions may sound difficult, but they soon become second nature – indeed, it becomes a kind of game!

Pumping the heads

Many heads have *very* long discharge pipes (ours is nearly 6 metres!). Measure how many pumps it takes to empty the pipe completely; and if you empty it thereafter at sea, you have a mini holding tank on arrival in the anchorage, and won't despoil your 'swimming pool'.

LIFE AT SEA

Because it's so vitally important to remember to open the engine-water inlet valve, Jimmy always stows the engine key by hanging it on the valve – then he can't forget to open it.

If we're likely to get in late and tired, we often get a chicken, potatoes and vegetables all ready to roast before leaving. We light up as we arrive, and there's our dinner busy cooking while we tie up – all we have to do is sit down with a drink until it's ready.

Avoiding seasickness

Going below is the thing that's most likely to make you ill. You won't want to go down and search for things when at sea, so get everything you might need ready beforehand.

Reading, bending over doing something awkward, nasty smells, and sitting thinking about how awful you feel are also to be avoided. The narrowest parts of the yacht tend to have the worst motion, ie the two ends (the bows being particularly bad), so avoid them. Fatty foods (eg bacon for breakfast) are also likely to cause sickness.

Always keep your seasickness tablets in your pocket when at sea, and on a convenient shelf handy to the companionway when in port; and be sure to take them *well before* you start feeling ill rather than putting it off and trying to be macho. You can chew the Kwells tablets if it's difficult to get a drink – they taste nice and start working quicker than if you swallow them straight down. If necessary, take a Kwell (or the brand that works best for you) the previous night, and before starting the day's sail.

If you *must* go down to the heads, take off as many clothes as possible in the cockpit where its easier. If it's rough, ask the skipper to do something to reduce the motion (eg turning away from the waves).

If you feel ill, sit where your can feel the wind in your face, and keep your eyes on the horizon. Keep active and warm. Steering is an excellent remedy, since it gives you something to do while looking at the horizon. Plain white bread with nothing on it is easiest on the stomach.

If you think you are actually going to *be* sick, be very careful not to fall overboard – wear a harness. And watch out that you don't lose your spectacles or dentures. If you have severe vomiting, drink plenty of fluids so you don't become dehydrated.

If you need to go and lie down, do this as quickly as possible, since you will feel better lying down with your eyes closed, wedged securely in a bunk, than unsteadily watching the cabin jump around. (Don't look out through the windows, because under these circumstances the horizon will appear to jump around too.)

Man-overboard prevention

- Remember the golden rule, 'One hand for yourself, and one for the ship' (ie *always* hold on).
- There should be an absolutely unbreakable rule that if anyone is alone on deck, they *never* go out of the cockpit without telling the person who's down below – even if that means waking them up.
- Men have the inestimable advantage of being able to relieve themselves without going below. However, this is apparently one of the most common causes of falling overboard. Therefore *always* clip on in rough weather, even though this may be difficult because of having to undress.
- If the boat is heeling, rig a line between the binnacle and the sprayhood on the lee side to prevent yourself from being thrown out of the cockpit.
- Wear a safety harness when going out of the cockpit when it's dark or rough – and *in* the cockpit if it's very rough. Keep it clipped on!

Blind spots

There are always bits of the horizon that are more difficult to see than other bits, hidden by sails, etc. But it's particularly important to check these blind spots, because if a ship on collision course should happen to be hidden in one, then she will remain in it until she hits you!

The most dangerous blind spot of all, because you don't know it's there, is the reflection-track of the sun. Your eyes automatically blink as they pass it, and you don't realise that you have failed to see what's hidden in it. So it's particularly important to shield your eyes and look carefully at this potential deathtrap each time you scan the horizon – sunglasses are useful here.

'Gentlemen never sail upwind'

But unfortunately one has to sail upwind (or motorsail, anyway) because the wind comes from ahead so much of the time. There are reasons for this:
- The wind finds it easiest to blow *along* the coast, making a reach unlikely if you are coast-hopping.
- Your forward speed adds a component of wind against you (of up to 7 knots), which brings the apparent wind farther ahead. When motoring, if the breeze is light even from astern, your apparent wind will come from ahead.

If you are motoring, it's worth always putting some mainsail up, hauled in tight, since this reduces rolling in a rough sea. Do this before leaving harbour.

VARIOUS PROBLEMS

Bad weather

Mooring in a surge This is where your snubbers will come into their own, stopping the boat jerking around too much. It is essential to moor with *single* lines when requiring snubbers (photos page 39); a line to the quay and back again prevents the snubber from working. However, you will also need extra lines for security under such circumstances; make sure these are long enough not to take any weight even when the snubbers are at full stretch, or this will cause a jerk.

If you need other mooring lines under tension (eg springs if you are moored alongside), you can reduce the jerk in these by increasing the length of the lines. Take them from the boat to the appropriate bollard ashore, but don't make fast. Instead, lead the line around the bollard, and on along the quay to a more distant one and make fast there (Fig 26). The extra length of line will absorb some of the jerk. However, the rope will move back and forth past the turning point, so guard against chafe.

Anchoring in a surge It's most uncomfortable when you're blown broadside on to the waves – if you anchor fore-and-aft, with the bow towards the swell, the yacht will ride it far more easily. However, you will have more windage moored this way, since you may then be broadside to the *wind*. It will also be more difficult to weigh anchor in an emergency.

Gales In the Mediterranean one can usually avoid gales at sea, but they are inevitable when you are moored. When in a marina, you don't have to do much more than put out extra fenders and ropes, and pull yourself a little farther from the quay. However, it is a different matter when at anchor:
- As soon as you get warning of high winds, consider whether you are already in a good position or whether you would do better to move – to a marina, to a safer harbour or anchorage, or perhaps just to a better position in the same one. If in harbour with a stern anchor, make sure you have sufficient scope out, and add a chum-weight if possible.

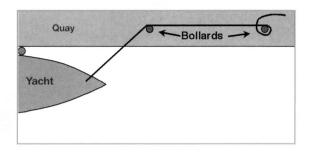

Fig 26 *When moored in a surge, if you haven't enough snubbers, try greatly increasing the length of your warps – they will then absorb some of the jerk.*

- If free anchored, you don't want to be immediately upwind of any dangers when the gale comes, in case of dragging. Try to avoid being downwind of any suspect boats (those with nasty spikes sticking out, those whose anchor tackle seems too light, etc); and remember that you (and they) will need much more swinging room.
- Let out more chain to ensure that it retains that essential horizontal pull on the anchor in spite of the extra wind strength, and consider whether a second bow anchor would be advisable. If we use one, we lay our Fortress in parallel with the main anchor – motoring forward at 45° to the main chain, dropping the kedge about level with the CQR, and then letting the boat drop back until both warps are pulling.
- Make sure you have adequate check bearings, so that you can tell if you start to drag. If there will be none that you can see in the dark, then take a careful note of your position relative to the other yachts.
- Take down wind scoops, awnings, etc.
- You will have to check frequently that you are not dragging, and that the boats upwind don't drag into you. Consider putting fenders out (an inflatable dinghy makes a good big one!). Have the engine ready to start at an instant's notice, and keep the horn handy in case you need to warn someone else that *they* are dragging.
- You may have to keep an anchor watch at night; put an anchor light on even if you don't do so normally; keep a torch handy; perhaps put on the depth alarm or the GPS alarm.

Thunderstorms Thunderstorms are usually brief, but can be quite severe. If you hear one coming it is wise to close all hatches, and generally prepare for a torrential downpour, a change in the direction of the wind (often a complete reversal), and a possibly violent increase in its strength. This is often up to force 6 or 7, and on one occasion in Greece we were nearly driven on the rocks when NW3 turned suddenly into a vicious easterly 8, gusting 9 or more.

Stand by the engine in case the anchor drags. Switch off and unplug any delicate electronics (eg computer). If you go far from the yacht in an area that is prone to thunderstorms, take precautions before you leave.

Salvage If you do have a severe problem at sea and need to call for help, remember that you will probably have to pay for things such as being towed to harbour. Do your utmost to agree on a reasonable fee before the start of the operation, or you my be charged for salvage. If this happens, get on to your insurance company immediately – *they* will need to do the negotiations.

Emergencies at home

If you have no mobile phone, there are three ways in which the family might be able to contact you in an emergency:

- Interpol (the International Police Organisation) could probably find you if you were in a marina.
- The BBC World Service can put out a call asking you to ring home (ring the BBC switchboard on 0207 240 3456 and explain the situation).
- If you were in the western Mediterranean, Monaco Radio could put out a call with the weather forecast (00377 9330 1313).

Medical problems

If you need a doctor urgently (eg for stitches), ask the harbourmaster for advice – the easiest option may well be to get a taxi and ask to be taken to the equivalent of Accident and Emergency. In Spain this is called the *Pac*, or *Centro Medico Urgencia* – it is open 24 hours a day and is part of the *Securidad Social*, and therefore free if you take your E111 form with you. In most countries many doctors are private, and their fees are not refundable.

Doctors in Spain will not stitch you more than six hours after the accident took place for fear of trapping infection in the wound. So it's best to treat it from the first as though you're not going to get there in time.

Pests

Mosquitoes These are most active during the evenings and nights, so your screens should be put in well before dusk, especially on still evenings (mosquitoes don't like wind). You will probably need to burn coils at times as well (available throughout much of the Mediterranean, though not in Spain), or use one of the electric killers. Mosquitoes are more of a problem in summer and autumn than during the cold weather, and are particularly prevalent in marshy areas.

Cockroaches You've a *real* problem if your boat gets infested with these, so it is very important to take precautions. First, try to stop them coming aboard: make sure that there aren't any small ones hiding in bunches of fruit you bring back; and since they often lay their eggs in the glue in cardboard boxes, you should *never* bring these aboard. Second, you need to deal immediately with any that do arrive before they multiply. Buy packets of cockroach traps (flat plastic boxes with poisoned bait inside) and hide them in dark places around the yacht – apparently the cockroaches walk in, eat the bait, then go home and die. If this doesn't work buy boracic acid powder from a chemist; mix to a paste with sweetened condensed milk and put lumps of this paste in sites around the yacht.

Rodents Another possible problem is getting a rat or mouse on board. These can be

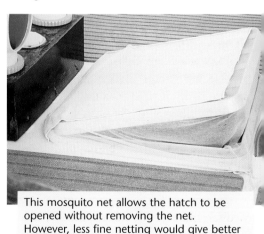

This mosquito net allows the hatch to be opened without removing the net. However, less fine netting would give better air flow.

very difficult to get rid of, so once again try to prevent them coming aboard. Avoid mooring alongside the kind of quay where they might live (marina cats keep them away beautifully). Avoid tatty old boats that look as though they have been left unattended for ages. When going ashore or to bed, leave the yacht in such a way that, if one should come aboard, it will not be able to get into the interior of the yacht – leave all hatches either shut or covered with mosquito screens, and block any entrances or finger-holes into the yacht (eg cockpit locker, chain locker, Dorade vents). If you are moored in a suspect place, check the deck over every morning (closing the companionway behind you) to make sure that there isn't one hiding somewhere (eg in the folded-up dinghy).

If you *do* end up with one taking passage with you, there are various ways of getting rid of them – mousetraps; mouseglue (you spread a ring of it on a piece of cardboard, with bait in the middle, and they get stuck in the glue); and poison (make sure you put this down in such a manner that you can remove it again afterwards). Which of these will work, if any, depends on how sophisticated your mouse or rat is.

Other problems

Shore power In many marinas the power supply is poor, and putting too much strain on it will trip the system – you will then have to switch on again in the box ashore. If it's your neighbours who are causing the problem, it's best to plug into a different box.

Water supply The water in most of the Mediterranean (both sea water and drinking water) is extremely hard, so equipment gets choked up with calcium deposits – it is possible for your toilets to become completely blocked. Buy dilute hydrochloric acid called *agua fuerte* in Spanish and *aqua forte* in Italian, and something sounding similar even in Greek! Empty the toilet bowl, pour in perhaps a pint of the liquid, pump it into the pipes and leave for ten minutes; then flush through with fresh water. Do this regularly, every week or two, and it will help keep your toilets clear. Occasionally put a large amount in, and gradually work it through the entire length of the pipe.

There are various liquids (called *anti-cal* in Spain) that you can buy to clear the scale from your kettle, but boiling, neat vinegar works nearly as well, and is cheaper. Don't use *agua fuerte*.

Dirty fenders Keep the fenders clean for otherwise they transfer dirt to the hull (and to your neighbours' hulls). Cif and a Scotch-Bright pad work wonders.

Outboards These frequently stop working, so *always* take oars as well.

WEATHER FORECASTS

Because of the convoluted nature of the Mediterranean (especially the eastern half), forecasts are not very accurate, but they will at least give an idea of the approximate direction and strength of wind – whether you can expect a hot, sunny, windless day; or unsettled weather with thunderstorms; or strong winds and a rough sea, etc. In our experience, the forecasts are much more accurate when strong winds are expected than when they are not. Most important of all, we have not yet (touch wood) had a gale there that has not been well forecast.

Our summary of radio forecasts in different areas

Area	Shortwave	VHF	Navtex
Spain	Poor availability, only moderate accuracy		Not tried
S France	Not tried recently	Good	Not tried
Monaco	Excellent	Not tried	Found nothing
Italy	Easily available but poor accuracy		Found nothing
Malta	Good	Good	Good
Croatia	Found nothing	Good, but muddled presentation	
Greece	Good	Not tried	Friends say ok
Turkey	We used Greek forecasts		
Tunisia	Found nothing – used Italy and Monaco		

Radio forecasts

Obtaining forecasts depends on getting good reception, and this can be drastically affected by interference from other electrical systems. If you are getting bad reception, it's worth turning off anything that might be affecting it – the wind generator, shore power, fridge, Navtex, engine, etc.

Short wave There are a number of coast radio stations all over the Mediterranean and on the way there, which provide forecasts in English, so long as you have a good SSB receiver (see Appendix 5 for details). Some forecasts are announced on 2182 SSB. Radio France International, though only in French, is particularly useful for Atlantic Spain and Portugal, since here one is getting out of range of the BBC shipping forecast. For the western Mediterranean basin, Monaco Radio (see Appendices 3 and 5) is *by far* the best (in French and English). They obtain their forecasts from Météo France, who have vast experience and many years of computer records to help them; we find them more accurate than anyone else.

I understand some of the German forecasts are pretty good, and may offer long-range forecasts that are particularly useful when planning a long passage – but these are only in German.

VHF forecasts In many countries, there are also forecasts available on VHF; these are often announced on channel 16, so if you haven't managed to get a forecast, it's worth keeping this on.

In the central Mediterranean there is a forecast in Italian and English on VHF channel 68. This is broadcast continuously, giving a 24-hour forecast with a 36-hour outlook. I think it is the same forecast as the national Italian one – and unfortunately it isn't very accurate, as can be seen from the fact that it changes considerably at every update. In Croatia (in summer) there is sometimes something similar on channel 67. Marinas in Croatia offer a long range forecast.

Navtex

As mentioned earlier, this is an up-and-coming method, but at present it is less widespread than radio. For example, in 2001 we could get nothing in Tunisia or southern Italy on our Target Navtex Pro (though I believe people with more powerful equipment could). However, in areas where there *is* coverage, Navtex is a lot easier – and we found it invaluable in Croatia (see table opposite) where there are no shortwave forecasts.

The internet

There are also shipping forecasts available on the internet, though this depends on access to an internet café. Weatheronline (at http://www.weatheronline.co.uk) offers a five-day shipping forecast, but I'm not sure how accurate it is.

CONCLUSIONS

Long-term cruising is a life of contrasts: leisurely afternoons at anchor, swimming and sitting watching the world go by; versus hectic work on marina visits, doing the shopping and the laundry, showering, washing the decks, and all the other tasks that require water and electricity. Blissful times in idyllic surroundings versus terrifying moments when you are dragging down on the rocks in a gale. The whole way of life is one of higher peaks and lower troughs than the humdrum life at home. But the peaks, without doubt, *more* than compensate for the troughs; and for those to whom it is suited, there is no better way of life.

Sunset over the town quay at Korcula on the island of the same name, Croatia.

Appendices

Appendix 1 • Packing and Modifications List

I have attempted to give a really useful, comprehensive list including all boat equipment – much of which will need to be built in, thus becoming more of a modification to the boat than part of a conventional packing list. I have found it hard to determine a cut-off point for things that should not be included, so this list aims to cover all you may need on the yacht – from an engine to a salt cellar! So all you need to add is your clothes, leisure and personal items and your list is complete. Where appropriate, each section covers modifications first, then equipment.

I am dividing much of the list into three categories of priority: 'essential' (strong yellow background); 'probably needed' (mid-yellow); and 'possible' (pale yellow); areas without tints have no particular priority – though since people's requirements vary, these are inevitably fairly flexible.

SAFETY EQUIPMENT
Modifications and
built-in equipment
Jackstays, U-bolts
Bilge pumps
Storm jib and means of
  rigging it
Fire extinguishers and fire
  blanket
Horseshoe lifebelt and holder
Danbuoy, whistle and
  automatic light
Extra hand rails
Spare tiller
Gas solenoid valve, or internal
  stopcock
VHF radio
Automatic fire extinguisher
  in engine room
Storm boards
Gas detector
Gas leak detector
Steering oar

Portable equipment
Liferaft *or* Tinker with
  survival kit
Safety harnesses
White flares
Fog horn

Radar reflector
Lifejackets
Wooden plugs for skin-fittings
Floating torch
Rigging shears
V-flag
Personal EPIRB
Trysail
Life-Sling
Emergency rope ladder
Storm anchor
Sea anchor

Permanent panic box items
(no priority)
Small, powerful torch (eg
  halogen)
Small compass
Long length of tough cord
Small mirror and penetrating
  whistle for signalling
Knife on a lanyard
Small baler and sponge
2 survival blankets (they fold
  up to the size of a large
  handkerchief)
Sunhats and/or warm head-
  scarves
Small roll-up bandage and
  triangular bandage

Antiseptic wipes, gauze swabs,
  plasters and Steristrips
Handkerchiefs and very small
  towel to dry yourselveswith
2 nesting plastic cups
Notebook and pencil

Perishable panic-box items
(renew each year)
Bottle of water (1½ litres)
Sweets
Torch batteries

Flares
4 red parachute
2 red hand
2 orange smoke, plus
4 + out-of-date red
  parachutes

Medicines
Anti-sickness tablets enough
  for 4 people for 4 days
Co-Codamol tablets (strong
  pain relief)
Germolene (antiseptic
  cream)
Anthisan (antihistamine cream)
Sun-protection cream

Extra panic bag
Handheld GPS (and instructions) and VHF
Extra flares and water
Personal essentials

DECK AND COCKPIT LOCKER
Modifications and built-in equipment
Mooring and access aboard
Bow anchor and cable
Bow windlass
Stern anchor, chain, warp and bucket(s)
Bow ladder or stern passerelle
Bathing platform and ladders
Modify pulpit
Pulley or windlass for stern anchor
Enlarge cleats and fairleads
Windicator
Bow passerelle

Other deck hardware
Sprayhood
Bimini awning
Powerful winches
Cockpit table
Gantry
Rigid kicker
Cockpit mug-rack
Bearing-out spar
Winter shelter
Transparent screen
Winter cover
Davits
Windvane steering

Portable equipment
Mooring and access aboard
Dinghy plus oars and pump
Two short warps
Two longer warps
One really long warp
Six sausage fenders
Spare ropes
Lifting-points on dinghy
Outboard engine
Plastic tubing on rails
Mooring gloves
2 snubbers
2 round flattened fenders
2+ large balloon fenders
Secure dinghy painter

Dinghy cover
Dinghy sailing kit
Chum-weight
Trip line + small float
Heaving line
Plank
Large bow/stern fender

Sails, awnings and other canvaswork
Mainsail
Roller-furling genoa
Side screens
Fore-and-aft screens
Mainsail cover
Over-boom awning(s)
Wind scoop(s)
Cockpit cushions
Cruising-chute/spinnaker
Snuffer for above
Guard wire spray dodgers

Other mast and deck oddments
Winch handles
Secure companionway lock
Long boathook
Long-handled mop and scrubber
Bosun's chair and/or mast ladder
Courtesy flags, ensign, Q flag
Lazyjacks or Stak-Pak
Boom preventers
Burgees
Sharp knife
Mainsheet snap shackle
Cabin lock (inside)
Sailboard
Fishing net

Cockpit locker
10-litre water cans
Hose, hose-ends
Pouring bucket, and 3+ other buckets
Shore-power lead + end-fittings
Diesel can
Spare Camping Gaz bottles
2 folding bikes (+ baskets, pumps, bike locks)
Hose connector
Pump-up garden spray or

black showerbag
Fishing and/or diving gear
Pick-up snap-hook
Antifouling and varnish
Polish (stainless, GRP)
Other bike accessories (repair kit, lights, bells, cycle clips)
Spinnaker sheets and blocks
Hose reel; end spray
Short (extra) boathook
Third anchor
Dinghy anchor
Jug for water

Gas locker
Camping Gaz
hurricane lamp oil
petrol can

ENGINES AND ELECTRICS
Modifications and built-in equipment
Yacht equipment
Diesel engine
Alternator
Shore-power charger
Electronic autopilot
Echo sounder + cockpit display
Navigation lights
Compass light
SSB radio receiver and/or Navtex
GPS
Diesel gauge
Rope cutter
Extra batteries
Battery monitor and/or ammeters and voltmeters
TWC/Adverc
Solar panels
Log speedo
Anchor light, cockpit light, instrument lights
Bow thruster
Wind generator
Petrol generator
SSB transmitter
Wind speed and direction indicator
Radar
Decklights, engine-room light

Domestic equipment
240-volt circuit
240- and 12-volt sockets
Refrigerator
Adequate cabin and reading
  lights
Freshwater electric pump
Calorifier
Immersion heater
12-volt fan (for hot weather)
Hi-fi radio/cassette player +
  cassettes
Diesel heater
Shower
External shower extension
Water-maker
240-volt saloon light
CD player + CDs

**Portable electrical
equipment**
Fan heater
Torch
Leads and regulators for
  equipment
Mobile phone, etc
Vacuum cleaner
Electric kettle
Table lamp (+shade, spare
  bulbs)
Fan with internal batteries
Low-power cockpit/anchor
  light
Inspection light on
  wandering lead
Calculator
240-volt inverter (from
  batteries)
Microwave oven
Slow cooker
TV/video
Electric razor and charger
Small tape recorder plus
  blank cassette(s)

Oddments
Multi-meter
Small screwdrivers
Insulating tape
Wirecutter/crimper/stripper
Hydrometer, plus distilled
  water, for lead-acid batteries
Adaptor for plugging continen-
  tal equipment into British

sockets (and/or vice versa)
Mains multi-outlet adaptors
Mains extension lead
Heavy-duty jump-leads
12-volt extension lead
Personal fans
Travelling iron
Hairdryer

Computer (if required)
Laptop computer
Mains and 12-volt charger
Floppy disks
Computer CDs
Printer with battery pack plus
  charger
CD rewriter
Anti-virus program
Other accessories
Palmtop computer and
  accessories
Zip or Clik! Drive and disks
Spare computer battery
Weatherfax program

Engine oddments
Engine manual and spares list
Engine oil and stern-tube
  grease
Any 'special' tools
Big diesel funnel with inbuilt
  strainer
Biocide and WD40
Workshop manual
Small funnel
Silicon spray
Old towels for cleaning
Disposable nappies
Wiring diagram

**INTERIOR YACHT
EQUIPMENT**
Built-in equipment
Adequate chart stowage
Extra insulation (fridge, deck,
  engine noise, etc)
Hatch modifications
Vice and workbench

**Portable navigational
equipment**
Charts
Parallel rulers
Dividers

Ruler
Pencils and rubber
Barometer
Binoculars
Hand-bearing compass
Navigator's Friend
Clock
Sunglasses
Sextant with dedicated
  calculator
Non-slip chart table cloth
Illuminated magnifier

Spares
Filters for oil, diesel and air
Cooling-water impellers
Alternator belts
Lamps for navigation lights
Batteries for important
  equipment
Appropriate fuses (including
  fridge)
Heads spares
Freshwater pump and shower
  pump or their service kits
Lamps for domestic lights
Gasket and valve for pressure
  cooker
Spare UK-style plugs
Bimini zips
Cooker burners
Seals for Porta-Potti
Cigar-lighter plugs and
  sockets
Stainless bolts, nuts and
  screws
Electrical connecting
  blocks/junction boxes
Various electric cables

Tools etc
Bosun'ry box including:
Split-pins and rigging tape
Shackles, snap shackles
Plenty of cord (of varying
  thicknesses)
Thick bungee/shock-cord
Hooks (metal and plastic)
Speedy Stitcher sewing awl
  (see address in Appendix 2)

Woodwork tools, perhaps:
Smoothing plane
Hammer and chisels

Hand drill and drill bits
Hand brace and bits
Electric drill, jigsaw and
  sander

Tool box, including:
Leatherman-type multi-tool
Tape measure
Sharp knife
Pliers
Hacksaw and spare blades
Screwdrivers (including
  Philips and short one)
Possibly: vice, pop riveter and
  staple gun

Spanners, including:
Set of socket spanners
Set of open-ended and ring
  spanners
Adjustable spanner
Mole grip

DOMESTIC EQUIPMENT
**Modifications and built-in
equipment**
Bedside shelf
Ventilation under mattress
Mirrors and towel hooks
Bookcases
Glass and mug stowages
Plate and bowl stowage
Bottle racks
Mug rack on stove
Jar and spice racks
Teak racks
Shelve cupboards
Shelf fiddles
Hanging lockers
Improve companionway
Bed headboard
Drawers
Holding tanks

General domestic
Rucksacks (perhaps 2 large,
1 small)
Non-slip matting
Ice-cream boxes
Coat-hangers (all-plastic)

Towel hooks or rings
Sewing kit
Self-seal bags + silica gel
String and Blu-Tak
Bubble-wrap
Big bags from Lakeland
Paper napkins (for guests)
Rubber floor mats
Sew-on Velcro
Sponge for removing bilge
  water (and portable hand
  pump)
(Max-min) thermometer
Small coat-hangers (if
  wardrobe small)
Plastic dress and blouse bags
  (Lakeland)
Tough bags for protecting
  bikes stored on deck
Scales (if you have a weight
  problem!)
Christmas decorations
Pictures and knick-knacks
Oil lamp for saloon
Safe candles
Carpeting

**Cleaning , toilet and 'bug'
deterrents**
Mosquito screens
Various mosquito killers
Fly swats (one per cabin +
  one in cockpit)
Cockroach traps (buy abroad)
Soap, washing-up liquid
Soap powder (hand and
  machine) in airtight pots
Clothes line
Clothes peg (storm, Mega-
  Pegs, etc)
Kitchen rolls and holder
Toilet rolls (we use 2/week)
  plus holders
Waste-bin, carrier bags as
  liners
Cif, bleach
Cleaning cloths (Lakeland's
  Soak-Ups are good)
Shoe-cleaning box
Dustpan and brush

Flyscreens for food
Washing-up brush
Pan scourer
Water purifying tablets
Rubber gloves (thick and/or
  disposable)
Conditioner
Soap holders (magnetic-type
  excellent)
Brillo***
Stiff upholstery brush
Nappy sacks***
Dustbin liners
Spot remover/solvent
Wood and metal polish
Polishing cloths
Duster (Lakeland's California is
  super)
Mosquito repellant (but do
  they work?)
Fly and mosquito spray
Ant powder
Porta-Potti (plus Aqua-Chem
  Green Water Freshener)**
Toilet brush
Universal sink plugs
Bottle brush
Kitchen and household Buddy
  (excellent cleaners, from
  Lakeland)
Pledge Soapy Wood-Cleaner
  (excellent)
Mould remover

First aid
Medicine box, containing:
Seasickness remedies
Co-Codamol for strong pain
  relief (tablets or effervescent
  type)
Aspirin for reducing fever, and
  for initial treatment of heart
  attacks
Paracetamol for fever (if you
  don't like aspirin)
Loperamide (Arrett) for
  diarrhoea
Lemsips
Tunes for a cough
Sore-throat lozenges (even in

---

*   = Available, but you have to search
**   = Difficult to obtain, except in some tourist resorts
*** = Impossible except perhaps in Gibraltar or Malta

the Med you can get colds
and flu!)
Thermometer

First-aid box, containing:
TCP (antiseptic liquid)
Germolene (antiseptic cream)
Burn cream (really cooling)
Anthisan (antihistamine
cream) for inset bites, etc
Mixed sizes of plasters +
knuckle plasters
Arnica (homeopathic remedy
for sprains and bruises –
wonderful stuff, especially if
put on immediately)
Mycil (medicated foot
powder)
Optrex eye lotion (for
inflamed eyes) + eye bath
(may come with the
Optrex)
Ibuprofen cream (for painful
muscles)
Antiseptic wipes (for cleaning
cuts)
Rolled elastic bandage (for
twisted ankles)

Serious injury kit
Sterile dressing pack (sterile
work surface)
Melolin packs of gauze swabs
Packs of Steristrips (for hold-
ing wounds together until
you can get them stitched)
Melolin packs of adhesive
wound dressings
Bactigras burn dressings (cool
and antiseptic)
More antiseptic wipes
Wood for splints
Sterile bandages (various sizes)
Adhesive strapping
Triangular bandages
Plastic finger stalls (various
sizes)
Sterile safety pins, scissors
and tweezers
'Toof Pegs' (temporarily
replaces lost fillings)
Eye pad and eye shade
Sterile, disposable rubber
gloves

Mouthpiece for giving artifi-
cial respiration (unpleasant
without)

Sleeping and linen
Light duvet + duvet covers
Sheets for both cabins
Pillows (4?) Pillow-cases (8?)
2 zipped sleeping bags
Lee cloths, curtains
Shower towels (2+ each)
Hand towels (3+ each)
Kitchen towels (4+)
Drying-up cloths (4+)
Oven gloves/squares (2+)
Roller blinds
Saloon cushions (+ covers)
Light rug
Napkins (4+)
Larger towels
Improved mattress
Cotton under-pillow-cases (6)
Shower curtain
Headrests for sitting with your
feet up (bunks and saloon)
Fitted soft covers for water-
proof cockpit cushions
Apron

GALLEY EQUIPMENT
Built-in equipment
Hand/foot pump(s) for water
Gas cooker with oven
Water gauge
In-line water filter
Galley strap
Seawater tap

Cookery equipment
Gas kettle
Pressure cooker (+ trivet)
Non-stick frying pan (plus lid)
Medium heavy-based
saucepan + lid
Small pan with pouring lip,+ lid
Matches
Roasting tin
Baking tray
Large plastic mixing bowl
Various Pyrex dishes
Large chopping board
Lemon squeezer
Grater
Large sieve and/or colander

Grill pan
Jam funnel (for pouring)
Whisk
Minute-timer for cooking
Second oven shelf
Smaller plastic bowl
Square lasagne dish
Other pans
Steamer
Small sieve
Scales
Casserole dish
Roasting bags***
Heat diffuser for hob top
Gravy skimmer
Meat thermometer
2 smaller dishes that fit in
oven together
Long matches if your oven is
difficult to light
Gas lighter
Hob toaster
Food processor (or Mouligrater)
Cake tin/bun tray, plus liners
Baster (useful for sucking
water from odd places)
Pie dish
Rolling pin
Xmas-pudding bowls
Egg poacher/pastry-cutting
ring
Garlic crusher
Barbecue or outdoor gas ring
(for hot weather)
Wok or stir-fry pan

Crockery
6 dinner plates and bowls
6 coffee mugs
4 beer mugs or glasses
6 wine glasses
6 general-purpose plastic
glasses
4 egg cups
Measuring jug
Teapot and strainer (or 3+
boule-à-thé)
6 side plates
Large serving and/or fruit dish
Other jugs, eg for milk
Cafetière and spare glass
Filter papers and funnel)
Airtight salt cellar with clip-on
lid over holes (Tupperware)

Metal plate
Other bowls
Small coffee cups
Small dishes for serving nuts, reheating, etc
Unbreakable glasses
Insulated butter dish
Jug with sealed lid

Cutlery
6 knives, forks, spoons and teaspoons
Large and small sharp knives
Carving fork
Large cooking spoon
Large scissors
Fish slice
Corkscrew
Beer-bottle opener
Tin opener
More teaspoons
Potato peeler
Wooden spoon/stirrer
Measuring spoons
Large slotted server (Lakeland)
Cocktail sticks
Frying tongs
Knife sharpener or stone
Long-handled serving spoon
Medium-sharp knife
Soup ladle
Pasta server
Pastry brush (scrapes lemon peel off grater)
Plastic bowl scraper
Tomato corer (Lakeland)
Herb cutter
Fine grater for nutmegs (ground nutmeg can be difficult to get)
Tongs and spikes for (organised) barbecues

General galley equipment
Klippits
Airtight storage boxes
Airtight boxes for leftover food
Airtight sandwich and biscuit boxes
6+ non-slip table mats and coasters

Draining rack (+ tray to collect water)
Large and small funnels (labelled 'clean')
Foil and clingfilm
Cutlery boxes (for galley drawers)
Bottle stoppers (Lakeland/ Ironmongers)
Pumps and seals (to pump bottles out and in)
Stay-fresh bags
Paper bags
Roll of food bags
2 flyscreens
Cool-bag
Small funnel for pouring oil, vinaigrette, etc
Bottle boxes
Spaghetti jar
Thermos
Rubber jar-gripper
Water-filter jug
Water can with tap
Open stacking boxes (for fridge, etc)
Cutlery drainer
Long bag for storing baguettes (from French bakers)
Breadboard
Mini cool-bags
Extra coasters (fairly large, or glasses tip off)
Fridge thermometer
Ice-cube tray
Variously sized bottles
Tray

FOOD AND DRINK
What one considers 'essential', in food, is a very personal thing, so all I can do is to divide the items according to my own views. I indicate where I know things are difficult to get abroad, so that you can stock up with these items before you leave. Where no asterisk is given, this means that I've had no problem (but this may be because I have never tried).

Long-life food
Rice, dried beans
Lentils (split red lentils unavailable in Spain)
Lasagne, spaghetti pasta bows (farfalle)
Tinned soups**
Tinned sardines and tuna (super in Spain/Portugal)
Tinned chopped tomatoes (for cooking)
Tinned sweetcorn (for salads)
Small tins of pineapple (for sweet and sour sauce)
Tinned fruit
Breakfast cereals**
Plain flour
Jam
White sugar
Biscuits
Marks & Spencer's tinned meals*** (Malta)
Pots of meat paste (Marks & Spencer's beef paste is excellent)
Packet soups
Fray Bentos-type tinned pies**
Small tins of mushrooms for stews
Crisps and sweets (snacks)
Penguin biscuits and chocolate bars for the trip down (they melt farther south!)
Salt-roast peanuts and pistachios (for apéritifs)
Round-grain pudding rice
Tinned rice pudding**
Tinned treacle/sponge puddings***
Dried apricots
Dried fruit, eg raisins (baking, curries, salads, aperitifs)
Marmalade*
Brown sugar*
Porridge** (super on cold mornings)
Uncle Ben's sauces**
Marks & Spencer's fried potatoes ***
Macaroni
Noodles
Brown rice

(For an explanation of the use of asterisks in these lists, see the note on page 185.)

Packets of suet***
Tinned red salmon (** and
    expensive)
Tinned broad beans (and
    other vegetables)
Baked beans
Cornflour and maizena (flour
    treated to dissolve in hot
    stews)
Salt-roast cashew nuts**
    (delicious in salads)
Strong plain flour (for bread)
Rolled oats** (for biscuits and
    muesli)
Muesli**
Treacle/golden syrup** (for
    making biscuits, and eating
    with bread)
UHT cream
Christmas puddings**

Flavourings etc
Wine vinegar (for cooking and
    vinaigrette)
Tubes of tomato purée*
Cooking oil
Cooking salt
Fine table salt
Black pepper
Mustard
Beef stock cubes**
Other stock cubes
Virgin olive oil for salad
    dressing
Vinaigrette or salad cream
Soy sauce
Marmite (to make gravy)**
Garlic granules
Baking powder* (for making
    biscuits and buns)
Allinson's Easy-Bake Dried
    Yeast
Balsamic vinegar (for salad
    dressing)
Tabasco*
Worcester sauce*
Chutney**
Gravy browning**
Vanilla essence
Tins of tomato purée
Ketchup
Brown sauce

You may want spices for making
curries (cardamoms,** chilli,
coriander, cumin, fenugreek,**
ginger, mace*, turmeric**);
other spices (cinnamon, cloves,
nutmeg, paprika, saffron); and
herbs (basil, bay, coriander
leaf,** dill, marjoram, mint,
parsley, rosemary, sage, thyme),
etc.)

Long-life drinks
6 x 1.5 litre bottles of
    drinking water
Tea*
Coffee
UHT Milk
Tins of soft drinks
Your favourite spirit/aperitif
Wine, to last until you can
    restock where cheaper
Beer (only lager available
    abroad)
Options chocolate drink***
Bovril**
Long-life fruit juice
Spirits for guests
Tonic and other mixers
Condensed milk
Sherry** (for cooking and
    drinking)
Orange squash**
Ribena***
Capuccino coffee sachets
Nesquik Hot Chocolate

**Fresh food and drink (last
minute packing)**
Bread
Margarine
Milk
Eggs
Cheese for lunch (some in
    vac-packs)
Bacon (ditto)
Meat for lunch (ditto)
Cooking cheese (grated,
    vac-pack)
Something for dinner
Potatoes, onions, carrots,
Tomatoes
Fruit

Fruit cake**
Buns
Yoghurt desserts
Lettuce
Other vegetables
Garlic
Ice (for drinks, and to cool
    the fridge)
Butter
Plain yoghurt
Drinking yoghurt
Other desserts
Sweet peppers
Cucumber
Fresh orange juice (to be kept
    in fridge)
Low fat margarine and/or
    cheese**

PAPERS
Yacht documents
Yacht registration document
Proof of ownership
Proof of VAT payment
Proof of insurance
Deviation curve
Radio licence
Radio operator's licence
Translations of insurance
Stowage plan
Port forms in different
    languages
Sight forms for astro-navigation

Personal documents
Euros
Credit/debit cards
Passports
Any necessary visas
PIN numbers and account
    numbers
International Certificate of
    Competence
Home money
Home cheque book and
    cheque card
Vaccination record cards
Card case
E111 form (and photocopies)
Other foreign currency
Hard currency or traveller's
    cheques for emergencies

(For an explanation of the use of asterisks in these lists, see the note on page 185.)

Receipts for new equipment	instructions	**Stationery**
Private medical insurance	Document wallets	Take a selection of your
Driving licences	Account book	preferred stationery, eg
	Notebook for cruise report	writing paper, envelopes,
Record books	Notebooks for weather-fore-	air-mail paper, notebooks,
Address book	cast frequencies, port	pencils, pens, Sellotape,
Logbook	information, etc	paper clips and other
Transfer book	Photo albums (+ photograph	fastenings etc.
Visitors' book	corners/invisible mounts,	
Calendar or pocket diary	negative-holders)	
Records book	Wallet containing family	
Diary to write account in	photos, etc	
Ring binder for equipment	Visiting cards	

Appendix 2 • Books

PILOTAGE BOOKS

Pilot guides
North Brittany
North Biscay
South Biscay
Atlantic Spain and Portugal
Costas del Sol and Blanca
Islas Baleares
Costas del Azahar, Dorada and Brava,
    Mediterranean France and Corsica
Italian Waters Pilot
Adriatic Pilot
Greek Waters Pilot
Turkish Waters and Cyprus Pilot
North Africa
    (All published by Imray)

Almanacs and Canal Guides
Imray Mediterranean Almanac
French Almanac *Votre Livre de Bord*
    (English/French versions): Channel/Biscay
    Edition, and Mediterranean Edition
List of Symbols and Abbreviations (Admiralty*)*
Paris by Boat (Adlard Coles Nautical)
Guides Navicarte (Editions Grafocarte)
Guides Vagnon (Les Editions du Plaisancier)
The European Waterways by Marian Martin
The RYA Book of EuroRegs for Inland Waterways
    by Marian Martin
European Canal and River Dues and Requirements
    (Pleasure Craft) Free to RYA members
For tide tables as far as Gibraltar, I suggest
    Macmillan Reed's Nautical Almanac or *The*
    Cruising Almanac (Imray); and *Tidal-Stream*
    Atlases (Channel and Biscay)

RECOMMENDED TITLES

Reference
Sailing, and technical subjects
Boat Owner's Mechanical and Electrical Manual
    by Nigel Calder (Adlard Coles Nautical) (an
    essential on-board manual). Consider also his
    Boatowner's Practical and Technical Cruising
    Manual (Adlard Coles Nautical).
Ocean Cruising on a Budget by Anne Hammick
    (Adlard Coles Nautical) (extremely useful
    reading when preparing for your cruise).
The Oxford Companion to Ships and the Sea by
    Peter Kemp (OUP).
Le Guide Marine de Météo-France.

The Mediterranean
Mediterranean Cruising Handbook by Rod Heikell
    (Imray).
First Eden by David Attenborough (Collins) (a
    fascinating account of the history of the
    Mediterranean and man).

Field guides
Field Guide to the Birds of Britain and Europe by
    John Gooders (Kingfisher).
Collins Bird Guide by Lars Svensson and Peter J.
    Grant (Collins).
Mediterranean Sea, Guide to the Underwater Life
    by Angelo Mojello (Swanhill Press).
Wild Flowers of the Mediterranean by David
    Burnie (Dorling Kindersley)
Insects of Great Britain and Western Europe by
    Michael Chinery (Collins).
Complete Mediterranean Wildlife Photoguide by
    Paul Sterry (Collins).

Language

For each country we visit, I get the *Collins Gem Dictionary*, and the *Rough Guide Dictionary/ Phrase Book*, or the *Berlitz Dictionary/Phrase Book* (plus cassettes.)

Other reference books

Collins Dictionary of People and Places
Foods that Harm, Foods that Heal (Reader's Digest).
How to Do Just About Anything on a Computer (Reader's Digest).
Using PCs on Board by Rob Buttress and Tim Thornton (Adlard Coles Nautical).
First Aid Companion by Dr Rob Hawarth
First Aid At Sea by Douglas Justins & Colin Berry

Narrative
Legends and history

The Odyssey (translation by E V Rieu) (Penguin Classics). An excellent translation of Homer into lively prose – though still a bit difficult because Homer's story isn't told in chrono-logical order.
The Wanderings of Odysseus: The Story of the Odyssey by Rosemary Sutcliff (Delacorte). A more readable version of the Odysseus story – designed for adolescents, but very good, and well illustrated.
Ulysses Found by Ernle Bradford (Hodder & Stoughton). An attempt to track the voyage of Odysseus, following the traditional identifica-tions of the places.
The Jason Voyage by Tim Severin (Simon & Schuster). A fascinating account of Tim's voyage in a contemporary galley, in (a success-ful!) search for the Golden Fleece.
The Ulysses Voyage by Tim Severin (E P Dutton). An equally fascinating account of Tim's subse-quent voyage, tracking the wanderings of Odysseus, and finding a completely new, perhaps more logical, set of places.
The RA Expeditions by Thor Heyerdahl (Unwin). The story of building an ancient Egyptian reed-boat, and sailing it across the Atlantic, to prove that the Pre-Mayan and Inca civilization could have been 'exported' from the Med.

Other true stories

Seraffyn's Mediterranean Adventure by Lin and Larry Pardey (Adlard Coles Nautical). The third book in a fascinating account of a round-the-world-voyage in a 24 foot yacht with no engine in the 1970s.

Brighton to the Med by David and Pat Teall (Adlard Coles Nautical).
The Leisurely Route to the Med by John Hartley and Pauline Drury (Go Publishing).

Relevant novels

My Brother Michael by Mary Stewart (Chivers Press). A beautiful romantic thriller about a visit to Delphi.
Madam, Will You Talk? by Mary Stewart (Hodder & Stoughton). Same as book above, but set in Provence.
The Dark Moment by Anne Bridge. Fascinating story about the Turkish Revolution and Mustafa Kemal Attaturk.
Illyrian Spring by Anne Bridge (Virago). A *delightful* story set along the Croatian coast.

Other useful reference books
RYA publications

The RYA offer a number of publications that are very useful when planning a Med cruise:
Planning a Foreign Cruise (Mediterranean Edition)
Cruising Yacht Safety
Buying a Second-Hand Yacht – The Legal Aspects
Buying a New Yacht – The Legal Aspects
VHF Radiotelephony for Yachtsmen (GMDSS Edition)
VHF Radio Operator Examinations (Syllabus and Test Questions)
The Seaway Code
The RYA Book of EuroRegs for Inland Waterways

Books on sailing, and technical books

Reed's/Macmillan's handbooks
The Art of Pilotage by John Mellor (David & Charles).
Short-Handed Seamanship by Conrad Dixon (Adlard Coles Nautical).
Blue-Water Countdown by Geoff Pack (Yachting Monthly).
Storm-Tactics Handbook by Lyn and Larry Pardey (Waterline).
Sell Up and Sail by Bill and Laurel Cooper (Adlard Coles Nautical).
The Happy Ship by Kitty Hampton (Faber & Faber).
Reed's Skipper's Handbook by Bo Streiffert

Books on the Mediterranean

The Turquoise Coast of Turkey by Rod Heikell (obtainable in Turkey).
Mediterranean Sailing by Rod Heikell (Adlard Coles Nautical).

The New Penguin Atlas of Ancient History (and also their medieval history title) by Colin McEvedy (Penguin).

Ancient Greece – Utopia and Reality by Pierre Leveque (Thames & Hudson).

The Myths of Greece and Rome by H A Guerber (Constable).

A Dictionary of Greek and Roman Mythology by Michael Stapleton (Hamlyn).

Field guides

The Rough Guide to Mediterranean Wildlife (Rough Guides) (indicates where various wildlife can be found, though only in specific areas of particular interest).

Birds of Prey (Collins Photo-Guide).

Mediterranean Wild Flowers by Marjory Blaney and Christopher Grey Wilson (Collins).

The Hamlyn Guide to Trees of Britain and Europe (Hamlyn).

Mammals of Britain and Europe by MacDonald and Barrett (Collins).

Field Guide to the Wild Flowers of Southern Europe by Paul Davies and Bob Gibbons (Crowood).

Whales and Dolphins (Collins Gem Series).

Other books in the Collins Gem Series:

World Atlas; Flags; Internet; Using Your Software; Home Emergency Guide; Ready Reference; Synonyms and Antonyms; Dictionary of Quotations.

Dictionaries and language books

Yachtsman's Ten Language Dictionary, ed. Michael Manton (Adlard Coles Nautical) (good on really technical subjects).

Pocket Oxford Dictionary

Cookery books

Cooking in Spain by Janet Mendel (Santana Books, see Appendix 2, available in Spain) (gives useful guidance on shopping for food in Spain, plus recipes).

Shopping for Food and Wine in Spain (Santana Books, see Appendix 2, available in Spain).

Greek Vegetarian Cookery by Jack Santa Maria (Rider).

Miscellaneous

Any necessary reference books relating to equipment (eg computer manuals).

Catalogues: eg Marineforce, ASAP Supplies, West Marine, Sea Chest Nautical Bookshop

Various maps and *Michelin Guides.*

Reed's Heavenly Bodies Astro-navigation tables (annual)

Possibly ephemeris and air tables for astro-nav; a Bible.

Narrative
Legends and history

The Nature of Alexander by Mary Renault (an interesting study, but difficult to follow if you don't have some knowledge of his life).

True stories

Watersteps Through France by Bill and Laurel Cooper (Adlard Coles Nautical) (interesting account of a trip through the main canals).

Gates of the Wind (Ef Stathiadu Gp SA) (sailing, building a house, and living, in the northern Sporades in the 1960s).

Small Boat in the Midi by Roger Pilkington

Appendix 3 • Useful Addresses

All the addresses and phone numbers listed here are in the UK unless otherwise stated. Numbers starting with a + sign may be dialled from abroad. If dialling from land lines in most countries, 00 should be substituted for the +. If dialling the UK from within the UK, 0 should be substituted for the +44.

Adlard Coles Nautical 37 Soho Sq, London W1D 3QZ. **Tel:** 020 7758 0222
  e-mail: acn@acblack.com
Air-Marine Wind Generators
  Tel: +44 1823 666 177

AOL **Tel:** 0800 376 5432 or 4444;
  Website: http://www.aol.co.uk
ASAP Supplies Beccles, Suffolk NR34 7TD.
  Tel: 01502 716 993; **Fax:** 01502 711 680
Besenzoni Besenzoni G & C snc, 24067 Sarnico

(BG), Italy. **Tel:** +39 35 910 456

Brompton Bicycles Ltd The Arches, 2A London Road, Brentford, Middlesex TW8 8JW. **Tel:** 081 847 0822

Bügelanker Rolf Kaczirek, Rotdornweg 15, D-24214 Gettorf, Germany. **Tel:** +49 4346 63477

CompuServe Tel: 0870 513 4819

Cruisermart (see **Marineforce**)

Cruising Association CA House, 1 Northey Street, Limehouse Basin, London E14 8BT. **Tel:** 020 7537 2828; **Fax:** 020 7537 2266; **e-mail:** office@cruising.org.uk

DHL International Carriers DHL International UK Ltd, 178/188 Great South West Road, Hounslow, Middlesex TW4 6JS. **Tel:** +44 8701 100 300; **Fax:** +44 20 828 34229

Drix Plastics Drix Plastics Ltd, Unit 3, Stanton Industrial Estate, Stanton Road, Shirley, Southampton SO1 4HU.

Get-Up Mast Ladder Hurst Marine, 20 Coppins Close, Chelmsford, Essex CM2 6AY. **Tel** and **Fax:** 1245 258 420; **e-mail:** gerry@hurst-marinefsnet.co.uk; **Website:** http://www.hurst-marinefsnet.co.uk

Hotmail Website: http://www.hotmail.com

Imray Wych House, The Broadway, St Ives, Huntingdon, Cambridgeshire PE17 4BT, UK. **Tel:** +44 1480 462; **Fax:** +44 1480 496; **e-mail:** ilnw@imray.com; **Website:** http://www.imray.com

Lakeland Ltd Alexandra Buildings, Windermere, Cumbria LA23 1BQ. **Tel:** 015 394 88100; **Fax:** 015 394 88300

Le Guide Marine (see **Météo France**)

Mailing Preference Service Department AM, Freepost 22, London W1E 7EZ

Marine Chart Services Thrift House, 60d Oxford Street, Wellingborough, Northants NN8 4JJ. **Tel:** +44 1933 441629; **Fax:** +44 1933 442662 **e-mail:**sales@marinechartservices.co.uk; **Website:** http://www.chartsales.co.uk/system/index. html

Marineforce (previously called **Cruisermart**) Unit 6, Waterloo Industrial Estate, Flanders Road, Hedge End, Southampton SO30 2QT. **Tel:** 01489 774 444; **Fax:** 01489 444 445; **e-mail:** sales@marineforce.com; **Website:** http://www.marineforce.com

Météo France 1 quai Branly, 75340 Paris Cedex 07, France. **Tel:** +33 1 556 7171

Monaco Radio Centre Radio Maritime Monaco Radio, 1 Chemin du Fort Antoine, 98000, M C Monaco. **Tel:** +377 9330 1313

Nauticalia Tel: 01932 253 333; **Fax:** 01932 241 679; **Website:** http://www.nauticalia.com

On Air Magazine BBC World Service, Bush House, PO Box 76, The Strand, London WC2B 4PH

Out-of-Print Book-Finding Service A & R Booksearch, High Close, Winnick Cross, Lanreath, Near Looe, Cornwall PL13 2PF. **Tel:** 01503 220 246; **Fax:** 01503 220 965; **e-mail:** robert.ronald@btinternet.com; **Website:** http://www.arbooks.com

Porta-Potti Thetford Ltd, Unit 6, Centrovell Industrial Estate, Caldwell Rd, Nuneaton, Warwickshire CV11 4UD. **Tel:** 024 7632 2700

Rod Heikell Website: http://www.medsail.nil-dram.co.uk/news/pilotage.htm

Rohan Rohan Designs Ltd, 30 Maryland Road, Tongwell, Milton Keynes MK15 8HN. **Tel:** 0870 601 2244

RYA RYA House, Romsey Road, Eastleigh, Hampshire SO50 9YA. **Tel:** +44 23 8062 7400; **Fax:** +44 23 8062 9924

Santana Books Ediciones Santana SL, Apartado 422, 29640 Fuengirola, Málaga, Spain. **Fax:** +34 9524 8536

Sea Chest Nautical Bookshop (World-wide mail-order catalogue and Admiralty chart agent) Dolphin Building, Queen Anne's Battery Marina, Plymouth, Devon PL4 0LP. **Tel:** +44 1752 222012; **Fax:** +44 1752 252679; **e-mail:** sales@seachest.co.uk; **Website:** www.seachest.co.uk

'Speedy Stitcher', from chandlers or: Stewart MFG Co, Northboro, Massachusetts 01532, USA.

Stazo Locks Pumpkin Marine. **Tel:** 0171 480 6630 or: Stazo Marine Equipment, PO Box 151, 3340 AD Hendrik Ido Ambacht, Netherlands.

Tinker Dinghies Henshaw Inflatables Ltd, Southgate Road, Wincanton, Somerset BA9 9RZ. **Tel:** +44 1963 33237; **Fax:** +44 1963 34578

Tupperware The Tupperware Company, 130 College Road, Harrow, Middlesex HA1 1BQ. **Tel:** 02082 041 906

Ventair 15 MMG Civil Engineering Systems Ltd, Vermuyden House, Wiggenhall St Germans, King's Lynn PE34 3ES. **Tel:** +44 1553 617 791; **Fax:** +44 1553 617 771

Virgin.net Tel: 0845 650 0000; **Website:** http://www.virgin.net

VNF Offices Bureau d'Affrètement de Bordeaux, Hangar B, face au No 4 Quai St Croix, 33800 Bordeaux, France. **Tel:** +33 5 5692 8141

Watski Website: www.watski.com

West Marine Catalogue Tel: 0800 895 473

Windrush Mill Windrush Mill Mail Order Warehouse, 214–6 Leconfield Industrial Estate, Cleaton Moor, Cumbria CA25 5PX. **Tel:** +44 1946 814 444; **Fax:** +44 1946 815 555

Appendix 4 • Weather Forecasts

ABBREVIATIONS

SSB	Single Side Band transmission	GMT	Greenwich Mean Time/Universal Time
USB	Upper Side Band transmission		
LSB	Lower Side Band transmission	LT	Local Time
N	Normal transmission	Ch	Channel

The most up-to-date information on Mediterranean and east-Atlantic forecasts is available from *La Guide marine de Météo-France*. Other sources are pilot guides, the *Imray Mediterranean Almanac*, *Votre Livre de Bord*, and the RYA Publication '*Planning a Foreign Cruise* (*Mediterranean Edition*). Up-to-date maps of the Atlantic and west Mediterranean forecast areas are given in both *Le Guide Marine* and *Votre Livre de Bord*. The following times and frequencies are those that I personally have successfully received – though, of course, things do change.

Atlantic coast forecasts

Station	Frequency	Time	Area covered	Language
Cross Corsen	1650 & 2677 SSB	0815 & 2015 LT	Channel and Biscay	French only
British Mobile Maritime NET	14303 SSB	1803 ± GMT	Atlantic coast and Mediterranean	English
BBC Shipping	198 kHz N	0048 0536 1201 1754 LT	Channel and Atlantic coast	English
Radio France International	15300 kHz N	1140 GMT	Whole of Atlantic	French only

Western Mediterranean basin forecasts

Station	Frequency	Time	Area covered	Language
Monaco	8728 & 8806 USB	0715 & 1830, GMT	Whole of western Mediterranean basin	French and English
Monaco	4363 USB	0903, 1403 & 1915 LT	North half of western Mediterranean basin	French and English
British Mobile Maritime NET	14303 SSB	1830 GMT	Atlantic coast and whole of Mediterranean	English
Various Coast Radio Stations	See Italian pilot guide		Local areas	Italian and English

Central Mediterranean basin forecasts

Station	Frequency	Time	Area covered	Language
From Italy	VHF Ch 68	Continuous	All Italian areas English	Italian and English
From Croatia	VHF Ch 67	Continuous	Croatia	Croatian, Italian and English
Crotone	2663 kHz SSB	0735 GMT	Adjacent areas	Italian and English
Kerkira (Corfu)	2830 kHz SSB		As Iraklion below	

(Note that Greece and Italy use different names for their Ionian forecast areas.)

Eastern Mediterranean basin forecasts

Station	Frequency	Time	Area covered	Language
Athens Radio	729 kHz N	0630 LT	All	Greek and English
Iraklion (Crete)	2799 kHz SSB	0703,	Greek waters	Greek
Rhodes	2624 kHz SSB	0903,	Greek waters	and
Limnos (Aegean)	2730 kHz SSB	1566 and 2133 GMT	Greek waters	English

Appendix 5 • Abbreviations and Conversions

ABBREVIATIONS

km	= kilometre	gal	= gallon	Br	= British
cm	= centimetre	pt	= pint	Imp	= Imperial
m	= metre	fl oz	= fluid ounce	US	= United States of America
mm	= millimetre	lb	= pound weight		
cc	= cubic centimetre	oz	= ounce	hr	= hour
kg	= kilogram	yd	= yard	min	= minute
gm	= gram	ft	= foot/feet	sec	= second
ml	= millilitre	in	= inch	NM	= nautical mile
M	= statute mile (land mile)	cu in	= cubic inch	kn	= knot = 1 NM/hr

CONVERSION TABLES
(Figures in brackets are convenient approximations)

Length

| 1km | = 1000m | 1m = 100cm | 1 cm = 10mm |
| 1M | = 1760yd | 1yd = 3ft | 1ft = 12in | 1 NM = 2027yd = 6080ft |

1 NM	1.1515 M	1 M	0.8684NM
1 km	0.540 NM	1 NM	1.852km
1 metre	3.28 ft = 39.37 in	1 foot	30.48cm ($\frac{1}{3}$m)
10 cm	3.937 (4) in	1 in	2.54 (2½)cm

Volume

1 litre = 1000 ml = 1000 cc   1 gallon = 8 pt
1 Imp (Br) pint = 20fl oz   So 1 Br gal = 160 fl oz = 277.4 cu in
But 1 US pint = 16fl oz   So 1 US gal = 128 fl oz = 231cu in

1 litre	0.220 Br gal	1 Br gal	4.54 (4½)litres
1 litre	1.76 (1¾) Br pints	1 Br pint	0.568 litres
100 ml	3.52fl oz	1 fl oz	28.375ml

Weight

1 litre of water weighs 1kg   1 Br gallon of water weighs 10 pounds
1 metric tonne = 1000kg   1 Br ton = 2240 pounds (US = 2000)
1kg = 1000gm   1 pound = 16 ounces

1kg	2.205 pounds	1 pound	454 grams
100 grams	3.528 ounces	1 ounce	28.375 grams
1 metric tonne	0.984 Br tons	1 Br ton	1.016 metric tonnes

Temperatures

0°C = 32°F   16°C = 61°F   28°C = 82°F   36.9°C = 98.4°F   100°C = 212°F

Time zones

Britain & Portugal	GMT (UTC)
Gibraltar, France, Spain, Italy	GMT + 1 hour
Tunisia, Malta & Croatia	GMT + 1 hour
Greece & Turkey	GMT + 2 hours

Everywhere except Tunisia uses Summer Time, ie:
Plus an extra hour, between last Sunday in March & last Sunday in October.

Other approximations

$\frac{5}{16}$ inch chain = 8mm $\frac{3}{8}$ inch chain = 10mm
25lb anchor = 11kg   35lb anchor = 16 kg   45lb anchor = 20kg

Index